MILITARY DECEPTION AND
STRATEGIC SURPRISE

MILITARY DECEPTION AND STRATEGIC SURPRISE

Edited by
John Gooch
and
Amos Perlmutter

Routledge
Taylor & Francis Group

LONDON AND NEW YORK

First published 1982 in Great Britain by
2 Park Square, Milton Park, Abingdon, Oxon, OX14 4RN
270 Madison Ave, New York NY 10016

Transferred to Digital Printing 2007

British Library Cataloguing in Publication Data

Military deception and strategic surprise.
1. Tactics 2. Military art and service
I. Gooch, John II. Perlmutter, Amos
355.4'2 U167

ISBN10: 0-7146-3202-3 (hbk)
ISBN10: 0-415-44933-2 (pbk)

ISBN13: 978–0–7146–3202–5 (hbk)
ISBN13: 978–0–415–44933–5 (pbk)

This group of studies first appeared in a Special Issue
on 'Military Deception and Strategic Surprise' of *The
Journal of Strategic Studies* Vol. 5. No. 1. published by
Routledge

Typeset by Cleer Typesetters, Hertford, Herts.

Publisher's Note
The publisher has gone to great lengths to ensure the quality of this
reprint but points out that some imperfections in the original
may be apparent

Contents

Notes on Contributors

Barton Whaley is Research Director of the International Center, Inc., Washington D.C., and former Associate Professor of World Politics at Fletcher School of Law and Diplomacy.

Michael Mihalka has been an employee at The Rand Corporation since 1977. He has written extensively on a wide range of national security issues including strategic studies, arms transfers, non-proliferation and conflict management.

Janice Gross Stein, Associate Professor of Political Science, McGill University, is co-author of *Rational Decision Making: Israel's Security Choices, 1967* (Ohio State University Press, 1980), and has published articles in *International Journal, Canadian Journal of Political Science, Journal of Conflict Resolution.*

Michael Handel received his Ph.D. from Harvard University in 1974. He is a research associate at the Harvard Center for International Affairs. Among his publications are *The Israeli Political-Military Doctrine* (1973); *Perception, Deception and Surprise: The Case of the Yom Kippur War* (1976); *The Study of War Termination* (1979); *Weak States in the International System* (1981); and *The Diplomacy of Surprise: Hitler, Stalin, Sadat* (1981).

Donald C. Daniel is Associate Professor of National Security Affairs at the Naval Postgraduate School and in 1981 was a guest scholar at the Brookings Institution in Washington, D.C. He is the editor of *International Perceptions of the Superpower Military Balance* (1978), a regular contributor to the *Soviet Armed Forces Review Annual,* and author of numerous articles, dealing mainly with naval affairs. He is a recent winner of a Ford Foundation grant and is completing a study on anti-submarine warfare and strategic stability. Together with Katherine Herbig, he recently co-edited *Strategic Military Deception* (1982).

Katherine L. Herbig is an Assistant Professor at the Naval Postgraduate School, where she teaches American and Modern European History in the Department of National Security Affairs, and undertakes historical research on military topics. In addition to work on deception, her current research interests include strategic theory and the problem of surprise attack. Together with Donald C. Daniel, she recently co-edited *Strategic Military Deception.*

Introduction

Deception is a conscious and rational effort deliberately to mislead an opponent. It seeks to create in the adversary a state of mind which will be conducive to exploitation by the deceiver. As such, deception is one of the oldest and most effective weapons of warfare. As a form of 'trickery' it has acquired a pejorative connotation: just as 'Gentlemen do not open each other's mail', so decent people should not engage in what is sometimes seen as an indecent activity. But strategic deception, far from being either ungentlemanly or random, is a systematic and consistent process in which success may bring substantial benefits.

As each of the authors in this collection demonstrates, deception is conceptually related to perception and misperception. In order to succeed, the deceiver must penetrate the inner mind of his opponent to identify the assumptions, expectations and aspirations of the adversary. He must then convey the notion of a partnership by convincing his opponent that his posture is 'genuine' or 'sincere'. The whole process of deception is an effort at self-projection designed to enhance the opponent's aspirations and thus make the deceived vulnerable to the deceiver.

Deception is frequently a weapon of the weak. The strong are generally more relaxed, unsystematic and arrogant in their approach to war against the weak, thus giving the latter a badly-needed advantage in the war of deception. Three case studies included here amply demonstrate this thesis: the Weimar Republic's circumspection in overcoming the restrictions of the Versailles Treaty; the Soviet missile inferiority (1962–1973); and the Egyptian air-missile/military inferiority to Israel between 1967 and 1973.

Barton Whaley, in the first contribution, deals with what can best be termed 'straightforward deception' in his analysis of Germany's evasion of the restrictions imposed upon her by the Paris peace treaty of 1919. Catering to a popular perception of a defeated, war-weary and pacific Germany, the political and military establishment engaged in cheating, lying, camouflaging, covert arms operations and concealments of infinite variety. The result was an operation whose success was due mainly to a well-conceived, efficiently organized and expertly co-ordinated programme of deception.

Michael Mihalka, in his paper on Russian deception, cements Whaley's thesis that for a deception to be successful it must be both wilful and systematic. In order to achieve strategic superiority and the modernization of Soviet nuclear missiles, the strategy of deception became one of persuading the United States that the Soviets did not want superiority but were, at worst, seeking parity, and at best wanted to stop the arms race. In reality the USSR wanted to modernize rapidly and forcefully without stimulating an equally dramatic United States response. The Soviet attempts to persuade the United States that arms reduction is a common aspiration of the two superpowers, and that the USSR seeks a military balance, have in the past depended in part at least upon a systematic deception.

Janice Gross Stein demonstrates in her paper that deception is an important element of surprise. Military and political deception is a force multiplier, and for Egypt between 1967 and 1973 it became a significant military asset. In order to overcome their obvious military inferiority, the Egyptians chose not to attempt to achieve military superiority but rather to deceive the Israelis. In this they were immensely aided by Israeli self-deception and over-confidence after the spectacular gains of the 1967 war. The Egyptians attempted to achieve limited military objectives such as crossing the 'Canal of Shame', which in turn brought them far greater political advantages than the limited tactical successes they achieved. The ambiguous line between the defensive and offensive, and the continuous Egyptian exercises between 1971 and 1973 finally succeeded in surprising the Israelis during the October War.

Michael Handel's contribution forms the bridge between practice and theory. With the aid of a range of historical examples he demonstrates both the positive and the negative faces of deception, and in so doing provides a critical link between the concrete and the conceptual, demonstrating also how analysis can lead to prescription.

Donald Daniel and Katherine Herbig display the systemic nature of deception by means of a concentric circle used as a model to explain the dynamic elements which it comprises. They demonstrate the key role in deception played by the withholding of information, which permits two types of ambiguity: increased ambiguity, which compounds uncertainty, and decreased ambiguity which enhances the attractiveness of false alternatives. They are, however, cautious about the overall importance of deception — a tool which may not be as powerful as some of its practitioners would have it to be.

Finally Barton Whaley makes a decisive step towards the formulation of a 'General Theory of Deception' by demonstrating the connection between magic and deception. Deception, like magic, is a distortion of perceived reality, and both seek to achieve the same behavioural result.

The strategic advantages and disadvantages of deception are many. The studies gathered together here represent a first step in exploration and analysis, resting on the pioneer efforts of their authors, on their originality and on their theoretical depth.

AMOS PERLMUTTER
JOHN GOOCH

Covert Rearmament in Germany 1919-1939: Deception and Misperception

Barton Whaley

I. Disarmament, 1918–1920

From 1918 until 1920, Germany was forcibly disarmed. Then, in January 1920, the Armistice was superseded by the Versailles Treaty. The formal constraints on German war potential were severe. The right bank of the Rhine was demilitarized. The strategic Kiel Canal and several rivers were internationalized. All overseas colonies were forfeit. Chunks of German territory were ceded to France, Belgium and Poland. The Saar, Danzig and Memel were placed under League of Nations supervision. And Germany was to pay huge reparations, a sum later set at $33 billion.

The German military was emasculated. Conscription was forbidden. The Army was limited to 100,000 troops (4,000 officers and 96,000 men). To prevent build-up of a reserve, officers had to sign on for 25 years, and enlisted men for 12. The Army was denied tanks, heavy artillery and poison gas. The Great General Staff was abolished and staff colleges and military academies closed. The Army was forbidden to have a field command echelon higher than that of corps. The Flying Corps was abolished and aircraft prohibited.

The Navy was limited to 15,000 sailors (1,500 officers and 13,500 ratings). It was left with obsolete warships, and was forbidden to build replacements over 10,000 tons. It was forbidden to have aircraft. It was forbidden to have or to build submarines. All production or importation of arms was prohibited, as well as the sending of military missions abroad. Even police were regulated; the national police force being restricted to 150,000, all of whom were to be lifetime employees to prevent the building of even a police reserve by rotation.

Germany was not trusted to keep the solemn Treaty provisions applied to disarmament. As a defeated (albeit not quite conquered) nation, she was required to accept on-site inspection to assure compliance. The official body set up for this purpose was the Inter-Allied Control Commission, established in September 1919 under the presidency of General Charles Nollet. The Control Commission comprised representatives of Great Britain, France, Italy, Belgium and Japan. It reported to and received higher policy direction from the specially created Allied Conference of Ambassadors that met irregularly in France. At the outset it numbered 373 professional military officers. This already impressive number was increased in 1920 to 383 officers and 737 men. (However, in the summer of 1921, the staff was reduced by almost half, leaving only 174 officers and 400 men.) Nor were these mere deskbound bureaucrats: over 800 on-site inspections, for example, were conducted in a six-week period in September/October 1924 alone.[1]

The Control Commission settled into Berlin's palatial Hotel Adlon. Headquarters staff comprised nine senior officers, four French, two British, one Italian, one Belgian and a Japanese colonel. The three subordinate echelons had responsibility for oversight, respectively, of armaments, personnel and fortifications. These echelons worked through 22 district commands covering all of Germany. Each district command was weighted in personnel: eleven for armaments, eight for personnel and three for fortifications. It was a simple, hierarchical structure, functionally well suited to its mission.[2]

Unfortunately the Control Commission committed a major strategic, political error at the very outset of its work, a blunder that was recognized and admitted by Generals Nollet, Morgan and their colleagues; but not until it was too late to reverse. This self-made trap was their own demand that the Germans provide a liaison committee to coordinate the disarmament process. The *Reichswehr* was astounded. It had assumed that the Control Commission would simply sweep into Germany in force, arbitrarily and ruthlessly confiscating, destroying and punishing any infractions of its orders. Instead, the *Reichswehr* was being *asked* to comply with military dictates and was handed the quite unexpected opportunity to appoint what, from its standpoint, would be a committee of obstruction. Accordingly, the German Defense Ministry created the Army Peace Commission (*Heeresfriedens-kommission*). Prussian General von Cramon was appointed its head. He was carefully selected, a vehement opponent of the *Versaillesdiktat* in all its onerous aspects. At the very first joint meeting with the Control Commission on 29 January 1920, Cramon demonstrated his intention that liaison did not mean cooperation, but rather power games, obfuscation and general obstruction.[3]

The key to German rearmament was the arms industry, and the key to the German arms industry was the giant industrial empire of Krupp. The Allies, fully aware of its crucial role, had ordered the destruction of Krupp's heavy arms production lines. Legal arms production was sharply restricted in numbers and closely watched by the Control Commission. Thus, Krupp was limited in 1921 to a single type of gun and could produce only four of these per year. Its production for the Navy of armor plate, ammunition hoists, gun mountings and cannon was limited to replacement of worn-out components in the obsolescent warships.[4]

To survive, it diversified, introducing peacetime lines that ranged from baby carriages and typewriters through motor scooters and optical instruments, up to such heavy gear as dredgers, agricultural machinery and locomotives. The government placed orders and generously covered some of the deficits. The more skilled and trusted engineers and workers of Essen were kept on or transferred to subsidiary plants throughout Germany and the world, ready for the day when Krupp could return to making arms.

This effort was applauded by both the government and the *Reichswehr*. Thus, immediately after the Armistice, the Army Chief, General von Seeckt, recognized that 'There is only one way in which we shall be able to provide for the arming of great masses of troops [and that is to make] suitable arrangements with the industrialists of the nation'.[5]

Personal initiative combined with discreet government support to preserve Fokker's famous aircraft factory. His superb F-7 biplane fighter was the only category of German equipment singled out by name in the Versailles Treaty for destruction. Thus forewarned, Tony Fokker immediately began plotting to save his fortune and his factory. His plan was to smuggle them out of Germany to his native Holland. His cash horde (nearly a quarter of his liquid assets) was eventually brought out in two consignments; one by sailboat and the other by rail in a decrepit suitcase concealed among privileged foreign diplomatic baggage. But rescuing the contents of his doomed Fokker-Flugzeugwerke mbH at Schwerin in northern Germany was another matter.

In a race against time in 1920 with the Control Commission inspectors, Fokker personally supervised the removal and concealment of over half his factory inventory in numerous remote barns, cellars, stables and sheds scattered over the surrounding countryside. The remaining planes, parts and equipment were left on open display for the Allied inspection team to find when they arrived at the factory. The inspecting officers did not realize they had been outwitted.

Fokker's next problem was to get this large inventory out of Germany. For that, he needed export licenses and transportation. Accordingly, his export manager, F. W. Seekatz, visited the Trade Ministry in Berlin. There he argued frankly that if this large stock of military aviation were transferred to Holland, it would be in a country that could be trusted to remain neutral. Germany would get much needed licensing fees and the Allies would be thwarted. The Trade Ministry officials agreed and quietly handed over export permits for nearly a half-million dollars' worth of material.

The transportation scheme was suggested, planned and arranged by Fokker's transportation department chief, Wilhelm Hahn. He obtained this from the state railway by a mix of appeals to patriotism, reminders of past favors and much outright bribery. Nearly a sixth of the hidden inventory was collected in trucks by trusted Fokker workers and driven to the waiting railway freight cars.[6]

With Hahn aboard, the train pulled out of the siding at Schwerin on the first stage of its 350-mile journey to Holland. The train was exactly 60 cars long, a length suggested by the bribed German railway customs officials who helpfully pointed out that they could then plausibly pass it directly through to Holland. Because the sidings at the frontier town of Saltzbergen could accommodate a maximum of only 40 cars, to hold up Hahn's extra long train would block the main line. Other careful arrangements were made to avoid delays so that no unwitting railway or customs official would have a chance to investigate. As the train neared Saltzbergen station, a report reached the joint Allied-German border patrol that a smuggling attempt was underway, but at a station further down the border. The report was true, but a ruse nevertheless, as Hahn had arranged for a diversionary party to lay a false trail. This simple diversion worked and the train crossed the border unchallenged.

In the next five weeks, an additional five trainloads managed to move the bulk of Fokker's hidden equipment. The precious, stripped-down airplane fuselages were carried on some 30 open flatcars in the last train; Fokker had not previously dared risk sending airframes because of their distinctive shape. Although camouflaged with wooden boards and metal tubing and covered with tarpaulin, the tarpaulins were boldly marked 'FOKKER-FLUGZEUG-WERKE' and 'SCHWERIN', for Hahn had run out of unmarked covers. Even so, this last shipment got through without unwanted notice.

The entire operation, from initial planning to final delivery, had taken less than seven weeks. Hahn had managed to smuggle out some 350 railway carloads carrying an amazing total of 220 airplanes (including 120 of the proscribed D-7 fighters), over 400 engines and considerable other material worth nearly $8 million. In all, Tony Fokker had salvaged enough cash and goods to reopen business in Holland as Nederlandische Vliegtuigenfabriek N.V., ready to play a continuing role in Germany's efforts to evade the *Versaillesdiktat*.[7]

Throughout the 1920s, Germany looked and, indeed, was substantially disarmed. But, if the letter of Versailles was being more or less observed, the intent was not. The *potential* for *rapid* rearmament was present and growing and so was the desire for it. The desire to rearm was a common bond between German politicians, soldiers and industrialists. As politicians, the government leaders resented the constraints placed on their power. As soldiers, the senior officers of the *Reichswehr* saw a need for an Army strong enough to back German foreign policy. As industrialists, the heads of Krupp, Stinnes, and I.G. Farben cherished continuing profits. And these purely professional desires and goals were complemented in no small measure by simple patriotism.

The various chancellors, chiefs of the *Reichswehr,* and captains of industry had, it is true, various motives for their desire to see a rearmed nation-state. Some, such as General von Seeckt, realistically feared aggression by Germany's new eastern neighbor, Poland. Others, such as industrialist Gustav Krupp von Bohlen, deeply resented a Treaty that he believed was designed to keep 'the German people ... enslaved forever'. Still others saw armaments variously as profits, national honor, a means to regain the surrendered German lands (perhaps even the colonies), and a renewed chance to gain predominance in Germany and the world. But whatever their separate motives, all shared the slogan 'military freedom' (*Wehrfreiheit*); and whatever its final purpose, all saw as its instrument a strong German Army and not the pathetic ersatz one of the detested *Versaillesdiktat*. This shared desire of 1919–1920 quickly led to a necessarily secret collaboration to evade the Treaty and rearm. This goal was so strongly held that it even overrode personal animosities (such as that between the cold aristocrat, Seeckt and the outgoing commoner, Stresemann) and the bitter infighting of bureaucracies (such as the continuing power competition between the *Reichswehr* and the Foreign Office).

II. Covert Arms Evasion, 1920–1926

The 1918–1919 period of disarmament was followed by one of arms evasion. Evasion throughout this new period, 1920–1926, was necessarily covert because it coincided with the presence of the large Inter-Allied Control Commission with its right of on-site inspection.

The Chief *(Chef)* of the *Reichswehr* was 54-year-old Colonel-General Hans von Seeckt. Seeckt set out to circumvent Treaty limitations in every way possible. The central control of the Imperial Army, the Great General Staff, had been abolished by the fiat of Versailles (Article 160) and was not to be reconstructed in any form. General von Seeckt neatly evaded this requirement in the low profile guise of the Troops Office (*Truppenamt*), ostensibly charged with overseeing *Reichswehr* organizational affairs. The *Truppenamt* had four sections: T-1, operations; T-2, organization; T-3, foreign armies; and T-4, training. Among those subsequently prominent officers who received their early general staff experience in this disguised General Staff, were Werner von Blomberg (later War Minister), Colonel Freiherr von Fritsch (later Commander in Chief of the Army), Colonel Walther von Brauchitsch (ditto), and Colonel Wilhelm Keitel (later Chief of Hitler's Supreme Command). Conscientious observance of the 12- and 25-year-old enlistment requirements (for officers and enlisted men, respectively) would have meant the Army could not even begin to build a trained reserve until after 1932, and even then only with troops all over 30 and officers over 43. But the *Reichswehr* was able to quickly accumulate a small but forbidden reserve by simply taking in a number of short-term enlistment recruits, the so-called *Zeitfreiwillige*.

Padding extended even to the police. The national police force exceeded the 150,000-man limit stipulated by the Allies. The police also introduced semi-military training and accumulated a trained reserve by adopting the *Reichswehr*'s 12-year enrollment policy in the face of an Allied lifetime employment requirement precisely to prevent development of a police reserve. Moreover, they managed to accumulate 25,000 of their force in barracks, as virtual light-infantry ready-response units.[8] The Allies were aware of all these measures. They complained, but the German government fought a successful delaying battle of negotiation.

The *Reichswehr* was allowed an Intelligence service of sorts. The Versailles Treaty did not explicitly prohibit it; indeed, the Treaty made no mention of the subject. Upon the Armistice, Section IIIb became the Intelligence Branch of the caretaker General Staff. Following general demobilization, it was reduced to an Intelligence Group. Colonel Nicolai, its head, was dumped into permanent leave status and replaced in 1919 by IIIb veteran Major Friedrich Gempp. Following the Treaty of Versailles, Gempp's unit simply followed the Great General Staff into its camouflaged form of the Troops Office (*Truppenamt*). For similar reasons of disguise, the Intelligence Office was renamed the *Abwehrabteilung* ('defense section') or, for short, *Abwehr*.

Gempp's tiny *Abwehr* had only four officers. Initially it developed Intelligence on the Russian Civil War and Russo-Polish Wars then raging uncomfortably close to Germany's eastern frontier. It went on to develop espionage networks, presumably against the main enemy, France.[9]

Although the Versailles Treaty explicitly permitted the signals detachment of each *Reichswehr* division to include a radio intercept unit, the Control Commission prohibited any cryptanalytic capability. However, at the beginning of 1919, 24-year-old ex-Lieutenant Erich Buschenhagen, who had worked in the Army radio intercept service during the Great War, went ahead on his own to set up a small intercept Intelligence unit for one of the Free Corps in Berlin. He called his unit the 'Volunteer Evaluation Office' and quietly installed it on the Friedrichstrasse. In the beginning, it merely translated plaintext intercepts from French, British, American and Russian sources as well as press reports sent by radio. But by May, after Buschenhagen had acquired his first few cryptanalysts, the unit was distributing some decodes, at least of Russian material. In February 1920, his twelve-man team was absorbed into the *Abwehr* as the Cipher Center (*Chieffrierstelle*), moving into the Army headquarters building on the Bendlerstrasse. Then, avoiding Control Commission inspectors just in time, the Cipher Center moved again to nearby Grunewald where it disguised itself as a newspaper translation and study group.[10]

In 1921 the *Reichswehr* secretly ordered expansion of the intercept service (*Horchdienst*), and assigned it to the Cipher Center. By late 1925 when Buschenhagen was transferred elsewhere, the Cipher Center had expanded to a staff of 32 plus 20 radiomen operating six radio interception posts, three or four of whose receivers were being monitored around the clock.[11]

The *Reichswehr* effectively supplemented its limit on troops by secretly equipping and/or funding several of the many private, paramilitary organizations that sprang up in the politically troubled times immediately following the Armistice. These groups were lightly armed to be sure, but soldiers nevertheless. Seeckt himself made only the narrow distinction between 'soldiers' and '*Reichswehr* soldiers'.

The secret transfer of large quantities of arms, equipment and ammunition from the *Reichswehr* to the paramilitaries was made possible by the long interval of 15 months between the time when the provisional *Reichswehr* learned of the 100,000-troop limit in the Versailles Treaty and the deadline for its implementation. The Allied Supreme Council originally intended to grant the provisional *Reichswehr* only three months (until summer 1919) to cut down to 100,000 troops and hand over its surplus war material, but the German delegates at the Treaty negotiations raised the quite real bogey that such speed risked a civil war in which a defenseless Weimar Republic could easily be swept away by Bolshevism. The British military delegation accepted this argument and urged it on the reluctant French, who yielded the point in the Supreme Council. Accordingly, the final Treaty provisions permitted the provisional *Reichswehr* to demobilize by stages, keeping 200,000 until 10 April 1920 (Article 163), that is, until three months after the Treaty went into effect. But this Article conflicted with another (Article 160) which set a 31 March 1920 deadline for the *Reichswehr* to cut back to its final 100,000 quota. To resolve this dilemma, the Supreme Council, on 19 February 1920, extended the deadline to 19 April for the 200,000 quota and to 10 July for the 100,000 quota. The overall effect of putting off these deadlines meant that the originally expected summer 1919 deadline for reduction to the 100,000 figure was delayed until the following summer. The *Reichswehr* was quick to take advantage of this windfall to conceal and transfer material to the paramilitaries in proportion as it gradually reduced its own force.[12]

The Allies rejected the German request to retain a single operational air squadron and eight airfields for internal security purposes and required the disbanding of the seven police air patrol squadrons established in 1919 in the provincial governments.[13] The Kaiser's Flying Corps had been abolished in 1920 by an ostensibly stern order of General von Seeckt, but Seeckt never intended that the Flying Corps 'die', only disappear, concealed, scattered in various guises until a time when it would be safe and politic to reconstitute it.

The first order of business was to maintain a hidden reserve of trained pilots, air crew and ground staff. The *Reichswehr* itself sheltered 120 former Army and 20 Navy officer pilots, although it proved much more difficult to keep together the NCOs and ground personnel. The second order of business was to maintain a viable aero-industry and keep it occupied with military R&D.

Seeckt also saw to it that his secret General Staff included an Aviation Staff (disguised as the Army Command Inspectorate of Weapons Schools). This was headed by Captain (later General) Helmut Wilberg, the very same air officer who had drafted Seeckt's order abolishing the Flying Corps.

The aircraft construction moratorium and Control Commission depradations combined to close most of Germany's 35 aircraft companies and 20 aero-engine manufacturers. When the moratorium was belatedly lifted in 1921, only four aircraft companies had survived: Junkers, Heinkel, Albatross and Dornier. In 1922 Dr Adolf Rohrbach opened the Rohrbach Metal Aircraft Company in Berlin with private finance and government subsidies. A branch office was established in Copenhagen, specifically to evade the Control Commission.

Many of the German airplane designers welcomed their secret orders from the *Reichswehr* as part of a battle of wits as well as profits. Adolf Rohrbach was one. Ernst Heinkel was another. Thus, Heinkel recalled that fulfilling a 1923 order from Major Kurt Student to build his first military plane involved 'an extremely risky game of hide-and-seek with the Allied Control Commission . . . , and I am bound to admit that it was a game that was bound to appeal strongly to a man who was given to taking risks'. To build his reconnaissance plane (the HD-17) and later military prototypes, Heinkel rented a workshop hangar outside his regular factory at Warnemünde. The Allied Control Commission inspectors only saw this hangar empty; because, hours before each inspection, all aircraft and components were loaded onto trucks and driven to hidden spots on the heath or among nearby sand dunes.[14]

During the 1923 Franco-German crisis in the Ruhr, the angered German government actually considered the possibility of military resistance to the threatened French occupation of the Ruhr. Accordingly, Captain Wilberg of the *Reichswehr*'s covert air staff, placed an immediate secret order for 100 fighter planes with the pro-German Fokker aircraft firm in Holland. By the time they were ready for delivery, the crisis had passed (and the German government had decided against any military resistance). Fokker sold half these planes to Rumania, but the other 50 units were eventually shipped in 1925, via Stettin and Leningrad, to the secret German air base established in Russia the previous year, as described below.[15]

The Ruhr Crisis also prompted the Defense Ministry's naval department to order ten seaplane fighters for the Navy. The components were designed and built at Heinkel's factory at Warnemünde, then shipped to Sweden for assembly. There, the ten Heinkel He-1 seaplanes received their British built Rolls-Royce Eagle IX engines and were testflown with Swedish markings before being packed in enormous crates and stored in bond by a Stockholm harbor warehouse firm owned by ex-German Navy Commander Bücker.

The German commercial airlines merged, at the beginning of 1926, to become the state controlled monopoly airline Deutsche Lufthansa. Prompted by General von Seeckt, the *Reichswehr* immediately began to blend in the desired military component. World War I pilot, Erhard Milch, became managing director and, working closely with the *Reichswehr*, soon built up a small reserve of combat airmen by including military instruction in Lufthansa's training program.

Some of the more restrictive provisions of the Versailles Treaty, as they applied to aircraft, were modified in the Pact of Paris of 1926. This kept the absolute ban on military aviation, but allowed the German aero-industry to build, under strict inspection, limited numbers of 'aircraft conforming to the aeronautical performance of current types of fighter aircraft' for use exclusively for flying competition and recordbreaking.[16] This, of course, was ideal for the *Reichswehr* because it permitted the public design, building and testing of the highest performance aircraft. Of course, some camouflage was still needed, but only to hide the more obvious signs of the intended military use of these aircraft. Thus the Navy's Seaplane Experimental Station was concealed within the civilian German Airlines Federation.

Willy Messerschmidt developed his Bf-108 'sporting monoplane', which was the immediate forerunner of the superb Bf-109 fighter of WWII. Hugo Junkers developed and sold large numbers of his Ju-52 trimotor that was designed, in fact, as a bomber but went on to become the workhorse transport of the *Luftwaffe*. Ernst Heinkel introduced his high-speed, slim and beautiful He-70 as a four-passenger 'mail carrier'; but it had been designed as a two-seater military reconnaissance and bomber plane, the forerunner of the He-111 medium bomber that would later smash Guernica and London.

The Pact of Paris further relaxed the Versailles Treaty to let the *Reichswehr* and Navy have a total of six officers receive flying instruction and serve as airmen. The Defense Ministry immediately took advantage of this opening to pad out the aviation ranks by secretly ordering that some 40 officer candidates per year receive flight training *prior* to call-up.

The relaxation, after 1926, of restrictions on commercial aircraft and sports planes had the equally important side benefit of permitting the open training of large numbers of pilots. The rudiments of flight were taught to large numbers of young men who now flocked to join glider clubs and graduated to the growing numbers of civilian flying schools. At least six of these included camouflaged military training facilities operated by the *Reichswehr*. All fully trained pilots and observers were then grouped together in so-called Publicity or Advertising Squadrons (*Reklamestaffeln*) that, in addition to hiring out their services for commercial skywriting and advertising, also helped out at *Reichswehr* maneuvers by target marking, reconnaissance and liaison. These Advertising Squadrons were, in fact, the first truly operational units of the new German airforce. By 1933, the *Reichswehr* had around 550 fully trained pilots, ready to man the airstaffs and regular formations that would soon be established.[17]

Although the successive Chiefs of the Treaty Navy[18] lacked Seeckt's single-minded loathing for the *Versaillesdiktat*, the Navy did manage similar, if smaller-scale, evasions. It lightly padded the 15,000-sailor limit and built a forbidden reserve by taking short-term volunteers and by integrating Naval organizations into 'civilian' ones. It also created secret arsenals and used proscribed weapons.[19] Evasion initially involved duping the national legislators during the annual naval budget fight in the Reichstag. The ruse used was vastly to overcharge for all items of equipment. This deceit was possible only with the collusion of the successive Weimar chancellors, defense ministers and certain other key senior government officials. The surplus obtained was then used to fund the Navy's numerous illegal projects.

Holland was the main haven for German U-boat development during the early 1920s. This took place in a Krupp subsidiary, the Siderius-owned shipyard of Ingenieur-Kantoor voor Scheepsbouw (I.v.S.) in the Hague, and was worked out jointly by Krupp, von Seeckt and Admiral Behncke, the Chief of the German Navy. Krupp initially sent 30 naval architects and engineers, accompanied by two German navy officers, to Holland to start production. I.v.S. sold submarine plans to Japan, Spain, Finland, Turkey and Holland itself; and additional German naval officers and marine engineers passed through the Hague to supervise construction in these other countries. Production began in Finland on the prototype of the German 250-ton submarines (U-1 to U-24) that would be used in World War II. Simultaneously, I.v.S. negotiated a secret contract with Spanish dictator, Primo de Rivera, to construct in Cadiz a 740-ton U-boat that became the prototype for the World War II 'flag subs', U-25 and U-26. Also Spain, Turkey and Finland let German commanders and crews put the submarines through their sea trials. This, as admitted later, permitted 'the training of camouflaged German naval personnel without diplomatic unpleasantness for the Reich'.[20]

Work in the shipyards of Finland, Holland and Spain had one even more remarkable and direct effect on the future German submarine fleet. By 1934 the prefabricated frame and parts for no less than 12 U-boats had been smuggled into the German naval base at Kiel, awaiting only the order to commence assembly.[21]

The Navy even managed to build a small air arm. It succeeded in purchasing six wartime seaplanes (Friedrichshaven FF-49s) before they could be seized by the Allies as reparations. For cover purposes they were maintained and serviced by the private air transport company of Aero-Lloyd (later Severa) at Kiel and Norderney; and used by the Navy for anti-aircraft gunnery practice, camouflage exercises, target towing and pilot training. The last of these ancient airplanes remained in service until 1934. The few former Great War naval pilots still in the Navy were enabled, from 1924 on, to take refresher flight training in greatest secrecy with Aerosport Company Ltd. at Warnemünde.[22]

Versailles (Art. 171) flatly prohibited tanks and, except for police use, armored cars as well. Consequently, the *Reichswehr* ostensibly contented itself with simulated tanks in its maneuvers — to the vast amusement of the foreign press, which featured photos and descriptions of these wood, canvas and cardboard makeshifts. The undercover reality was less comical, as the *Reichswehr* and German industry were busily designing, building and testing tanks and armored cars throughout this period.

The few armored cars permitted to the German police were of several makes but all of similar (and antiquated) design. Then the Boulogne Note of 23 July 1920 permitted an increase in number to 150 armored cars for police use and allowed a total of 105 for the *Reichswehr* — 15 for each motor transport battalion attached to each of the seven infantry divisions. Vehicle design was to be approved by the Control Commission and construction was to be subject to their inspection. These provisions insured that the Daimler and Erhardt models of 1919–21 were obsolete when built.[23] In any event, the Germans did not cheat in the armored car category until after the withdrawal of the Control Commission in early 1927.

Although Seeckt was committed to mobile warfare, he favored cavalry over armor to achieve it. Still, he and the *Truppenamt* gave limited support to mechanized development, perhaps simply because it was forbidden. Accordingly, as early as 1919, the *Truppenamt* established a small special section to study armored warfare. By 1921 the Inspectorate of Motorized Troops coordinated and directed all mechanized units, including the shadow tank forces.

The consequence of the pioneering work by Joseph Vollmer, Germany's only significant designer and manufacturer of tanks during the Great War, and the Krupp designers was, as stated in a later Krupp memo, that: 'With the exception of the hydraulic safety switch, the basic principles of armament and turret design for tanks had already been worked out in 1926.'[24] In 1926 a German engineer named Ernst Kniepkamp joined the *Heereswaffenamt* for the express purpose of coordinating the various industrial firms engaged in secret armored R&D.

Designs now gave way to prototype production and the scene shifted to Russia where rigorous field testing could take place behind a curtain of secrecy. The site was the Red Army's tank center at Kazan. After a reconnaissance there by a German officer in 1922, at the very beginning of the Russo-German military collaboration, German technicians were permanently stationed at Kazan from 1926 on. And beginning in 1927, several makes of tanks and armored cars were tested there.[25]

Secret orders were placed with German industry in 1926 for the production of tank and armored car prototypes. Ford and Opel were explicitly excluded as potential manufacturers because their American affiliations were thought to make them too insecure for such a delicate undertaking. Production began in earnest and many of these prototypes were immediately smuggled to Kazan for their equally secret testing. First off the mark was Daimler-Benz in 1927 with its so-called Grosstraktor I ('Heavy Tractor'), this being its 'concealed purpose' name to disguise this heavy tank as a hunk of agricultural machinery. Designed by Dr Ferdinand Porsche, this tank was noteworthy for its large 75mm turret-mounted gun. Rheinmetall and Krupp were next, in 1928, with their VK.31 'Light Tractors' of 9.5 tons mounting a 37mm gun in a Swedish-type turret.[26]

Armored cars were produced in the same period. Daimler-Benz Büssing and Magirus entered the field first in 1927. Maffei joined the next year, BMW in 1929, Rheinmetall in 1932 and Demag in 1934. (Krupp did not enter the armored car race until 1936.)

The Swedish Army collaborated secretly with the German covert General Staff on tank development just as it had earlier with aircraft. Thus in 1929, at the age of 40, Major Heinz Guderian, now with the Transport Section of the Operations Department of the *Truppenamt,* drove his first tank as a guest of the Swedish Army's lone tank company. Appropriately, his machine was one of Vollmer's smuggled ex-German alias M-21s.[27]

As Sweden had proved a safe and discreet haven for German rearmament, Krupp acquired a second dummy company there in addition to its Bofors cannon subsidiary. The new Krupp affiliate was the old machinery firm of A.B. Landsverk, located at Landskrona in southern Sweden. It produced its first tank design by 1929 and its first production tank, the fine 11.5 ton L-10 light tank with 37mm gun, appeared in 1931 and entered Swedish service in 1934. A succession of excellent tank and armored car models flowed from Landsverk which now dominated Sweden's armored vehicle industry. These models foreshadowed several of the features that would later appear in the tanks of Germany and Russia, a clear proof of the fruitful collaborative German-Russo-Swedish cross-fertilization.[28]

The Control Commission ended its long surveillance of the Krupp works when it withdrew from Essen in March 1926. Foreign Minister Stresemann now pressed hard for the withdrawal of the Control Commission from all Germany. His timing was excellent for his French and British counterparts, Aristide Briand and Austin Chamberlain, both welcomed an accommodation. They were impatient with the Intelligence from their military advisors that Germany was violating numerous points of disarmament. Briand declared that 'he had no intention of bothering with such petty detail'; he wanted to focus only on 'the larger issues'. Stresemann deliberately dragged out these negotiations to avoid as many concessions as possible. His delaying strategy succeeded. On 11 December, Briand and Chamberlain decided to withdraw the Control Commission the following month, despite their own ambassadors' reports the previous day that Germany was not meeting its disarmament obligations.[29]

On 31 January 1927, as scheduled, the Inter-Allied Military Control Commission was withdrawn from Germany. The Commission's final, detailed report concluded that: 'Germany had never disarmed, had never had the intention of disarming, and for seven years had done everything in her power to deceive and "counter-control" the Commission appointed to control her disarmament.' This report was deliberately ignored and suppressed.[30]

Allied efforts had sometimes penetrated German camouflage. As early as May 1921, only 14 months after Krupp had taken its first steps toward covert rearmament, US Army Intelligence officers concluded from a study of Krupp patents that 26 were for artillery control devices, 18 for electrical fire control apparatus, nine for fuses and shells, 17 for field guns and 14 for heavy railway cannon. Although the US Secretary of War made these details available to the press, they were ignored.[31]

If the Control Commission's snoopers were occasionally successful in ferreting out evidence of evasions by German industry, foreign journalists were not. As Gustav Krupp gleefully put it, the visiting foreign correspondents had been 'hoodwinked' to a man. If they had pooled their individually meager investigative resources, they might have noticed suspicious patterns. For example, all saw various parts of Krupp (after all, it was huge) but none saw certain corners. Moreover, those who brought cameras subsequently found their film rolls overexposed. Before leaving the Krupp works, they had been graciously treated to a luncheon snack at a particular canteen, part of the always *gemütlicher* reception that so impressed journalists such as the *Literary Digest*'s correspondent. While they dined, their cameras were irradiated. Krupp's security men took this extraordinary precaution, not because they feared that the visitors would see, much less understand, anything embarrassing (their conducted tour avoided *those* parts), but because their photos may have inadvertently included drawing board plans that experts at home might recognize for what they actually were.[32]

The Control Commission had the power to inspect, including 'snap' or spot inspections, and the skilled personnel to do this. However the *Abwehr* (and/or Krupp's own security staff) had penetrated the Control Commission and gave ample warning of unannounced snap inspections so that embarrassing paperwork could be hidden. Only rarely did German counter-intelligence fail to warn of snap inspections. Once, for example, Control Commission inspectors managed a genuine surprise visit to the Rohrbach aircraft factory. Unable to remove a Rohrbach 'Roland' experimental three-engine 'transport' (i.e. bomber) in which machine guns had been installed in extra long engine pods, the workmen had only time to move it to the center of the hangar and clutter it up so much with dust covers, staging, ladders and other bits of gear, that it looked like a pile of discarded equipment. The inspectors passed it by without notice.[33]

Some exposés of these numerous Versailles Treaty evasions did appear in the world's press. The earliest serious effort to enlighten the British public about the threat of German rearmament was a long article published with official permission by Brigadier-General Morgan in late 1924, immediately after his resignation from the Control Commision.[34]

As might be suspected, some Control Commission inspectors had been mere time servers or, as in the case of some of the British, actually welcomed German rearmament as a counterweight to France. Thus, one of the senior departing naval inspectors, Commander Fanshawe, told retired Lieutenant Renken, his German opposite number: 'It is now time for us to separate. Both you and I are glad that we are leaving. Your task was unpleasant and so was mine. One thing I should point out. You should not feel that we believed what you told us. Not one word you uttered was true, but you delivered your information in such a clever way that we were in a position to believe you. I want to thank you for this.'[35]

Had arms inspection failed? Did the numerous evasions escape the notice of the Control Commission? Clearly not. The memoirs of Brigadier-General Morgan, for four years a member of the Commission, make plain that much was noticed and the rest suspected, at least by some perceptive members of the Commission.[36] French military Intelligence, the famed Deuxième Bureau, was also reporting many evasions.[37] So too was British military Intelligence, particularly from Holland; the Military Attaché there, A. C. Temperley, was able to piece together a general picture of the Versailles evasions during his four-year tour (1920–1925) in his listening post at the Hague.

The failure had been one not so much of the Control Commission, much less of Intelligence services, but rather of apathy on the part of the Allied governments behind the Commission. As Winston Churchill later commented, strict enforcement 'was neglected while the infringements remained petty, and shunned as they assumed serious proportions'.[38] And Nobel Peace Laureate, Philip Noel-Baker, summing up this sordid episode of treaty evasion, concluded that it proved '*Not* that the system of inspection failed in Germany, but simply that after 1925 it was never enforced'.[39]

III. Clandestine Rearmament, 1927–1935

The Inter-Allied Control Commission had left Germany at the beginning of 1927 and the Conference of Ambassadors sent its final report to the League of Nations Council on 22 July. Henceforward, the League Council would be the only agency authorized to inquire into German disarmament violations. But the League of Nations could only inquire and complain; the Germans easily dragged such matters out by protracted debates and negotiations. Without Control Commission inspectors, the League was blind; without an Army of Occupation, it was powerless.

The withdrawal of the Control Commission did not, however, mean that Germany could immediately begin rearmament; the political climate was not yet ripe. It only meant that design, testing and training could proceed under thinner, less hampering cover. The more cumbersome bits of camouflage could now be dispensed with. Having surrendered their rights of inspection and verification, the Allies were henceforward limited for information to their small, inter-war Intelligence and espionage services. German counter-intelligence and security could cope with much of that; and a judicious mix of official lying and thin cover stories usually sufficed to deceive the foreign press and diplomatic corps.

Krupp now launched a period of so-called 'black production' (*schwarze Produktion*). Manufacture was stepped up on self-propelled guns, torpedo launching tubes, periscopes, armor plate, remote control devices for naval guns and primitive rocket design. The prototype of the magnificent 88-mm AA/AT gun emerged from the drawing board. As one inter-office memo said: 'Of the guns which were being used in 1939–41, the most important were already fully developed in 1933.' So, too, with tanks, which went into production in 1928. Except for the hydraulic safety switch, all other tank components had been worked out by 1926. Artillery test firing ranges went full blast in 1929. And Krupp acquired an enormous, 15,000-ton press, suitable only for making giant cannon.[40]

The *Abwehr* remained under the command of Gempp until 23 June 1927 when he was promoted out and succeeded by Major Günther Schwantes, a cavalryman who had been in the *Abwehr* only a year. Then, the conniving empire-building inside the Defense Ministry by General Kurt von Schleicher led the Ministry to grab the *Abwehr* from the *Truppenamt*. First, in 1928, appropriately on April Fools' Day, Schleicher persuaded his boss, Defense Minister General Wilhelm Groener, to create an *Abwehr* Branch as 'the Defense Ministry's sole Intelligence-acquisition post'. This centralized service combined the *Abwehr* and its Cipher Center, appropriated from the *Truppenamt,* and the small naval Intelligence section, appropriated simultaneously from the Navy. The next year, on 1 March 1929 the *Abwehr* Branch was incorporated, along with several other Ministry offices, into a newly created Minister's Department headed, not surprisingly, by the ambitious Schleicher himself. This administrative shuffle made the *Abwehr* the supraservice military Intelligence agency that it henceforward remained.

To ensure his closest control over the flow of information, Schleicher relieved Schwantes as head of the *Abwehr* Branch and replaced him at the end of 1929 with Lieutenant Colonel Kurt von Bredow, a trusted friend and protégé whose only other qualification was that he had briefly served as an *Abwehr* field officer eight years earlier. Bredow somewhat reorganized and enlarged the *Abwehr* Branch, recruiting employees of German arms firms as agents and travelling to France and Belgium.

Bredow remained chief of the *Abwehr* Branch until June 1932 when Schleicher, who had become Defense Minister, moved Bredow up to replace him in the Minister's Department. Three days later, on 27 June, Schliecher broke with a 66-year-old tradition by appointing a naval officer to head military Intelligence. This new Chief of the *Abwehr,* Commander Conrad Patzig, had been head of the *Abwehr*'s naval group since 1929.

An unusual contribution, literally above and beyond the call of duty, to the *Abwehr/Reichswehr*'s secret capabilities was made at this time. Theodor Rowehl had been a reconnaissance pilot in the Great War, credited with several cross-Channel missions to observe England. Now, he became concerned by the possible threat posed by the new fortifications that Poland was building along the German and East Prussian frontiers. A 1929 treaty between Germany and Poland expressly forbade unauthorized military or civilian overflights of each other's territory and required special permission for aerial cameras. Nevertheless, Rowehl decided to attempt to photograph the forts at a sufficiently high altitude, he hoped, to avoid detection. As a 26-year-old civilian, entirely on his own, he hired a private plane on Sundays and holidays and flew it over the prohibited areas at 13,000 feet. The flights went unchallenged and when he felt he had obtained adequate photo coverage, Rowehl presented his intelligence to astonished government officials. He argued that he could do much more, if money were given to supplement his own slender, private means. The officials were delighted to arrange this service and in 1930 the audacious young patriot became a civilian contract employee of the *Abwehr*.[41]

Rowehl promptly chartered a single aircraft; a singularly suitable one. It was the unique Junkers W-34, the very plane that had the previous year (26 May 1929) set a world's altitude record of 41,800 feet. For the next four years Rowehl flew this superb machine along the Polish border taking oblique photos; and over the target country itself, covering mainly forts and harbors. As before, these sorties attracted no attention and Rowehl's successive *Abwehr* chiefs, Bredow and Patzig, winked away this illegality under the 1929 German-Polish agreement.

Hitler was appointed Chancellor by President Hindenburg on 30 January 1933. His views on 'revenge' against the so-called *Versaillesdiktat* were well known to his intimates; and quiet, verbal understandings were sufficient substitutes for blatant contracts between government officers and arms companies. In anticipation of arms orders, the production of steel soared and stockpiles of strategic metals grew rapidly, including imports of Brazilian zircon ore used only for gun steel.

With the experimental and training air bases in Russia closing down, Göring cast about for a suitable substitute. Mussolini agreed to permit selected German fighter pilots to train with the Regia Aeronautica, at that time one of the world's largest, most modern and efficient air forces.

The first group of the selected pilots were already serving in Lufthansa. They travelled secretly in 1933 to Italy and, posing as South Tyrolean soldiers, were escorted to various Italian Air Force airfields. There they were issued Italian Air Force uniforms and enrolled as students in combat aviation. One of these young pilots, the 21-year-old Adolf Galland, was the future General of Fighters in the *Luftwaffe*.

Training was intensive and included realistic ground attack and support exercises held jointly with the Italian Army. When the course ended a half-year later, in fall 1933, the now highly trained fighter pilots returned to Germany as Lufthansa commercial pilots. Early in 1934 they were placed on the German Air Force active list and a year later, most, including Galland, were commissioned officers in the *Luftwaffe*. The bases in Italy had only been a brief stop-gap to bridge the closing of air bases in Russia and the large-scale opening of new bases in Germany now about to take place.

Conscription into the *Reichswehr* was, of course, forbidden by Versailles, but the Treaty said nothing about a National Labor Service because it did not exist. Therefore, in 1934, Hitler created the National Labor Service (*Reichs-arbeitdienst*) and made it obligatory for all 18-year-old males to spend six months in this rigidly disciplined, mass, national organization, complete with close-order drill with shovels. A reserve Army was also prohibited, but, in July 1933 Hitler authorized the *Reichswehr* to take military jurisdiction of the private, paramilitary Stalhelm and the Nazi SA and SS organizations. Specifically, the *Reichswehr* undertook to train 250,000 SA members as an army reserve.

In April 1933 the Reich Commission for Air Transport became the Ministry of Air Transport (*Reichsluftfährtministerium*) and Hermann Göring was appointed Air Transport Minister, a title designed to perpetuate the fraud that it was a purely civilian occupation, although within a month the Army began handing over its secret military aviation component.

The Paris Air Pact (1926) had relaxed the provisions of Versailles to permit Germany to have 'air police' units and aerial defense. Göring now invoked this to create the German Air Defense Union which gave him control of anti-aircraft artillery and civil air-raid defense.

Hitler wanted something to whip up popular support for his rearmament plans, something that would simultaneously seem to justify to the world the German need for increased arms, albeit 'defense' arms. Göring needed something similar that could give him a military role in the air. The imaginative Propaganda Minister, Dr Joseph Goebbels, therefore, manufactured a suitable 'big lie', an aerial equivalent of Hitler's political 'Reichstag Fire' hoax. Accordingly, on 24 June 1933, the official Nazi newspaper, *Völkischer Beobachter,* bannerheadlined 'FOREIGN AIRCRAFT OVER BERLIN!'. The lead story, which covered the front page, told a dramatic tale of how, the previous day, a formation of several unidentified foreign bombers had violated German airspace, penetrated to Berlin and circled the German capital, dropping insulting leaflets before making their return flights to the east. The implication was that the warplanes were Soviet Russian. The article pointed out that interception had been impossible because the Air Police had no aircraft.[42] Göring, feigning outraged innocence, complained to the British Embassy of Germany's defenselessness against air attack, and pleaded that Britain grant export licenses for enough engines to equip 'a few police planes'. As a result, the Armstrong-Siddeley works shipped over 85 engines from England. By early 1934, the secret air force was operating 44 units from 42 airfields throughout Germany, disguised by civilian cover names.

In January 1934, Hitler astonished the world by signing a ten-year non-aggression pact with Poland. A secret clause of the pact enjoined each party not to engage in espionage on the other's territory. The *Abwehr* Chief, Navy Captain Patzig, summoned his department heads to apprise them of the secret clause, but concluded with the remark: 'It goes without saying that we continue our work.'[43]

Thus, Rowehl's overflights of Poland continued, unnoticed until October, when Defense Minister General Werner von Blomberg made an inspection visit to Kiel-Holtenau airfield. There he innocently asked about an aircraft standing outside one of the hangars and was told it was an *Abwehr* plane used for photo-reconnaissance over Poland. Appalled to learn of flights that risked disrupting Hitler's cherished pact with Poland, Blomberg immediately terminated Rowehl's operations against Poland and soon dismissed Patzig as *Abwehr* Chief.

At this point Rowehl had collected five aircraft and about as many pilots and formally joined the *Reichswehr* as an officer. His small *Abwehr* unit was given the camouflage title of Experimental Post for High Altitude Flights and transferred from Keil-Holtenau to Berlin-Staaken. Prohibited from over-flying Poland, Rowehl turned his cameras on other potential *Luftwaffe* targets. By the end of 1934 his aircraft had begun photographic cover of the USSR, penetrating to the Kronstadt naval yard at Leningrad and the industrial regions around Pskov and Minsk. Other flights were soon exploring the fortified border regions of France and Czechoslovakia.[44]

The armed forces were now given a blank check, the *Wehrmacht* and Navy being told to prepare their own budgets, the government undertaking full responsibility to find the money. An order was placed for six submarines with a sub-a-month program to follow. The naval architects and craftsmen who had been squirreled away in Dutch shipyards returned. Tractor-drawn, quick-firing howitzers were tested and manufacture of armor plate and the great guns was begun for the Navy's battleships whose keels were now laid.

On 4 April 1934, Hitler secretly ordered rearmament, creating the Central Bureau for German Rearmament to coordinate the effort. This not only helped assure the fidelity of the *Reichswehr* chiefs, but firmly cemented his relationship with German industrialists. But camouflage was still the order of the day. Amidst a fanfare of Goebbels' orchestrated propaganda about Hitler's 5.4 billion-mark public works program, the 21 billion for arms went unmentioned. This enormous rearmament budget was skillfully concealed by Economic Minister Hjalmar Schacht's elaborate financial legerdemain. The 'Old Wizard''s main trick was to pay the industrialists special IOUs, called 'Mefo bills', that were accepted in Berlin by a dummy corporation, Metal-lurgische Forschungsgesellschaft, GmbH, representing four private concerns and two ministries that were, in turn, backed by the national treasury. Since the Central Bank eventually rediscounted all the 'Mefo' IOUs, all creditors were paid without a single mark appearing on the record. From 1934 through 1937 Schacht's 'Mefo bills' totalled 12 billion marks all used to finance rearmament. This amount constituted 33 to 38 per cent of the total military expenditures in that crucial period.

Hitler now placed an order with Krupp for the first hundred new tanks, all light models, to be delivered by March 1934 with 650 more to follow a year later. The German engineers and foremen who had been serving quietly with Landsverk in Sweden were recalled. The blueprints were brought out of hiding, the Krupp truck assembly line at Krawa shut down to retool and tank production began. By October 1935 the first three Panzer divisions had come into existence; a fact duly reported by agents of French Military Intelligence.[45]

By withdrawing their arms inspectors, early in 1927, the Allies had cut themselves off from their best source of intelligence about German military developments. The foreign press corps was, as we have seen, hardly a paragon of aggressive investigative journalism. The international business community contributed little information because the German arms industry limited its foreign contacts to German-controlled companies (as in Holland and Sweden) or ones that benefited from continued secrecy (as in Spain, Finland and Russia). Leaks to and public disclosures in the Reichstag also diminished. And the *Reichswehr* and its collaborators in industry and government had improved their security following the occasional embarrassing disclosures of the early 1920s.

The Allies and other concerned governments were left with only two regular sources of information on German arms: official German statements and their own Intelligence services. But these various inter-war organizations were understaffed following demobilization in 1918 and underbudgeted after the start of the Great Depression in 1929. Only the Russians maintained large services, but their size was not reflected in efficiency and, besides, they were targeted mainly on Britain and the United States. The French maintained perhaps the best services and their reduced effort was at least concentrated on Germany. The British services were also highly professional but were very thin on the ground in Germany. The Americans operated mere skeleton services, dependent for data on military attachés and foreign service political officers who, with very rare exceptions, lacked Intelligence training. The Poles operated a centralized Intelligence service (the world's first) but it was targeted on Russia, as well as Germany. Czechoslovak Military Intelligence had only 20 men, $120,000 per annum and no current Intelligence on Germany. Consequently, even when suspicions about German activities were raised by rumors, reports or leaks, the various Intelligence and espionage services were seldom able to mount the sort of intensive search effort necessary for verification.

With the Allied inspectors (and their right of 'snap' inspection) gone, the task of maintaining security eased considerably for the Germans. It was no longer necessary to work under such deep cover, or to hide plans and documents. A bold '*Geheim*' ('Secret') stamped on the papers usually sufficed to keep them from prying eyes. For example, after 1932 the Reich Defense Ministry simply stopped publishing its lists of active military officers. Unlike British, French and American practice they now treated this list as secret information. As well they might, for these lists contained two forbidden facts: one, the services had exceeded the 4,000 *Reichswehr* and 1,500 *Reichsmarine* officer limits (albeit by only small amounts) — British Military Intelligence suspected this but could not prove it; and two, rapidly increasing numbers of officers had received pilot training. The overworked French Military Intelligence had been trying to monitor precisely such biographical detail but was, henceforward, severely hampered by the lack of these officer lists.

Occasional Intelligence coups were, however, still possible. For instance, the French Deuxième Bureau was able to learn from close study of the German government budgets that the *Reichswehr* and *Reichsmarine* were being permitted to overspend their already large proportion (40 per cent in 1929–30) of government funds. Valuable input to these fiscal analyses were supplied by the published texts of speeches made by opposition deputies during Reichstag debates.[46] Other Versailles evasions, such as the training of pilots in Russia, were also partly known to the British and French Intelligence services and duly reported by them to their governments. However, the governments themselves chose to keep most of this Intelligence secret.[47]

A secret French dossier reported the *Reichswehr*'s concealed short-service enlistments, the enormous (technically legal) proportion of NCOs, of whom there were something like one for every two privates, the illegal General Staff (*Truppenamt*), the large numbers of militarized police in barracks, the training and equipping of various paramilitary units, the secret arming with forbidden weapons, the covert training of pilots in Russia and the existence of the 'Black Luftwaffe'. The dossier also outlined the scheme of industrial mobilization. Despite such comprehensive and believed Intelligence, political considerations prevailed and on 8 September 1926 Germany was admitted to the League of Nations.

IV. Overt Rearmament and Bluff, 1935–1939

In the spring of 1935 Hitler took the political decision unilaterally to abrogate the Versailles Treaty and publicly to display German rearmament. This did not mean, however, that deception was at an end. It only changed its form.

On Saturday 16 March 1935, the eve of Germany's Memorial Day, the Führer decreed universal military conscription and proclaimed his intention to build up the existing 10-division, 100,000-man Army to 36 divisions with a strength of 550,000. Two months later, Hitler secretly promulgated the Reich Defense Law. The *Reichswehr* was superseded by the Wehrmacht. The *Truppenamt* came out of hiding to become publicly the *Generalstab*. The naval *Reichsmarine* was renamed *Kriegsmarine*. And the Defense Ministry became the War Ministry. The 'defense' forces were now openly a war machine.

Göring soon took jealous note of the impressive successes of the *Abwehr*'s photo-reconnaissance unit headed by Theodor Rowehl. Accordingly, in 1936 Rowehl and his small unit were plucked whole from the *Abwehr* and placed in the *Luftwaffe* General Staff as the Special Purposes Squadron of the Fifth (Intelligence) Branch. It quickly grew in size to a full squadron of about a dozen planes with improved cameras, photo-interpretation staff and hand-picked aircrew. Rowehl also had his choice of aircraft types and the superb single-engined He-70 'Blitz' was soon replaced by the He-111 that Heinkel had just unveiled as the world's fastest passenger aircraft. With a crew of four, this fine, twin-engined machine had a cruising range of 2,000 miles and a ceiling of 28,000 feet. They flew against Czechoslovakia and England in violation of air treaties with those two countries and against France and Russia as well. Rowehl's planes flew disguised as commercial aircraft, their crews in mufti. Over public targets, such as cities, they operated at normal altitudes while pretending to test possible new commercial routes; against military targets they flew at maximum altitude to avoid detection and, if detected (by sound or condensation trails), identification. Even when one He-111 went down in the

USSR, the Russians did not complain; perhaps its 'civilian' disguise enabled Stalin to avoid embarrassment.[48]

The year 1935 marked a new stage in German propaganda policy. It produced a new myth and introduced a period of bluff. The myth was that the *Luftwaffe* had been conjured into existence out of nothing but the sheer will of the Führer and the genius of Göring and German industry and engineers. The more than 15 years of careful, secret preparation (design, prototypes, testing, recruiting and training) was officially forgotten. The sole purpose of this myth was to exaggerate the achievement and potency of Hitler's Third Reich at the expense of the solid progress under the Weimar Republic. Henceforward, there was no fear of publicizing the existence of the *Luftwaffe* and Army.

The only German fear, now that the Army and *Luftwaffe* were brought into the open, was that they would be seen for what they were, weak instruments of Hitler's aggressive foreign policy. The *Wehrmacht* timetable estimated 1942 or 1943 as the first year when it would be ready to go to war. Consequently, deception was continued. Now, however, it switched from dissimulative deception that concealed the facts of secret preparations to simulative deception that concealed weakness.[49]

Hitler's policy switch from shy concealment to intimidating bluff in the diplomatic arena was coordinated with Göring who paralleled it in public announcements. Just as Hitler used Eden as his channel, Göring used Mr Ward Price as his. Price was the bemonocled roving correspondent for Lord Rothermere's London *Daily Mail*. Göring had chosen well, as both Price and his newspaper proved most accommodating to the Nazi regime throughout the mid and late 1930s, uncritically publishing all the disinformation that the top German leaders were pleased to provide them. In the first stage, in February 1934, Göring told Price and his readers that Germany possessed a grand total of only 300 aircraft, of which many were obsolete and none were capable of being used in a military role. He added that the aviation industry was so weak that at least two years would be required before it would even be possible to start building an air force, one that he assured Price would be purely defensive. Only 13 months later, on 9 March 1935, Göring summoned Price to give him the scoop of the year, proclaiming the existence of the *Luftwaffe*.[50] That same day, Göring also summoned the British and French air attachés to give them, officially, the same news.

The sharp contrast between these two successive policies of concealment and bluff is epitomized by Hitler's personal assurances to Anthony Eden, who was then Lord Privy Seal. In February 1934, on the occasion of Eden's first meeting with the German Chancellor, Hitler flatly asserted that Germany was defenseless in the air; that having no desire for aggression she had no need of offensive weapons and was prepared to renounce all military aircraft if other nations would do the same. He promised to limit the *Luftwaffe* to 30 per cent of the number of planes of its combined neighbours, but in no case to exceed 50 per cent of the French Armée de l'Air and to comprise purely short-range defensive aircraft, no bombers. Then, just 13 months later, on 26 March 1935, only 16 days after Göring had publicly unveiled the *Luftwaffe*, Hitler informed Eden that the *Luftwaffe* had already achieved 'parity' with the RAF. To illustrate this, Hitler displayed a table that put British air strength at 2,100 machines, including reserves. Knowing that actual RAF firstline strength in Britain was only 453, plus 130 auxiliaries, the Foreign Office queried the German Air Ministry about the precise meaning of Hitler's claim to 'parity'. The disturbing reply was that Germany had 900 planes. Foreign Secretary Simon read this as a 30 per cent *superiority* for the Germans.[51]

The essence of the new propaganda was bluff, to portray a force far stronger than it was. Accordingly, it was shown off at its best in photo magazines that caught the world's attention; at the vast Nazi rallies at Nuremberg; by entering souped-up, prototype aircraft in international airshows (1936-1939); and by giving carefully planned conducted tours to visiting British, French and American experts (1936-1938). All the military attachés and selected foreign dignitaries were invited to the first, full-scale maneuvers (1937); maneuvers and tours specially designed to imply more than was shown. The Condor Legion fighting in Spain (1936-1939) was publicized to prove the excellence of German 'volunteers' and equipment.

The new *Wehrmaht* was a gigantic bluff, but a bluff that served Hitler's purposes superbly. His immediate goal was to recover the borderlands that had been lost at Versailles; and for three-and-a-half years, from early 1936 until final confrontation in late 1939, the *Wehrmacht* gave him a series of bloodless victories over relatively stronger armies.

Hitler's first target was the Rhineland demilitarized buffer zone. On 7 March 1936, in violation of both Versailles and the Locarno Treaty, the *Wehrmacht* reoccupied the Rhineland. This coup was achieved by the *Wehrmacht*'s single division of infantry, marching under strict orders to retreat literally on the mere first sight of any French Army patrol. Such extraordinary orders were based on wisdom, not cowardice, for although Hitler had threatened publicly to send 'six extra divisions into the Rhineland', the *Wehrmacht*'s entire combat strength mustered only four brigades against 30 French *divisions*. (The *Wehrmaht had* had ten divisions, but they were broken up five months earlier to provide the cadre for the projected 36-division Army.)[52]

Although the *Wehrmacht* had deployed only its one division and placed three battalions, totalling 3,000 men across the Rhine, British Intelligence showed four divisions totaling 35,000 troops on its Rhineland enemy order of battle map. William L. Shirer, Berlin bureau chief for Universal Service, accepted a figure of four divisions, or about 50,000 men. Incredibly, French Intelligence believed the German strength *inside* the Rhineland to be 265,000.

On their part, the French simply stood back, their Army refusing to march unless the British marched with them. Britain refused. It was an astonishing victory. As Hitler later admitted, 'we would have had to withdraw with our tails between our legs, for the military resources at our disposal would have been wholly inadequate for even a moderate resistance'. Among the most astonished were the *Wehrmacht* commanders who had expected defeat.

Luftwaffe deployment comprised three squadrons of fighters (armed but with unsynchronized and, therefore, useless guns) and three squadrons of dive bombers (newly organized and inadequately trained).[53] However, Galland's view that it was a 'bluff' force still holds. The British were still deluded by Hitler's year-old claim that the *Luftwaffe* had achieved parity with the RAF.

Beginning in the fiscal year 1935–36, the *Luftwaffe* was ready to begin mass production. The budget had grown rapidly from $30 million, in the fiscal year 1933–34, to $52 million in the fiscal year 1934–35. Now, in the fiscal year 1935–36 it was allotted $85 million in its official budget. However, that year it also received $750 million in a special black fund financed by interest-bearing notes sold secretly by the government to the *Reichsbank*. This elaborate scheme to circumvent public debate in the Reichstag was the invention of *Reichsbank* President Schacht. His intention was to keep these transactions secret to escape both inflation inside Germany and loss of confidence in the Reichsmark abroad.

Göring's Air Ministry understood that efficient mass production required selecting a few promising types from among the numerous aircraft prototypes currently being test flown. For its medium bomber, it chose Ernst Heinkel's He-111, which had its first test flight on 24 February 1935. Like its He-70 predecessor, it was a bomber camouflaged as a civil transport. In this mufti version, the He-111 carried ten passengers, four forward and six aft, separated by an empty compartment amidship that Lufthansa advertised as a smoking lounge. In fact, it was the bomb bay. Series production began, but the first ten proved unwieldy in flight and were rejected by the *Luftwaffe*. (Heinkel later sold them at a handsome profit to Chiang K'ai-shek.) An improved version quickly followed that was accepted by the *Luftwaffe* and serial production started in earnest.

The civil transport version of the He-111 was unveiled to the public at the Berlin-Templehof airfield in January 1936. However, Lufthansa was not destined to receive this high-performance aircraft. Instead it went to Theodor Rowehl's secret, high-altitude, photo-reconnaissance squadron of the *Luftwaffe* as replacement for its He-70s.

At this point, the Air Ministry decided to adopt the He-111 as its main medium bomber and mass production was ordered. Accordingly, Colonel Fritz Loeb, from Colonel Wilhelm Wimmer's Technical Office, informed Ernst Heinkel that the Air Ministry wanted him to build a separate factory that would produce exclusively He-111s and at the then prodigious rate of 100 per month. The astounded Herr Heinkel balked at the enormous cost, coming as it did before he had paid off his new factory at Marienehe. Colonel Loeb, aware of the secret funds available in the 1935–36 *Luftwaffe* budget, announced that the *Luftwaffe* would underwrite the entire costs of Heinkel's new plant. It was to be ultramodern with carefully dispersed sections to minimize its vulnerability to enemy air attack, its own air raid shelters, and a self-contained fire department. When Heinkel pointed out that dispersal reduced production efficiency and hence lowered profits, Colonel Loeb merely answered: 'Don't worry about it, it isn't your money.' Heinkel agreed, and a suitable site was found at Oranienburg. Plans were completed at the beginning of April 1936 and ground was broken on 4 May.[54]

Exactly one year later, on 4 May 1937, the first Oranienburg-built He-111 bomber taxied off the assembly line to be greeted by a cheering throng of thousands of workers and guests. Oranienburg was, henceforth, the public display case of the new German aircraft industry. The *Luftwaffe* used it freely to impress, and intimidate, foreign visitors.

Göring, with Hitler's permission, took the occasion of the Fourth International Military Air Competition held at Dübendorf, Zürich, Switzerland, in the last week of July 1937, as a fine opportunity to propagandize his new *Luftwaffe*. The crowd, which included air force observers from many countries, was awed by the apparent display of German aerial strength. The superb little combat observation and liaison Fiesler 'Storch' hovered at 32 mph without stalling; but it was merely a pre-production model. The beautiful, streamlined Heinkel He-112 fighter flashed past; but it had already been rejected by the *Luftwaffe*. A team of five Messerschmidt Me-109s easily captured first, second and third places in the 228-mile race; took first in the 31.4 mile circuit and another first in the climb-and-dive contest. A sleek, silver, twin-engine Dornier Do-17 'Flying Pencil' medium bomber, complete with military markings won the Alpine Circuit with a 280 mph performance; an amazing 30 mph faster than any non-German *fighters* present. It seemed an uncatchable bomber. The stunned French and British observers did not know the crucial fact that this 'bomber was only a handmade, specially souped-up, single plane'; the real production models were being turned out with smaller engines that gave a top speed 30 mph under that displayed at Zürich.

The Air Ministry had conducted a series of comparative test flights at Travemünde, back in October 1935, to determine the one fighter plane that would be adopted for mass production. The winner was Willy Messerschmidt's easy-to-assemble Bf-109. It was a clear choice over the runner-up He-112, which was a more promising performer but grossly over-engineered with 2,885 separate parts and 26,864 rivets. This defeat for his He-112 only served to spur Ernst Heinkel, who considered Messerschmidt an upstart, to go back to the drawing board and return with a winner. The result was the magnificent He-100. It had only a third as many parts and half the rivets of its He-112 forebear. It was first flown on 22 January 1938 and on 5 June, with the head of the *Luftwaffe*'s Technical Office, General Ernst Udet at the controls, it set a new world air speed record at 394.6 mph; a spectacular 50 mph faster than the then current record held by Italy.

The next day every major newspaper in Europe featured the German air triumph. Some careful readers were no doubt alarmed that Propaganda Minister Goebbels' press release had declared this custom-built, experimental model to be the production version of the long-discarded He-112 or the 'He-112U', a design that, in fact, existed only in Goebbels' imagination.

Hitler's best opportunity to portray the illusory German might was offered in 1936 by the Civil War in Spain. It also enabled the *Luftwaffe*, Army and Navy to give their pilots and other military specialists some real combat blooding and to battle-test their latest equipment. It was a showcase operation, but one that represented a proportionately far greater drain on Germany's available strength, a point not widely appreciated. Moreover, because she made a recognized contribution to Franco's victory, and because Russia ended among the losers, Germany received a grudging recognition from the fearful world that she was a major military power.

In addition, the *Luftwaffe* and *Wehrmacht* gained nearly 14,000 combat experienced pilots, aircrewmen, tankmen and anti-aircraft crewmen in the 32 months of battle. They tested a number of new weapon systems, such as the Messerschmidt Bf-109 fighter, the Junkers Ju-87 'Stuka' dive bomber and the superb dual-purpose 88mm anti-tank/anti-aircraft gun. All these would become major weapons in the upcoming World War II. They tried out several new tactics, such as air-ground support and 'carpet' (saturation) bombing. And commanders learned some strategic lessons, as when in 1937, Condor Legion Commander 'Sander' (General Hugo von Sperrle) gutted the Basque town of Guernica with his He-111 medium bombers. This was the same weapon and tactic that three years later, as General-Fieldmarshal commanding Air Fleet 3, he would deploy against London.

While the Spanish Civil War continued with German aid, Hitler launched a further series of land grabs. In each case the then current mix of allied states possessed a combined strength quite sufficient to have called Hitler's bluff with relative impunity. But, mesmerized by the German propaganda that exaggerated the strength of the *Wehrmacht* and *Luftwaffe*, and hoping to appease Hitler's appetite, they failed to move. Hitler did so instead. In March 1938 he annexed Austria by a bloodless invasion. In September, at the Munich meeting, he bulldozed France and Britain into surrendering the Czechoslovak border region to Germany.

Munich was not only a failure of Anglo-French nerve, it was an enormous failure of Intelligence. We now know two things that were, at best, uncertain at the time. Hitler himself was not bluffing. At this juncture he fully intended to invade Czechoslovakia. But the *Wehrmacht was* bluffing, it almost certainly could not have succeeded against Czechoslovakia and France, not even counting Britain and possibly the USSR. The French Deuxième Bureau counted 90 German divisions (plus 30 reserve) when, in fact, the *Wehrmacht* had only 42 divisions (plus seven reserve). The French had 65 (plus 35 reserve) and the Czechs a crack, well-entrenched force of 32 (plus six reserve). Thus, French Intelligence reported an uncomfortable parity when the real order of battle gave the Allies a better than two-to-one advantage. Similar Allied Intelligence miscalculations applied to the *Luftwaffe* and armor, to deployments and mobilization levels. The Allies succumbed to a combination of fear, self-delusion and German deception.[55]

Two specific examples can be given to show how the Germans directed their campaigns of disinformation by using visiting experts to carry back tales of German invincibility. The primary target of intimidation was the French. Accordingly, in August 1938, as the Czechoslovak crisis was heating up under Hitler's pressure, Hermann Göring invited the chiefs of the French Armée de l'Air to an inspection tour of the *Luftwaffe*. General Joseph Vuillemin, Chief of the Air General Staff, promptly accepted and brought along several key members of his staff. His guide, General Milch, showed Vuillemin huge and well-furnished *Luftwaffe* barracks. A mass bombing display was laid on. He took him to Berlin-Döberitz to view the pampered Richthofen Wing, where Vuillemin was walked past long rows of brand new Messerschmidt Me-109 fighters; their tall, stern pilots in full battle dress drawn up at attention by their planes. All this was mere conditioning for the final act of the tour, one in which the Germans had laid a careful trap.

Vuillemin and his staff were now conducted about the busy, ultra-modern Heinkel works at Oranienburg by Milch, Udet and Heinkel himself. Dozens of He-111 medium bombers were flowing off the mass production assembly line. He saw the immaculate air-raid shelters, deep underground with 'everything in readiness, even down to ten sharpened pencils on every desk'. He watched an He-111 pushed to its limit on a single engine. Udet then took Vuillemin up in his personal courier plane to view the sprawling factory. As Udet brought the slow plane in at near stalling speed, the moment he had carefully planned with Milch and Heinkel for his passenger's benefit arrived. Suddenly a Heinkel He-100 streaked past at full throttle, a mere blur and a hiss. Both planes landed and the Germans took their startled French visitors over to inspect the sleek 'He-112U'. Milch explained that the aircraft (one of only three He-100s ever built) was the *Luftwaffe*'s latest production fighter. 'Tell me, Udet,' Milch asked with feigned casualness, 'how far along are we with mass production?' Udet, on cue, replied, 'Oh, the second production line is ready and the third will be within two weeks'. Vuillemin looked crestfallen and blurted out to Milch that he was 'shattered'. Later, in the privacy of their limousine, Vuillemin confided to François-Poinçet that he was depressed by what he had seen of the *Luftwaffe* and glumly predicted that: 'should war break out as you expect late in September, there won't be a single French plane left within a fortnight!'[56]

The French air delegation returned to Paris with the defeatist word that the *Luftwaffe* was unbeatable, but this opinion was not fully shared by the resident Deuxième Bureau officer in Berlin, Assistant Air Attaché Paul Stehlin who observed that: 'The Germans set out to make a great impression on him [Vuillemin]. They succeeded and Vuillemin's opinions had more effect than they deserved upon the decisions of our government.'[57] Stehlin was less gullible, but Vuillemin had the rank and influence.

The other noteworthy instance of German disinformation was directed against American and, indeed, world opinion. The unwitting instrument was Colonel Charles A. Lindbergh who, beginning in 1936 made three trips to Germany at the request of American military Intelligence. Lindbergh was brought in by US military attaché Truman Smith specifically to ferret out better Intelligence on the *Luftwaffe*. On its part, the *Luftwaffe*, from Göring and Milch and Udet down, were charming hosts. Literally 'charming', for Lindbergh accepted their false production figures, future plans that were never fulfilled and their pretense that the *Luftwaffe* was already, in 1936, the world's most powerful air force. After his second visit to the Reich, in October 1937, Lindbergh reported that the *Luftwaffe* had a vast airfleet of 10,000 (of which 5,000 were serviceable bombers) and was building between 500 and 800 planes per month (with a capability of 20,000 per year); statistics that, he pointed out, made the *Luftwaffe* 'stronger than that of all other European countries combined'. The truth was that the *Luftwaffe* then totalled only 3,315 aircraft (of which only 1,246 were serviceable bombers); and during the Munich crisis, the *Luftwaffe* was actually able to mobilize only 1,230 first-line aircraft (including 600 bombers and 400 fighters). Production was, in fact, way below 300 planes per month. But Lindbergh's misinformation circulated on the eve of Munich throughout the US, Britain and France, where it was accepted credulously by such persons as French Air Minister Guy la Chambre, French Foreign Minister Georges Bonnet and US Ambassador to Britain Joseph P. Kennedy. When British Prime Minister Neville Chamberlain flew to Germany the week before Munich he carried a summary of Lindbergh's report. Two weeks after Munich a grateful Göring presented Lindbergh with the Service Cross of the German Eagle.[58]

During March 1939 the *Wehrmacht* occupied the rest of Czechoslovakia, again without resistance. Later that same month the port city of Memel was also simply annexed from Lithuania by the German Navy. In June the Danzig Free State was virtually occupied by German forces thinly disguised as local, volunteer 'Free Corps'.

At 4.45 a.m., dawn on 1 September 1939, the *Wehrmacht* launched its surprise invasion of Poland. Despite the existing Anglo-French treaty guarantees to Poland, Hitler still hoped that France and Britain, particularly Britain, would remain as irresolute as they had over Czechoslovakia. In his speech delivered at 10 a.m. that same day to the Reichstag and simultaneously broadcast to the world he said: 'For more than six years now, I have been engaged in building up the German Armed Forces. During this period more than ninety billion Reichsmarks were spent building up the *Wehrmacht*. Today, ours are the best equipped armed forces in the world, and they are superior to those of 1914. My confidence in them can never be shaken.'[59]

Hitler's 90 billion Reichsmarks claim was a gross exaggeration, if not a deliberate lie, to encourage his people and to overawe his enemies. Nonetheless, it was widely credited. Although the amount is not entirely fictitious, it is a misrepresentation. Actually, it was the approximate *total* government expenditure for the period; only about 50 billion Reichsmarks having been spent on armaments. As one postwar German economist remarked: 'Public views of the scale of armament were very much exaggerated. The German government at the time did nothing to contradict the exaggerated ideas; on the contrary they were desirable propaganda, producing the illusion of a warlike strength which in reality was not available on that scale.'[60]

Hitler's luck in bluffing appeared to have run out with the Polish invasion in September 1939 when the Poles chose to fight and after two days of ragged indecision, Britain and France joined the battle. However, his luck still held to the degree that the powerful Franco-British forces limited themselves to mere pinprick attacks. Incredibly, they still thought they could do business with Hitler during the half-year period they called the 'phoney war'. Meanwhile, the *Wehrmacht* had six months' grace to build its strength at a more rapid rate than either Britain or France.

Finally, in April 1940, Hitler invaded Denmark and Norway and the following month, by his all-out onslaught into France, shattered the last illusions about his aggressive intentions. But only those illusions concerning his intentions were shattered, for the illusion of *Wehrmacht* might was actually enhanced by the blitzkrieg victory in France.

Even that late in her German rearmament program Germany had only just managed to reach overall parity with her combined enemies in order of battle. French Military Intelligence reported a total of 190 German divisions in April when, in fact, five months later the *Wehrmacht* had managed to mobilize only 157 divisions. In fact, German production began its prodigious growth only after mid-1942, when Albert Speer took over as an effective Minister of Armaments. By then it was already too late, as Allied production had been outstripping that of Germany since 1939. Even the shaky French war economy was catching up in the race with Germany after having slipped suddenly behind after 1935; British aircraft production was also gaining on that of Germany and would achieve parity the following year. And in naval warship construction, British, US and even French production exceeded that of Germany by 1939.

How had this situation, one that boded ill for German hopes of victory, come about? It arose from basically two circumstances: deliberate policy plus self-deception. Hitler's policy was, from the outset, to portray the maximum of publicly visible strength, even when this portrayal was at the price of real military strength. In other words, the bluff policy required that 'armament depth', that is, long-term investment in strategic raw material stockpiles, expansion of military production capacity and buildup of military spare parts take a lower priority than 'armament breadth', that is, the stress on sheer numbers of planes, tanks, guns, troops, divisions, etcetera, that would show up most impressively on the order of battle charts of Germany's opponents. The consequence of choosing this latter option was that on the outbreak of war in 1939 the *Wehrmacht* had only enough ammunition for six weeks of war, the *Luftwaffe* bombs enough for only three months, and the war economy as a whole, raw material stockpiles for only nine to twelve months.

By opting for show over substance, Hitler deliberately made the better choice for a strategy of bluff but the poorer one in the event of war. Success, initially in bluff and later in quick battlefield victories, fostered hubris, that insidious arrogance fed by excessive pride. Convinced of his own infallibility, Hitler finally overreached in 1941, attacking Russia and then declaring war on the US. In the end, it seems that the German leadership had also succeeded in deceiving itself.

V. Covert German-Soviet Military Collaboration 1921–1933

During the years between 1919 and Hitler's assumption of power in 1933, an intimate, continuing and entirely covert collaboration, masked as 'commercial' relations or other subterfuges, existed between the *Reichswehr* and the Red Army. Beginning, slowly and cautiously, with feelers as early as 1919, this collaboration became quite close in 1921, well before the Russo-German Rapallo Pact of 1922. The Soviet Union enabled Germany to evade the Versailles prohibition against training artillery and tank officers and developing aviation, naval and chemical warfare by having the Red Army provide secret training and experimental facilities to German officers on

Soviet territory in return for German military expertise and supervision in arms factories. The closest secrecy was observed by both parties; the Germans to avoid diplomatic embarrassment under the Versailles Treaty, the Russians to avoid both international complications and undercutting the anti-*Reichswehr* propaganda of the German Communist Party (KPD).[61]

Formal Russo-German relations were opened by the signing in April 1921 of a Trade Agreement. As a result, talks were begun on the economic and technical aspects of the military situation and Seeckt even sent two envoys to Russia. Then, early in 1922, the former Allies called a conference in Genoa to ponder the problems of German war debt and Russian status. However, the Germans and Russians pre-empted by pulling out of Genoa and hastily convening their own bilateral conference at Rapallo in neutral Switzerland. The Russo-German Treaty concluded at Rapallo in April specified friendly relations and economic agreements.

This published treaty was merely the most superficial manifestation of a still largely concealed policy and active collaborative operation which remained undetected by nearly 600 Allied inspectors of German disarmament. Because of the peculiar circumstances surrounding the publication of the Rapallo Treaty, the foreign press and governments openly speculated about possible secret political or military clauses. Soviet Foreign Commissar Chicherin promptly denied this in a note to his French counterpart, declaring 'in the most categorical terms that the treaty of Rapallo does not contain a single secret clause, military or political, nor any such kind of clause whatever, and that the Russian Government is not a party to any act the operation of which is directed against the interests of France or of any other nation'.[62]

The secret German organization for military collaboration with Russia was directed out of Berlin, jointly, by the Defense Office of the *Reichswehr* Ministry and the *Truppenamt*. These two offices directed the three *Reichswehr* bases in Russia: the Air Training Center, established in 1924 north of Voronezh at Lipetsk; the School of Gas Warfare, opened in 1927 or 1928 at 'Tomka', an invented covername for Torski near Saratov on the lower Volga; and the Tank Corps School at Kazan on the middle Volga, created by 1926. Liaison was maintained through both the German Embassy and a special *Reichswehr* office in Moscow, the Zentrale Moskau ('Z.Mo.').

The initial contingents of men and materiel were smuggled aboard Russian vessels at Stettin and other German Baltic ports and shipped to Leningrad. *Reichswehr* personnel traveled in civilian clothes with faked passports and assumed names. Transit was arranged by two ostensible commercial trading companies, actually disguised *Reichswehr* offices. Items of military equipment that could not be effectively hidden or camouflaged, such as new types of bombs, were smuggled across the Baltic at night, or in foggy weather by *Reichswehr* officers in small sailing vessels. Aircraft were flown, usually at night, at high altitudes and in one hop. After their tour in Russia, the German soldiers and civilians returned as passengers on Russian ships from Leningrad, landing unobserved by climbing over the dikes of the Kiel Canal at night.[63]

This smuggling organization was so efficient that after 1925 it even managed on a routine basis to return the British-made aero-engines to their home factory for overhaul and then back to Russia without the deception being spotted. These were the 450-horsepower Napier-Lion engines carried by the 50 Fokker D-13s and the eight Heinkel HD-17s at Lipetsk. As its time came for periodic overhaul, each engine was crated and shipped via Holland to the British Napier factory. After repair, the engines were sent back to Lipetsk by the reverse route. British Napier simply assumed the work was being done for the Dutch who were regular customers. Later, when the necessary non-metric tools had been imported and mechanics specially trained, the British engines were repaired on site in the workshops at Lipetsk itself.

Increasing numbers of German officers passed through Moscow Central, particularly after 1927, and included more high ranking officers (such as Colonels Keitel and von Brauchitsch from the *Truppenamt*) to tour the arms factories and testing/training centers at Lipetsk, Kazan and Torski. These senior visitors, Junker aristocrats and other conservatives to a man, traveled in mufti and, ironically, as the 'Communist German Workers' Delegations'.[64]

The Air Training Center opened in 1924 at the underused Russian aerodrome at Lipetsk, located about 250 miles SSW of Moscow and north of Voronezh. From 1925 to 1930, the mixed military and civilian staff numbered about 200 Germans, of whom some 50 ran the military training courses. After 1930, the staff grew to about 300 to handle the enlarged program of technical trials of aircraft and equipment. The annual cost of running Lipetsk was two million marks (200,000 British pounds), a sum carefully concealed in the *Reichswehr* Ministry's budget.

In addition to the numerous German-built prototype aircraft tested at Lipetsk, the air training school there had initially 52 military aircraft in 1925 which were increased to 66 in 1929. These were of German, Dutch or Swedish manufacture and all flew without national markings. Trainees arrived from Germany with a six-month preliminary course in tactical theory and radio operation. Then, at Lipetsk, they received a one-year course in navigation, a six-month course in radio, gunnery and bombing and a 20- to 22-week course as fighter pilots. Some experience was also obtained in joint operations with the Red Army and Air Force. By the time the School closed in late 1933 it had trained 120 fighter pilots, over 300 air and ground crewmen (mostly officers) and nearly 450 highly qualified administrative and training staff. Some 100 of the officer-pilots had also received additional specialized training as artillery observers.

Despite the intensive, ramified and lengthy duration of the Soviet-German military collaboration during this period, the two governments succeeded for several years in maintaining general secrecy and, when finally exposed, managed quite well to evade all but the most meek repercussions from the League of Nations, foreign powers, the German Communist Party and the Moscow Comintern. Seemingly, all members of the KPD were excluded from this plan, and on the Comintern side, apparently only Karl Radek was fully involved.[65]

Despite the false rumors of secret political and military clauses in the Rapallo Treaty and the occasional authentic press and Intelligence leaks,[66] the detailed story of Russo-German collaboration was first broken only on 3 December 1926 in the *Manchester Guardian.* Two days later, the *Vorwärts,* official newspaper of the German Social Democratic Party (SPD) reprinted the *Guardian*'s account and provided additional details. On the 16th a *Pravda* editorial and an article by Radek in *Izvestiya* admitted the existence of German-built factories in Russia, but denied any Soviet arms aid to the *Reichswehr.* Subsequent debates in the Reichstag in 1926 and 1928 centered on Social Democratic charges and frank government admissions of the military and industrial alliance. Finally in June 1932 British journalist Cecil Melville published a detailed and nearly full account in book form.

Subsequent memoirs by intimate participants, such as German General von Seeckt and Soviet chemist, General V. N. Ipatiev, as well as the German archives seized after WWII, all confirm the essential accuracy of the early spectacular and detailed charges which were once received with great skepticism, if not outright disbelief. Following the flurry of public revelations in 1926, the Germans and Russians tightened their security, and little more leaked out about their continuing collaboration.

It was Hitler who, during the first three years of his dictatorship, dissolved all material and policy links between the Red Army and the *Reichswehr.* In mid-1933, on Hitler's orders, the training courses and factories in Russia were shut down and the few residual collaborative links were terminated by the signing on 25 November 1935 of the German-Japanese Anti-Comintern Pact with its secret provisions — soon revealed to the Kremlin by a GRU Intelligence coup — pointing aggressively toward Russia.

VI. International Arms Cheating: The Naval Tonnage Example

The architects of navies desire to build warships and fleets that are more powerful than those of their opposition; but on the other hand, they recognize that to do so will only provoke the opposition to follow, or, worse, anticipate this growth with still larger ships and numbers. Even great powers often shy away from the economic costs of arms races; and most naval limitation treaties are, in large part, an effort to limit such mutually costly competition. One possible solution to this dilemma is deception; to design and build the desired larger classes of warships but to conceal this fact from the opponent.

Even in those times, it was difficult if not virtually impossible to conceal the *numbers* of large warships being built. It was also difficult to hide the size of the main armament. But it was comparatively easy to fake on displacement.[67] The tonnage of a ship can be estimated closely from its dimensions (length, beam and draft), taken together with certain (easy) assumptions about its type and (more difficult) estimates of thickness and/or weight of armor. Length and beam are easily verified by aerial photography and unusual variations are immediate cause for suspicion. However, draft and armor thickness needed to be verified by either physical inspection (frogmen or a camera shot while afloat) or by access to plans or specifications (espionage). Consequently, most cases of tonnage deception involved either draft or armor.

It is the nature of naval architecture that certain slight weight variations from design often occur without any intention to deceive. This amount of excess tonnage can run as much as three or four per cent.[68] But figures of nine per cent and over furnish strong indications of deliberate cheating and were cause for alarm as they could give the ship a significant if not decisive advantage over potential opponents in its class.

All the major naval powers faked warship tonnages between the two world wars. Germany, chafing under the constraints of Versailles, led the pack. Permitted to replace obsolescent vessels according to a fixed schedule of age and tonnage, Germany started cheating in the early 1920s with the light cruiser, *Emden,* which exceeded her permitted 6,000-ton limit. So did the handful of other light cruisers that followed. Indeed, all German warships built in that period exceeded their displacement limits.

Japan was next in the game, with her *Atago*-class heavy cruisers that were fully 45 per cent larger than their announced 9,850 tons. Four of these ships were laid down in 1927 at the beginning of Japan's effort to modernize her fleet while pretending to keep within the limits of the 1922 Washington Agreement.

Germany followed suit two years later in 1929 when the first of three *Deutschland*-class 'pocket-battleships' was laid down at Kiel. Designed in 1927 and authorized in 1928, this class ostensibly honored the Versailles 10,000-ton limit while being a fine compromise that was faster than battle-ships but more heavily gunned than cruisers. It was called, officially, an 'armor-clad' (*Panzerschiffe*) to conform to the Versailles Treaty text, but was popularly and appropriately dubbed a 'pocket-battleship'. Also, it weighed 11,700 tons, 17 per cent over its permitted and announced weight.

The British Admiralty accepted German assurances that these pocket-battleships did not exceed the 10,000-ton Treaty limit. Because they were, in fact, heavier, this led the Admiralty correspondingly to underestimate their strength on the (correct) collateral assumption that it was impossible to pack massive 11-inch guns *and* plenty of ammunition *and* powerful engines *and* strong armor into a hull no weightier than a heavy cruiser. When the *Deutschland*-class *Admiral Graf Spee* managed to fight a virtual draw against a British team of one heavy and two light cruisers (totalling 22,400 tons), at the Battle of the River Plate in December 1939, the Admiralty marvelled at *Graf Spee*'s strength and still failed to question her tonnage.[69]

Germany got back into the game in June 1934 when Hitler authorized construction of the two *Scharnhorst*-class battleships. These were then planned as 25,000 to 26,000-ton ships, but Hitler personally told Navy chief Admiral Raeder, that they were to be referred to only as 'improved 10,000-ton ships' to conceal the fact that they were 16,000 tons over the Versailles limit. Next year, when the Anglo-German Naval Treaty accepted a 25,000-ton limit on future battleships, Hitler was free to admit the 'real' tonnage as 26,000. In fact *Scharnhorst* was then 31,850 tons, 23 per cent more than announced.[70]

In 1935 *Admiral Hipper,* first of a class of four heavy cruisers, was laid down. Announced as 10,000 tons, it was actually 14,475, an enormous 45 per cent overweight.[71] This degree of cheat was equalled only by the Japanese heavy cruiser *Atago* already mentioned, and exceeded only by the huge Japanese

Yamato-class battleships, which at 68,200 tons were 95 per cent over their pretended 35,000 tons.

In 1936 the Washington Naval Limitation Agreement of 1922 expired and was immediately replaced by the London Naval Treaty ratified in March 1936 by Britain, the United States and France, with Germany and the USSR joining later. This new Treaty retained the 'Washington Displacement' limit of 35,000 tons for battleships, but specified an odd discontinuity in displacements so that no warships could be built between 8,000 and 17,500 tons. This clause was clearly designed to block further construction of Germany's unique '10,000-ton' *Deutschland*-class pocket-battleships. In fact, the Germans had already switched to building the larger, *Scharnhorst*-class and were planning the full-scale *Bismarck*-class battleships. All this was now technically legal. Not legal was Germany's failure to disclose that her four *Hipper*-class heavy cruisers, which had been laid down in 1934, were designed to run 45 per cent over their pretended tonnage of 10,000.

The great German battleship *Bismarck* was laid down at the Blohm and Voss shipyard in Hamburg on 1 July 1936. When commissioned four years and one month later, she weighed in at 41,700 tons, making her the world's best armored and second largest warship.[72] Britain did not even begin to match her strength until four months later, when *King George V* was commissioned at 38,000 tons. Both nations had lied about these displacements — the Germans by 19, the British by nine per cent — but the British fudged later and less. This gave *Bismarck* a decisive margin when, in May 1941, she outfought the combined, 80,500-ton team of the old and thinly armored battlecruiser *Hood* and the *King George V*'s brand-new but under-gunned sister ship, *Prince of Wales*.

The entire *Kriegsmarine* had only 35 per cent of the total tonnage of the Royal Navy. The British negotiators for the 1935 Anglo-German Naval Treaty had thought, by obtaining agreement to this 35 per cent limit, to assure the Royal Navy's preponderance over the *Kriegsmarine*. Germany, however, by building bigger, single ships that would require the British Admiralty to deploy two or three even to match them, effectively wiped out the supposed fruits of the Treaty. They had hoodwinked the British. How?

The day *Bismarck* was laid down, the German Embassy in London disclosed, in confidence to the British Foreign Office, that this battleship would be 792 feet long, 118 feet wide and would mount 15-inch guns. These data were true, but the dimensions seemed rather more (by about 14 and 15 feet, respectively) than might reasonably be expected of its professed 35,000 tons. Reassurance was there, however, in the other vital statistics: a 26-foot draft, nine inches for the thickest armor, 80,000 horsepower and a flank speed of 27 knots. All of these latter figures were deliberate understatements, but the British Director of Naval Construction merely commented that the shallow draft compensated for the extra wide beam. The Admiralty Plans Division added its judgment: 'The present design of German capital ships appears to show that Germany is looking towards the Baltic with its shallow approaches more than in the past.' Thus, Plans falsely inferred *Bismarck*'s target to be the Soviet Navy rather than the British.

Meanwhile, in Berlin, Captain Thomas Troubridge had stepped in as Naval Attaché in 1936. He pondered his predecessor's opinion that Germany Navy chief Admiral Raeder was a liar, and soon had his own doubts about Raeder's 'earnestness and apparent sincerity'. In his annual, year-end report, Troubridge concluded that: 'The Anglo-German naval agreement was one of the master strokes of policy which have characterized Germany's dealing with her ex-enemies since the war. When the time is ripe, as history shows, it will unquestionably go the same way as other agreements: but the time is not yet.'

This prescient report went to the Ambassador who deleted Troubridge's final, disturbing sentence from his own annual report to Chamberlain's Foreign Office. However, copies of Troubridge's full report went to the Director of Naval Intelligence who circulated it for comment.

Troubridge's report was thrashed out early next year (February 1937). The German Section at Naval Intelligence Division (NID), which also held to the healthy but unpopular assumption that the Nazis might lie, questioned the *Bismarck* statistics. The Director of Plans, however, dampened these existing doubts with the depressing conclusion that: 'Our principal safeguard against such an infraction of treaty obligations lies in the good faith of the signatories.'

Tom Phillips had, as Director of Plans, been closely involved in negotiating the various naval limitations agreements. He had personally taken part in negotiation of the Anglo-German Naval Treaty. Donald McLachlan, the semi-official historian of British Naval Intelligence, concludes that Phillips was the victim of an affliction common to many negotiators; namely, having sincerely negotiated the best terms of which he was capable, he developed an unwarranted faith in the final agreement. McLachlan writes: 'Who is to blame Phillips for this attitude when the Whitehall line, set by the politicians and by what they believed to be the mood of the voters, was to hope for the best and give the dictators a little more rope to hang themselves? Plans Division's job was not to argue against the treaties, but to make the best plans they could within their limits.' Phillips' delusion, once acquired, persisted; subsequently, when he was a member of the Admiralty Board, he was still 'inclined to underrate the size of the *Bismarck* … and the capacity of the [*Deutschland*-class] pocket-battleships [precisely] because he had negotiated the tonnage limits which they had infringed'.[73]

In any case, Phillips found ready support against the wary skepticism of Troubridge and the NID's German Section from both the NID's own Technical Section and the Director of Naval Construction. DNC remained as complacent as before, conceding only that: 'The figures given are not in themselves sufficient to warrant the conclusion that the standard displacement of 35,000 tons is being purposely exceeded … [The] designers of the [*Bismarck*] would not be blamed if the displacement on completion was 36,000 tons, and such a figure would be more in line with the length and beam reported than 35,000 tons.'

Shortly after *Bismarck*'s launching on 14 February 1939, the British vice-consul in Hamburg reported to Naval Attaché Troubridge that 'she was drawing a good deal more than she should'. Although this new Intelligence cried out for verification, none was attempted and the old, false estimates stood unchallenged.[74] So that was it. Naval Intelligence Division did not realize that it had been deceived by the draft, armor, horsepower and speed of the *Bismarck* until October 1941, when it completed its examination of the ship's captured notebook and the interrogation of her 115 survivors. Even so, this conclusion of their own Intelligence Service was not accepted by the British Admiralty until 12 months later, when the Soviet Admiralty handed over *its* Intelligence estimate. At that point, six years *after Bismarck* had been laid down and 17 months after she was sunk the mystery of her 'shallow draft' was finally solved. She did not draw the proclaimed 26 feet, but 34 feet, an amount identical to the *King George V* class. Only now did the Admiralty recognize that those extra feet of length and beam concealed a much more heavily armored ship.

VII. Lessons to be Learned

The story of secret German rearmament carries perhaps seven main lessons:[75]

1: National political leaders tend to be unwilling to heed Intelligence that has awkward political implications.

2: Negotiators, having negotiated a difficult agreement to mutual satisfaction, tend to place unwarranted faith in that agreement. They 'lose the skepticism which is part of vigilance'.

3: Arms limitation agreements tend to leave out automatic sanctions that would significantly raise the costs of any evasion. Credible and potent sanctions might better deter evasions and swiftly punish those that do occur.

4: Technical experts tend to discount Intelligence suggesting that their opposites have accomplished something that they, themelves, have not achieved or have not thought of doing. In such cases, the technicians and engineers 'may not be the best judges of enemy intentions and achievement'.

5: Intelligence services tend to be under enormous bureaucratic political pressure to report (or at least stress) data that is in line with the prejudices and needs of their clientele and to suppress (or at least de-emphasize) that which is not.

6: 'Money', as British Major General Temperley concluded from his long experience with the German case, 'is the key to increased armaments and a careful scrutiny of any upward trend would justify a demand for explanations.' However, any such economic analysis must go beyond publicly professed budgets to probe deeply for fiscal deception. And it is not only the target government's books that must be open to skilled auditors, but those of plausible or suspected contractors including those in other countries.

7: Evidence of arms evasion is likely to be ambiguous to some (perhaps a large) degree — the familiar problem of 'signal to noise ratio'. Though it is possible to find evidence of sharp and strikingly prophetic judgments in a retrospective examination of the Intelligence data presented to decision-makers of the period it is likewise possible to find grossly inaccurate assessments and 'facts'. In such a situation the preconceptions of the decision-makers together with other (e.g. domestic) considerations loomed more significant than the evidence before them.

By failing to understand the first two lessons, the national leaders were easy prey for deception. By failing to demand rigorous verification of alleged infractions they showed apathy. By failing to apply sanctions when Intelligence did occasionally bring undeniable proof of infractions to their attention they showed themselves impotent as well. And the opponent's perception of this impotence was a spur to ever more audacious infractions.

NOTES

1. J. H. Morgan, *Assize of Arms* (New York: Oxford University Press, 1946); H. M. Mason, *The Rise of the Luftwaffe: Forging the Secret German Weapon, 1918-1940* (New York: Dial Press, 1973), 85; Hans W. Gatzke, *Stresemann and the Rearmament of Germany* (Baltimore: The Johns Hopkins Press, 1954), 27.

2. Mason (1973), 77.

3. Morgan (1946), 30, 63-64; Mason (1973), 77-79.

4. William Manchester, *The Arms of Krupp; 1887-1968* (Boston: Little, Brown, 1968), 345.

5. Ibid., 350.

6. Anthony H. G. Fokker and Bruce Gould, *Flying Dutchman* (New York: Holt, 1931), 13, 215-244. The derivative account in Mason (1973), 74-76, contains numerous errors.

7. As we shall see below, although Fokker's autobiography omits any such mention. Within a short time, the Fokker operation became the third largest industry in Holland. Fokker (1931), 244.

8. Gatzke (1954), 29, 41, 54. See also Robert J. O'Neill, *The German Army and the Nazi Party, 1933-1939* (London: Cassell, 1966), 7.

9. David Kahn, *Hitler's Spies: German Military Intelligence in World War II* (New York: Macmillan, 1978), 224. This carefully researched book gives the best published account of the *Abwehr* prior to Navy Captain Canaris' arrival at the helm in 1935. The earlier works by Abshagen, Leverkuehn, Colvin, Whiting and Brissaud are not only very skimpy on this period, but hopeless jumbles of inaccurate facts.

10. Ibid., 190-191, 224; and David Kahn, *The Codebreakers* (New York: Macmillan, 1967), 454.

11. Kahn (1967), 454; Kahn (1978), 198.

12. J. Benoist-Mechin, *History of the German Army since the Armistice,* Vol. I (Zürich: Scientia, 1939), 308-310.

13. Hanfried Schliephake, *The Birth of the Luftwaffe* (Chicago: Regnery, 1972), 12.

14. Schliephake (1972), 15; Mason (1973), 118-119.

15. Mason (1973), 125, 126; Schliephake (1972), 14.

16. Schliephake (1972), 23.

17. Ibid., 29.

18. Namely, Admirals Paul Behncke (1920-24), Hans Zenker (1924-28), and Erich Raeder (1928-43).

19. David Woodward, *The Tirpitz and the Battle for the North Atlantic* (New York: Norton, 1954), 36-49.

20. Manchester (1968), 353-354.

21. William L. Shirer, *The Rise and Fall of the Third Reich* (New York: Simon and Schuster, 1960), 281. See also *NCA*, VI, 1018.

22. Schliephake (1972), 15–16.

23. Duncan Crow and Robert J. Icks, *Encyclopedia of Armoured Cars and Half-tracks* (Secaucus, N.J.: Chartwell Books, 1976), 75.

24. Manchester (1968), 355.

25. Crow and Icks (1976), 75.

26. Duncan Crow and Robert J. Icks, *Encyclopedia of Tanks* (Secaucus, N.J.: Chartwell Books, 1975), 142, 144–146; Peter Chamberlain and Chris Ellis, *Pictorial History of Tanks of the World, 1915–45* (Harrisburg, Penn.: Galahad Books, 1972), 43, 47–48; and F. M. von Senger und Etterlin, *German Tanks of World War II* (New York: Galahad Books, 1973), 21 and figures 8–10.

27. Kenneth Macksey, *Guderian* (New York: Stein and Day, 1976), 47, where however he errs in calling the Swedish tank company a 'battalion'.

28. Crow and Icks (1975), 208; Chamberlain and Ellis (1972), 158–159.

29. Gatzke (1954), 46–71.

30. John W. Wheeler-Bennet, *The Nemesis of Power* (London: Macmillan, 1953), 185–186.

31. Manchester (1968), 348.

32. Ibid., 345, 346.

33. Schliephake (1972), 20.

34. J. H. Morgan, 'The Disarmament of Germany and After', *Quarterly Review,* October 1924, 415–57.

35. An alternate translation is given by Woodward (1954), 38.

36. J. H. Morgan, *The Present State of Germany* (1924); and Morgan (1946).

37. Philip John Stead, *Second Bureau* (London: Evans, 1959), 12.

38. Winston S. Churchill, *The Second World War,* Vol. I (Boston: Houghton Mifflin, 1948), 16.

39. Philip Noel-Baker, *The Arms Race* (London: Stevens, 1958), 535–536.

40. Manchester (1968), 355–356.

41. Kahn (1978), 115–116.

42. *Völkische Beobachter,* 24 June 1933, 1; Mason (1973), 176.

43. Ian Colvin, *Chief of Intelligence* (London: Gollancz, 1951), 14, quoting the recollections of Richard Protze, ex-*Abwehr* Chief of Counter-Intelligence.

44. Kahn (1978), 116.

45. Georges Castellan, *Le Réarmement Clandestin du Reich, 1930–1935* (Paris: Plon, 1954), 137.

46. Stead (1959), 13.

47. Major General A. C. Temperley, *The Whispering Gallery of Europe* (London: Collins, 1938), 221.

48. Kahn (1978), 116–19; Schliephake (1972), 35.

49. The explicit, helpful equations that dissimulation yields underestimation and simulation yields overestimation were formulated 28 July 1978 by Lewis Reich.

50. Castellan (1954), 164; Mason (1973), 189.

51. Anthony Eden, *Facing the Dictators* (Boston: Houghton Mifflin, 1962), 69, 73, 157, 204, 205.

52. Mason (1973), 210–11.

53. See Schliephake (1972), 41.

54. Mason (1973), 196–7.

55. Frantisek Moravec, *Master of Spies: The Memoirs of General Frantisek Moravec* (Garden City, N.Y.: Doubleday, 1975), 121–125 for actual order-of-battle; and Stead (1957), 18–19 for French Second Bureau's German order-of-battle estimate.

56. André François-Ponçet, *The Fateful Years: Memoirs of a French Ambassador in Berlin, 1931-1938* (New York: 1949; reprinted New York: Fertig, 1972), 264-5.

57. Leonard Mosley, *Lindbergh: A Biography* (Garden City, New York: Doubleday, 1976), 224.

58. Ibid., 208–245, 414; and Wayne S. Cole, *Charles A. Lindbergh and the Battle Against American Intervention in World War II* (New York: Harcourt Brace Jovanovich, 1974), 31–61.

59. As translated from the *Völkischer Beobachter* of 2 September 1939 in *NCA*, VI (1946), 420.

60. Rolf Wagenfuehr, as quoted by Burton H. Klein, *Germany's Economic Preparations for War* (Cambridge: Harvard University Press, 1959), 17.

61. The extensive trade and German capital investment which also developed during this period was an independent occurrence and not, as suggested by some writers, such as Manchester (1958), 329, an integral part of the quid pro quo. W. G. Krivitsky, *In Stalin's Secret Service* (New York: Harper, 1939), 4–7, 10, 19; Ruth Fischer, *Stalin and German Communism* (Cambridge: Harvard University Press, 1948), 527–36; Cecil F. Melville, *The Russian Face of Germany: An Account of the Secret Military Relations Between the German and Soviet-Russian Governments* (London: Wishart, 1932). This material is summarized by E. J. Gumbel, 'Disarmament and Clandestine Rearmament under the Weimar Republic', in Seymour Melman (ed.) *Inspection for Disarmament* (New York: Columbia University Press, 1958), 203–219; and Golo Mann, 'Rapallo: The Vanishing Dream', *Survey*, No. 44/45 (October 1962), 74–88. F. L. Carsten, 'The Reichswehr and the Red Army, 1920–1933', *Survey*, No. 44/45 (October 1962), 114–132, provides the most detailed and best documented account. For the intensive collaboration in military and civil aviation see Robert A. Kilmarx, *A History of Soviet Air Power* (New York: Praeger, 1962), 65–74, 90–91, 99. For an excellent bibliographical essay on this question see Robert M. Slusser and Jan F. Triska, *A Calendar of Soviet Treaties, 1917–1957* (Stanford: Stanford University Press, 1959), 403–12, 427–28.

62. Text of letter in Jane Degras (ed.), *Soviet Documents on Foreign Policy*, Vol. I (London: Oxford U.P. 1951), 304–5.

63. Schliephake (1972), 19; Mason (1973), 158–159.

64. Gatzke (1954), 87–8.

65. On Radek's role see H. Schurer, 'Radek and the German Revolution, Part II', *Survey*, No. 55 (April 1965), 126–40.

66. For example, reports of secret German-Soviet military agreements appeared in the British and French Press in May 1922 and in French, Polish and US intelligence reports between 1920 and 1928. These specific accounts of agreements attracted little attention at the time and many of them are now known to be fabrications, at best based indirectly on distorted rumors. See Slusser and Triska (1959), 407, 427–8.

67. All tonnage figures in this paper are in 'standard displacement'. This measure is the one conventionally used in treaties and is lower than the 'full load' figures often mentioned in the literature. Thus, *Bismarck* was 41,700 tons standard and 45,000 full load. Historians often slip the larger figure in unspecified to impress their readers.

68. Donald McLachlan, *Room 39: A Study in Naval Intelligence* (New York: Atheneum, 1968), 137.

69. Dudley Pope, *Graf Spee: The Life and Death of a Raider* (Philadelphia: Lippincott, 1957), 84n; and McLachlan (1968), 360.

70. *NCA*, I, 431. See also McLachlan (1968), 398.

71. *Jane's Fighting Ships*, 1939, 1944–45; McLachlan (1968), 398.

72. First was the old British battle cruiser *Hood*, which following her second reconversion in 1940 displaced 42,462 tons.

73. McLachlan (1968), 136, 137, 360.

74. Ibid., 140.

75. Lessons 1), 2) and 4) are those Rear Admiral John Godfrey, British Director of Naval Intelligence, 1939–43, drew specifically from the *Bismarck* case. See McLachlan (1968), 142. The two phrases quoted in lessons two and four are Godfrey's.

Soviet Strategic Deception, 1955-1981

Michael Mihalka

An evaluation of Soviet strategic deception must compare the stated objectives of Soviet policy with the development and deployment of weapons that the Soviets consider strategic. Unlike the information that has become available on Nazi Germany, little direct material has appeared on the strategic objectives that the Soviets have pursued in the post-war period. Therefore, we must infer Soviet strategic intentions by evaluating not only their statements, but also their actions and their preparations. In the strategic arena, we need to compare their actual forces and their deployment with public claims about their numbers and capabilities.

The debate over the pursuit of strategic superiority provides the backdrop for examining Soviet procurement of and claims about nuclear weapons and their accompanying delivery systems. Strategic superiority implies that one side can assure victory in a nuclear conflict. The Soviets have traditionally characterized the West and particularly the US as pursuing the chimera of superiority. Soviet claims about superiority seem to vary inversely with their capability (or with Western intelligence about that capability) and provide an important piece of evidence supporting the argument that the Soviets have engaged in systematic strategic deception since the end of the Stalin era.

Strategic Deception as Policy

Strategic deception occurs whenever a country continues over a period of time deliberately to mislead another regarding its strategic objectives or the forces designed to achieve those objectives. Deceptions of intent leave much less of a trace than deceptions about capabilities. Evidence that a country indicated that it intended one thing when it subsequently did another may simply reflect a shift in policy. Often statesmen disguise their true intent from others and memoirs after the fact often betray greater vision than the confusion of the actual moment suggested. Actual plans or programs for deception should have limited circulation and thus should rarely enter the public domain.

Limited evidence that the Soviets have engaged in or encouraged systematic strategic deception has appeared in the memoirs of a former head of the Czechoslovakian disinformation section, Ladislav Bittman:

> For disinformation campaigns to be successful, they must at least partially correspond to reality or generally accepted views. A rational core is especially important when the recipient enemy or victim is a seasoned veteran in such matters, because without a considerable degree

of plausible, verifiable information and facts it is impossible to gain his confidence. Not until this rational skeleton has been established is it fleshed with the relevant disinformation. In 1963 for example, the general staff of the Czechoslovak army, with the help of the intelligence and counter-intelligence services, developed a long-range military disinformation operation in order to deceive NATO countries about the military strength of the Czechoslovak army. It was in fact a part of the Warsaw Pact disinformation program, and it can be assumed that similar techniques have been used by other members of the pact as well.

The general staff supplied Czechoslovak media with purposely distorted information on the Czechoslovak military, assuming that NATO analysts would pick it up. At the same time hundreds of double agents on Czechoslovak territory working both for Czechoslovak counter-intelligence and Western intelligence services were supplied with disinformation material on the Czechoslovak military that would fit with the published information. It was a very costly operation because the general staff had to finance the construction of deceptive missile ramps and organize a false transfer of army units in order to support the correct mixture of disinformation.

After 1964, the Czechoslovak disinformation service helped to develop this long-range project further, without knowing, however, whether or not the desired effects had been achieved. The NATO military command had not reacted, but our department had at least one indication of success: the Russians insisted that we continue. it is quite possible that this operation is still being conducted [Bittman:20–21].

This episode remains one of the few that directly implicates the Soviet Union in a plan systematically to deceive the West. The Soviet forgery offensive and the current disinformation efforts over the location of long-range theater nuclear weapons provide more tangible evidence of Soviet deception. However strong the evidence that the Soviets use deception to support their foreign policy, little has appeared to connect their strategic deployments and pronouncements directly to a program of deception. Nevertheless, a clear pattern of systematic deception emerges. The Soviets have consistently disguised the true strength of their strategic nuclear intercontinental forces: when weak, feigning strength; when strong, feigning parity.

Depending on the context, deception can serve a number of purposes. Hitler sowed confusion about the size of his military forces. Deception allowed Hitler to achieve what his rearmament program had not succeeded in doing, deterring intervention by third parties in his succession of diplomatic coups in the mid- to late 1930s. Deception may also serve peaceful purposes by deterring attack. Exaggeration can lead to reaction as the target feels a need to meet the threat posed by the enemy. In the late 1930s, the Germans, realizing that the inflated figures about German forces appearing in the British press were exerting pressure on the British to rearm, initiated a deception that indicated that the rate of German rearmament would just match the current British program. Thus, a deception campaign must not only succeed in achieving short-term goals, but it must also prevent a response which defeats the policy in the long run. Soviet strategic deception since 1955 shares the features of both boasting when weak and downplaying when strong.

As Bittman notes, all deception must possess a kernel of truth. Any discussion of Soviet deception generally turns on protestations of US self-deception. Many seem more inclined to admit that the US has fooled itself than the Soviets have fooled the US. Such an attitude, of course, facilitates Soviet deception by providing a ready explanation for any Soviet behavior that appears deceptive. Reinforcing preconceived notions represents one of the easier tactics of deception. Homilies and half-truths about Soviet behavior also provide a ready basis for deception (for example, Soviet technological inferiority, Soviet 'defensive' posture, etc.). The pluralist nature of the American political process provides a ready market for virtually any Soviet deception, just as Churchill became an unwitting agent of exaggerated German claims in the mid-1930s. The leak and counter-leak system of bureaucratic infighting provides additional fertile ground for Soviet manipulation. Soviet attempts to disrupt the American political process may not necessarily reflect any conscious program other than confusion.

The true test of Soviet deception lies in their deployments and their public statements of intent and capabilities. Unfortunately much of the information about Soviet deployments must come from US public assessments of the threat posed by the Soviets, in part discredited by repeated Soviet attempts to fool US intelligence resources and by the many uses to which parts of the government put intelligence. Thus, the internal consistency of Soviet claims and military demonstrations must bear close scrutiny. Because the Soviets betray little about their strategic intentions (other than the general desire to deter an attack on their homeland, and Russian and Soviet historic expansionism), claims that they have made for their forces and their rationale in justifying them provide the best basis for evaluating Soviet deception.

Some deceptions possess elements that do not allow an easy distinction between strategic and operational. A government may disguise its forces to complicate the military planning of its opponents. For example, a country may construct dummy missile sites in an attempt to divert attacks on actual missiles. Such an operational deception assumes strategic implications if the country then argues that the number of missiles it has deployed conveys some advantage. If that country has engaged in some process with its major opponent in which quantity or quality, per se, has attained strategic significance, then that country need not even draw attention to the number of missiles in order for the deception to assume strategic status. The dialogue between the US and the Soviet Union has placed extraordinary importance on the quantity and quality of nuclear intercontinental systems. Thus, any attempt to disguise the quantity or quality of those systems, even without drawing attention to that disguise, represents strategic deception. Before the SALT process began, Soviet operational deceptions involving their nuclear intercontinental systems did not, ipso facto, constitute strategic deception. Now they do.

Some operational deceptions do not assume strategic importance because they have failed to enter the US-Soviet dialogue. For example, if the Soviets constructed dummy SAM sites or prepared camouflaged airfields for their interceptors to complicate US bomber route planning, they would not have engaged in a strategic deception. If the Soviets then made claims about the capability of their strategic air defenses that they did not believe, then they would have perpetrated a strategic deception. Sophisticated analyses have not appeared about the effectiveness of Soviet air defenses and even within the US controversy surrounds assessments because of the need to evaluate weapons programs. Unfortunately, the nature of the procurement process (at least in the United States) lends itself to deception directed more internally than externally. Occasionally, a vested interest will point with pride at (and exaggerate) current capabilities and view with alarm (and understate) future capabilities.

The controversy over major weapons decisions does not play itself out in the Soviet popular press as it does in the US. Nevertheless the Soviets may cite capabilities in vitro. Boasts in isolation may reflect the give and take of justifying a particular weapons program or the pride of technological development. Repeated references to a capability yet to appear indicate more than simply pride of parenthood; they reflect a conscious desire to trade prestige on that capability. Goebbels understood the dangers of boasting about untried capabilities in wartime. He threatened the British with the V-1 long before it had achieved an operational status. His propaganda backfired as the German people wondered why the state did not use the weapon and the British launched a counter campaign to embarrass the German government. In Soviet practice claims about future capabilities fade away as they fail to materialize or fail to strike a resonating chord in the West. (Johnson apparently asserted that the US possessed an ASAT capability at the time development began.)

Shifts in the capabilities of systems also pose a problem for identifying strategic deception, especially in the light of initial claims that later testing proves false or when the opponent adopts measures which effectively nullify the initial advantages of the system. For example, the Soviets may boast that no planes can effectively penetrate their air defense, as they did when they shot down the U-2. Tactics such as low-flying penetration may defeat an air defense designed to counter the high-flying threat. Similarly, a ballistic missile defense may succeed against a small number of re-entry vehicles which have low ballistic coefficients (that is, high drag so that the RV remains in the atmosphere longer) but become quickly saturated with large-scale attacks. As the threat changes so should claims about the capability of defenses. Isolated claims probably mean little. Claims sustained over a number of years without a corresponding capability suggest strategic deception.

Just as a system may fail owing to countermeasures, it may succeed owing to incremental technological improvement. Thus, a defense originally designed to cope with low beta RVs in small numbers may fail against high beta RVs in large numbers and beome relegated to a high altitude defense against aircraft. Gradual technological improvement may gain some capability against the high beta RV threat. In the absence of an arms control agreement that identifies ABM systems, a country need not tout its recently acquired capability and thus not perpetrate a strategic deception. If the arms control agreement does outlaw upgrades, then the upgrade does qualify as a strategic deception, especially because silence identifies a system as an air defense.

Preparations for breakout from an arms control agreement pose a special problem in identifying strategic deception. The Soviet Union presumably wishes to do as little as possible to limit its war-fighting capability. Therefore, the Soviets should design agreements that allow them maximum flexibility with respect to breakout. If the Soviets view war as inevitable, then the arms control agreement means little (since it was designed to manage the peace). To enhance their ability to achieve breakout does not violate the spirit of the agreement, per se. Unilateral statements about breakout by the other party to the agreement represent more naiveté and self-deception than Soviet strategic deception. Nevertheless, if the Soviets adopt measures that aid in the breakout process and also violate the letter of the agreement, then they engage in strategic deception.

OPPORTUNITIES FOR DECEPTION

The German pattern suggests that the Soviets should exaggerate their capabilities when low and downplay them when high. The specifics of the deception should depend on the dynamic between Soviet and US capabilities. Thus, the Soviets should pursue an overall program of deception with the specifics left to the interplay of technological progress and policy of the moment. The preconceptions of the US strategists and military should provide the most fruitful ground for deception.

I: Exaggeration to 1962

After the death of Stalin, the Soviets found themselves at a distinct strategic disadvantage. Stalin had left the Soviet military with a military doctrine ill-suited to the technological changes already underway with nuclear weapons and the prospects of intercontinental ballistic missiles. Their major opponent possessed weapons and bases with which to strike deeply within the heart of the Soviet Union and yet remain unscathed itself. Apparent Soviet weakness could little serve a forward policy in Europe. Two paths seemed open: one, to forsake a capability against the United States, per se, and concentrate on the pressure that the Soviets could exert on Europe with local forces; the other, to expand the arena of conflict by pushing the new missile technology, realizing that geography and the massive industrial base of the US for producing bombers would lead the Soviets to the short end of the strategic competition.

Two doctrines presented themselves, one more consistent with the diversion of heavy industrial resources to broader economic purposes than simply military. The belief that nuclear war meant the end of mankind and that each side need possess only enough weapons to assure that destruction appeared early. The other view that technology did not fundamentally change the nature of warfare (and by extension, the class struggle) required forces sufficient to defeat the enemy. A minimalist approach to nuclear weapons would require merely that the Soviets guarantee that the US suffer if it should attack. Exaggeration of limited Soviet forces would help, but convincing the US of the need to restrict its nuclear capability would help even more. The maximalist approach required that the Soviets exaggerate their forces, because it admits that superiority conveys strategic advantage. Thus, the weakness of Soviet forces necessitated that Khrushchev pursue a policy of strategic deception to achieve his global forward policy. Hitler, faced with similar choices in the early 1930s, adopted a very similar policy-deception to compensate for strategic weakness.

MALENKOV AND HIS REPUDIATION

On 12 March 1954, Premier Malenkov argued that nuclear war would mean 'the destruction of world civilization' [H&R:25]. Such a view leaves little room for the pursuit of 'military-technological superiority' and Malenkov moved to reduce military expenditures. Opposed by the views of Bulganin that only imperialism faced destruction, Malenkov reversed his position the next month. Addressing the Supreme Soviet in late April, Malenkov claimed:

> The Soviet Armed Forces have at their disposal and will have at their disposal everything that is necessary for carrying out their lofty mission — to stand guard over the defense of the motherland and be ready always to deliver a crushing rebuff to an aggressor who would want to disrupt the peaceful toil of the peoples of our country! [H&R:20–21].

Nevertheless, the Malenkov faction continued to downplay the need for greater military effort, but lost the struggle finally with the ouster of Malenkov in February 1955. Khrushchev argued that a call for more consumer goods was 'particularly intolerable ... when the imperialist powers are stepping up wild preparations for war'. The journal *Kommunist* disparaged the notion that the imperialists would not initiate a nuclear war. Such a view would lull one side into complacency and being ripe for a surprise attack. After Malenkov's purge, the Soviets moved quickly to increase military expenditures [H&R:27].

THE BOMBER DECEPTION

During their Aviation Day display in July, the Soviets resorted to an old trick to impress Western visitors about the size of their intercontinental bomber force. Twenty-nine planes, in three flights, passed the reviewing stand. Later estimates indicated that the Soviets possessed only ten operational bombers at the time [H&R:27–28; F:65–66]. This display reinforced Western projections that the Soviets would invest heavily in a intercontinental bomber force.

 Despite their display, the Soviet leaders said little about the size and capability of their bomber force. Neither before nor after the Aviation Day display did the Soviets advance any claims that linked the Soviet strategic capability to bombers, preferring instead to emphasize the still unproven ballistic missiles.

When General Twining visited the Soviet Union in 1956, the Soviets tried to disabuse him of Western inflated estimates of Soviet bombers. In fact, the Twining visit seemed designed to impress upon the US the defensive and peaceful nature of Soviet aviation. The single Soviet aerial demonstration contained just seven heavy bombers, three Bison jets and four Bear turboprops. The Soviets took the Twining group (which included the Deputy Chiefs of Staff for Operations, Development, and Material) to an obsolescent air engine facility and a transport plant. Unlike the Germans in the 1930s, the Soviets showed their older plants and none which displayed the production of combat aircraft. To a query about why the Soviets showed so few bombers, Marshal Zhukov responded, 'Oh, they are in production, but we are a peaceful people. We do not want to boast about our offensive weapons and offensive capability' [AF, July 1956:60].

The Soviets clearly wished to undermine the impression created by the Bison flyby during the 1955 Aviation Day displays. They intended with the Twining visit to undercut the impressions of a massive program for bomber production. Thus, they either wished to correct the impression created by the earlier visit or their overall policy had changed with the success of the Khrushchev faction. Their continuing emphasis on rockets in their public pronouncements and their failure to harvest the fruit of the 1955 display would suggest that the Bison flyby did not reflect overall Soviet policy and that they deliberately designed the Twining visit to affect US projections of Soviet strategic capabilities. From the misguided bomber deception (and indeed their own experience with the Germans in the 1930s) the Soviets had learned the power of military demonstrations.

THE MISSILE DECEPTION

The lull in Soviet claims between the 1955 aerial display and the announcement of the the ICBM test in 1957, punctuated by the Twining visit in 1956, suggests that the Soviets were applying the lessons of strategic surprise to the international image of their strategic capabilities. In late August 1957, the Soviets claimed that they had successfully launched an ICBM which allowed them to strike any location in the world. After the Sputnik launch in October, Khrushchev claimed: 'We now have all the rockets we need: long-range rockets, intermediate-range rockets and short-range rockets.' Despite launching a public relations campaign directed in part at Western journalists (again reminiscent of Hitler's use of non-German journalists), Khrushchev made claims only about the scientific, technological, and military superiority of the Soviet Union. Instead, Soviet commentary emphasized that the Soviet Union now possessed the means to deny the US the strategic advantages it had previously held [H&R:48–49].

In November 1958, Khrushchev began making claims about placing ICBMs in production. In his speech to the 21st Party Congress in February 1959, Khrushchev emphasized: 'When we say that we have organized the serial production of intercontinental ballistic missiles, it is not just to hear ourselves talk.' From an intelligence standpoint, claims regarding production capabilities carry much greater weight. Defense Minister Marshal Malinovsky, at the same meeting, thanked those who had 'equipped the armed forces with a whole series of military ballistic missiles, [including] intercontinental'. The Soviets wished to convey the impression that their military had received operational missiles. Nevertheless, the Soviets still did not claim superiority, instead arguing that the Soviet Union possessed 'no less force and capabilities' than the US [H&R:50–53].

In mid-1959, Khrushchev disparaged the claims of some in the US that

> ... the Soviet Union has few intercontinental rockets ... But this, after all, is what the American military men assert. It should be said, however, that it is always better to count the money in your own pocket than that in the other fellow's. I might say, incidentally, that we have enough rockets for America, too, should war be unleashed against us.

In November 1959, Khrushchev boasted: 'We now have stockpiled so many rockets, so many atomic and hydrogen warheads, that, if we were attacked, we would wipe from the face of the earth all of our probable opponents' [H&R:58]. In January 1960, Khrushchev continued this theme:

> I stress once again that we have already enough nuclear weapons — atomic and hydrogen — and the corresponding rockets to deliver these weapons to the territory of a possible aggressor, [so] that if some madman stirred up an attack on our state or on other socialist states we could literally wipe from the face of the earth the country or countries that attacked us [H&R:59].

The Soviets continued to contest the claims made by those in the US who suggested that the Soviets possessed considerably fewer ICBMs:

> We declare openly that the 'data' at the disposal of A. Dulles are of little interest to us. To calculate in Washington the number of rockets and other types of Soviet arms is of as little use as counting crows on the fence. Why does the master director bother at all? We are prepared to answer his question. How many rockets do we have? Enough! Enough to wipe out from the face of the earth any country which dares to attack the Soviet Union. N. Khrushchev frankly and openly declared this at the January session of the USSR Supreme Soviet [H&R:62].

To complicate US ability to estimate the size of the Soviet ICBM even further, Malinovsky and Khrushchev argued that they could easily conceal the ICBM locations. Malinovsky claimed: 'The building of large expensive airfields with complicated equipment is not required for launching rockets. It is far easier to camouflage and even completely conceal rocket-launch positions; this guarantees a higher degree of security and invulnerability for rocket weapons.' Consistent with earlier practice in World War II and the continuing treatment of deception in the Soviet military literature, we should have also seen in this period dummy mockups of Soviet ICBMs and M/IRBMs. The Soviets emphasize the need to make dummy installations look real and real installations look like dummies. Dummy rockets would have reinforced Soviet claims if they believed that the US would receive only photographic intelligence. Human intelligence would have revealed, albeit in a fragmentary way, the nature of the Soviet deception.

The revelations of the U-2 affair make it appear that the Soviets did not construct dummy ICBMs, either because they felt that the US lacked capability to photograph deep within Soviet territory or the claims at the higher levels did not trickle to actual deceptions at the local levels. Physical deceptions to reinforce verbal claims clearly mark a strategic deception. After the downing of the U-2 in May 1960, Khrushchev began to back off his previous claims of superiority. He began to echo Malenkov's comments, that nuclear war would represent a catastrophe for both sides. General Talensky argued that 'a future war, if the aggressors succeed in unleashing it, will lead to such an increase in human losses on both sides that its consequences for mankind might be a catastrophe' [H&R:79]. Khrushchev instead emphasized the value of the Soviet air defense, asserting that 'not a single bomber could get through to its target' and that the 'whole military concept of attack on the Soviet Union based on the use of bomber planes [has] been shattered' [H&R:80–81]. As he did at the UN in September 1960, Khrushchev continued to claim that the Soviet Union remained 'superior in the most effective means of delivering nuclear weapons, intercontinental ballistic missiles'.

Kennedy had made much political capital out of the 'missile gap' during the fall 1960 campaign. Once in office, he discovered (as Nixon and the Eisenhower administration knew from the U-2 flights) that the Soviets had decided not to deploy the difficult first-generation SS-6 in great numbers. By October 1961, administration spokesmen and their favored journalists began to reverse the image of Soviet strategic superiority. Soviet reaction became almost defensive. Malinovsky claimed in January 1962:

> US President John Kennedy once admitted that our strength is equal. This was a more or less correct acknowledgement, and it is high time that the American military leaders drew appropriate conclusions from it. I hold that today the socialist camp is stronger than these countries [NATO], but let us presume that the forces are equal. We are ready to agree to this so as not to take part in stirring up a war psychosis. But since our forces are equal the American leaders should come to correct conclusions and pursue a reasonable policy [H&R:88].

In May 1962, Khrushchev indirectly alluded to US claims that he had exaggerated Soviet capabilities:

> Our strength today is not illusory but is enormous and real. The President of the United States himself said to me that our military forces are equal. I made no objections to this although we are in fact stronger

than imperialism, because our forces include not only the socialist states
but all progressive and peace-loving peoples on earth, all people who
hold peace dear. These peace-loving forces are greater than the forces of
imperialism [H&R:86].

Soviet superiority no longer rested on its military-technological capabilities
but on its ideological purity. Nevertheless, the Soviets did not retreat from
their quest for superiority.

The Soviets clearly engaged in a campaign to impress the US with the
capability and size of their ICBM force. Claims by some authors recently that
the Soviets were merely touting their burgeoning 'strategic' capabilities
(which would include the M/IRBMs deployed in this period) do not square
with the clear Soviet emphasis on rockets of intercontinental range [Aspin and
Lee in *Strategic Review,* Summer 1980]. Presumably, the Soviets lacked a
proper appreciation of the reconnaissance capabilities of the U-2. The
seemingly slow build-up towards the superiority claims in 1959 suggest the
Soviets could, if they had chosen, deploy dummy missiles to support their
public claims. They decided not to and reaped the embarrassment of the
deflated missile gap and the US strategic build-up.

THE CUBAN MISSILE DECEPTION

The Soviets clearly engaged in dissimulation in the months preceding the
Cuban Missile Crisis. The revelations of strategic inferiority had embarrassed
Khrushchev and threatened his policy (backed before by claims of strategic
superiority). To correct the strategic deficiency quickly, Khrushchev needed
to emplace missiles in Cuba before the US discovery to establish a fait
accompli. The Soviets apparently had no satisfactory ICBMs in production.
The SS-6 had proved an operational nightmare. Thus, Cuba would provide
the basis for Soviet forward base systems. The SS-4 and SS-5 would restore the
nuclear correlation of forces on Cuban soil.

To plan to emplace missiles in Cuba required elaborate concealment and
deception procedures. Khrushchev would announce the presence of the
missiles sometime during his planned visit to the US after the US Congressional elections. The Soviets needed to keep the missile deployment secret
until they became operational The failure of the Soviet plan suggests that they
had not developed a proper appreciation of the U-2 capabilities, revealed to
stunning effect when Kennedy announced that the Soviets had begun to place
the missiles in Cuba.

Kennedy had come under fire because of the increased Soviet activity in
Cuba. During the early days of September, Soviet Ambassador Dobrynin
gave repeated assurances:

> Nothing will be undertaken before the American congressional elections
> that would complicate the international situation or aggravate the
> tension in the relations between our two countries ... The Chairman
> does not wish to become involved in your internal affairs [A:40].

Despite such reassurance, Kennedy explicitly and publicly warned against the introduction of offensive missiles in Cuba. He received through back channels a message from Khrushchev that read: 'No missile capable of reaching the United States would be placed in Cuba' [A:40]. To cap these private communications, the Soviets expressed public denials through *Tass* on 11 September 1962:

> The Government of the Soviet Union authorized *Tass* to state that there is no need for the Soviet Union to shift its weapons for the repulsion of aggression, for a retaliatory blow, to any other country, for instance Cuba. Our nuclear weapons are so powerful in their explosive force and the Soviet Union has such powerful rockets to carry these nuclear warheads, that there is no need to search for sites for them beyond the boundaries of the Soviet Union [A:40].

The first Soviet ship carrying MRBMs had already arrived, on 8 September. Construction would begin by the 15th [A:103–117].

Thus, the Soviets had given private and public assurances that they would not emplace missiles in Cuba. They claimed that they would make no trouble for the US prior to the elections. Yet the U-2 flights had discovered the missiles, uncamouflaged and deployed with the SAMs in the same four-slice pattern used in the Soviet Union [A:56]. Nevertheless, the Soviets had used great care in transporting the missiles from the Soviet Union and in moving them to the deployment sites. The failure to camouflage the sites (analogous to the Soviet failure to construct dummy missiles to buttress the early missile claims) suggests that the Soviets had failed to develop a completely coordinated plan (the deception planners only covered the transportation phase) and/or that the Strategic Rocket Force construction teams had not yet realized the need to alter their practices to fool the U-2 capabilities (probably because, in the segmented world of Soviet intelligence, no one had told the SRF of the U-2's capabilities). The Soviets only began to camouflage the missiles after the US had imposed the blockade.

The Cuban Missile deception continued the general thrust of Soviet strategic deception. The initial missile deception had failed. To redress the balance, Khrushchev decided to emplace missiles in Cuba. Only by deceiving the US could Khrushchev pull off the coup. Perhaps the Soviets failed to appreciate the capabilities of the U-2. But perhaps the Soviets were more impressed by the electoral venality of American politicians. Perhaps they thought that Kennedy would have no stomach for an international crisis immediately before the election and would call off U-2 flights over Cuba. But such theorizing presumes too much. The failure of the Cuban Missile deception left the Soviets, for the second time but with much more impressive evidence, in a compromising position of clear strategic inferiority.

II: Compensating for Weakness to 1968

The Cuban Missile crisis left Soviet policy in a shambles. The crisis not only confirmed Soviet strategic inferiority but also underscored the political importance of strategic advantage. Khrushchev's bragging had reaped not only the embarrassment of the crisis but also an invigorated US armament program that included US advancement in both strategic offensive and defensive systems. Mere words would not compensate for Soviet weakness, but they needed a program that would at least give the West pause in some of its more adventurist excesses. The Soviets turned from an emphasis on quantity to quality in their public statements. They launched a massive armament program which would find them with over 1,400 ICBM launchers by 1970.

Although Khrushchev fell from grace in 1963, the policy pursued by Brezhnev differed more in style than in substance. The qualitative deceptions begun by Khrushchev continued under Brezhnev who realized that he needed to compensate for weakness as the US launched new global offensives in Indochina and the Dominican Republic. At the same time, Brezhnev realized that he could not directly threaten the US as Khrushchev had done. Thus, Brezhnev and Khrushchev before him seized on US statements that emphasized Soviet-US parity. Qualitative comparisons carried the day.

Many of the Soviet attempts to manipulate US perceptions during this period invite two interpretations. The Soviets may have simply been boasting about capabilities that they thought they would have: the ABM, the mobile missile, and the global rocket. Khrushchev had made early claims about the ABM and the global rocket, but only under Brezhnev did they appear in parades. Towards the end of the sixties, the Soviets ceased making claims about both the ABM related capabilities for the SA-5 and the intercontinental features of the mobile missile. They actually tested the operational capability for the global rocket, otherwise known as Fractional Orbital Bombardment System (FOBS), but the failure of the US to deploy its ABM left the global rocket without a strategic purpose. For whatever reason, the Soviets did not deploy its first generation mobile systems, the SS-13, SS-14, and SS-15. Nevertheless, the Soviets did exploit the implications of the mobile systems long after they knew that they would not deploy them. They did treat as operational systems such as the global rocket which they had not yet tested. By inference, they later denied with the ABM treaty that the SA-5 system possessed any of the ABM capabilities that they had earlier claimed. They confused the distinction between SSBNs and nuclear attack submarines to enhance perceptions of their capability.

The period between the Cuban Missile Crisis and SALT has the Soviets trying to achieve at least technological parity by leaving the impression that they had deployed systems which they still had in the development phase. They even attempted to convey the impression of equal numbers. Repeated references to systems that had not yet achieved operational status and their appearance in parades combined with the Soviet need to compensate for real and perceived weakness suggest strategic deception not simply a pointing with pride at future capabilities.

THE ABM DECEPTION, PART ONE

The first ABM deception followed closely the exposure of Soviet exaggerated claims about the numbers and capabilities of their ICBM force. The second ABM deception forms part of the coordinated effort that parallels and exploits the SALT process. (This section relies heavily on Greenwood.)

The Soviets did little to exploit the extent of their ABM development work until after the collapse of the missile deception. Apparently, the Soviets began work at their range at Sary Shagan in the late 1950s. The U-2 photographed an early prototype of the Hen House radar. The US radar in Turkey, used to cover Soviet ICBM tests, lacked the range to detect any interceptor activity at Sary Shagan. Photographs could not readily distinguish between air and missile defense missiles. A primitive phased array radar like the early Hen House could serve the function of early warning. Even if the Soviets were not working on an ABM, they could have staged an ABM deception in the late 1950s. Instead they chose the missile deception to deter a possible US missile attack (the downing of the U-2 provided the necessary propaganda about the effectiveness of the Soviet air defense). The ABM defense, once deployed, would 'surprise' and thwart the US attack. In fact, Soviet commentators emphasized that nothing could stop a missile attack. In October 1960, Major General Talensky wrote, 'So far there is no practical way of repulsing a nuclear rocket attack' [G:172]. Despite the Soviet low profile on the ABM, the Assistant Secretary of the Army (Research and Development) concluded in February 1961, 'It is my opinion, based on my information, that the Russians have a large, very large antimissile effort and have had for some time.'

Atmospheric tests in September 1961 led to widespread speculation that the Soviets had substantially increased their understanding of how to manage an ABM system. High-altitude tests provide critical information about the effects of nuclear explosions on radars and radio communications and the kill radius of an antimissile warhead [see *NYT*, 3/3/62:2]. In justifying the resumption of US tests, Kennedy argued:

> We are spending great sums of money on radar to alert our defenses and to develop antimissile systems — on the communications which enable our command and control centers to direct a response — on hardening our missile sites, shielding our missiles and their warheads from defensive actions and providing them with electronic guidance systems to find their targets. But we cannot be certain how much of this preparation will turn out to be useless blacked out, paralyzed or destroyed by the complex effects of nuclear explosions ... [U]ntil we measure the effects of actual explosions in the atmosphere under realistic conditions, we will not know precisely how to equip our future defenses, how best to equip our missiles or penetrate an antimissile system, and whether it is possible to achieve such a system ourselves.

In October 1961, the Soviets claimed that missile defense no longer posed a problem. Marshal Malinovsky, in addressing the Communist party congress, announced: 'I must report to you especially that the problem of destroying missiles in flight has been successfully solved' [*NYT*, 10/24/61]. During 1961, US intelligence interpreted construction in the Leningrad area as the beginnings of an ABM system. This system never became operational.

In July 1962, Khrushchev claimed that the Soviet Union had developed an antimissile missile [*NYT,* 7/11/62:4] and a 'global' rocket. A week later he claimed that the antimissile missile could 'hit a fly in outer space'. He also disparaged the recent US high altitude tests by claiming that 'we actually have a global rocket that cannot be destroyed by any anti-rocket means and I know, if anybody knows, what anti-rocket means are because we do have them'. [The 'global rocket' eventually appeared as the FOBS system on the SS-9, another example of Soviet deception] [*NYT,* 7/17/62:1]. In December 1962, following the débâcle of the Cuban Missile Crisis, Marshal Biryuzov, Commander-in-Chief of the Soviet Rocket Forces, claimed: 'The USSR has proved her superiority over the United States in the field of antimisile defenses' [*NYT,* 12/11/62].

The resumption of Soviet testing in early 1963 confirmed earlier conjecture. Hanson Baldwin reported:

> In the most recent series of tests in the Arctic, Moscow is believed to have accumulated considerable data on antimissile defenses. A number of high altitude shots were fired, and the effects upon radio and radar noted. In one test a multimegaton thermonuclear warhead, detonated presumably above the atmosphere, destroyed two ballistic missiles [*NYT,* 4/5/63, 8:1].

In February, Marshal Biryuzov continued the claim that 'the problem of destroying enemy rockets in flight has been successfully solved in our country' [*NYT,* 2/22/63].

In November, the parade honoring the anniversary of the Bolshevik revolution contained a missile that Marshal Biryuzov claimed on radio could destroy 'the enemy's rockets in the air'. Other Soviet commentators indicated that this was the missile that Khrushchev had credited with the ability to hit 'a fly in space'. *Tass* touted the missile as able to thwart 'any modern means of air-space attack'. Nevertheless, Western analysts thought the Griffon interceptor merely a larger variant of other Soviet SAMs [*NYT,* 11/8/63].

The display of the Griffon in November 1963 seems designed to shore up the reputation of the Leningrad system with which it had been deployed beginning in 1961. In August 1963, Harold Brown, then Director of Defense Research and Engineering, had argued, 'Any deployed system which the Soviets are likely to have now, or in the near future does not appear to be as effective, almost certainly not more effective, than the Nike-Zeus'. His predecessor, Herbert York, went even further, 'Anybody can put some missiles around and say, "I have got an anti-ballistic missile system". It is quite a different thing to have one that would work. I stand on my belief that it won't work' [F:91]. York may have stumbled upon the true purpose of the initial Leningrad system, to deceive the West into believing that the Soviets possessed an operational ABM. By 1964 the Soviets had begun to dismantle the Leningrad system, replacing it with the Tallinn line. The confusion over the Griffon served several purposes, the most important of which was to confuse in the minds of the West the differences between the Soviet air and missile defenses. This confusion carried over into the SALT period.

The Soviets began constructing an ABM system around Moscow in 1962. The Try Add missile tracking radars followed closely upon construction of the interceptor complexes [G:173]. The Galosh interceptor appeared for the first time in the November 1964 parade. Confusion reigned over whether the Galosh had an endo- or exo-atmospheric mission, but Soviet sources claimed it could hit enemy missiles 'hundreds of miles' from defended targets. The long range of the Galosh suggested an area defense. Construction also began on the Hen House radars designed to provide early warning with some capability to track missiles. Unlike the Tallinn line, the Moscow system seemed clearly designed to perform the ABM mission.

The Soviets continued to claim that they had solved the missile defense problem. In February 1965, Marshal Sokolovsky claimed, 'We have successfully solved the complex and extremely important problem of intercepting and destroying enemy rockets in flight' [NYT, 2/18/65]. In May, the Soviets again displayed the antimissile missile [NYT, 5/10/65]. To reinforce the impression of an effective ABM, the Soviets broadcast a program on television which showed an ABM installation and the intercept of an ICBM [NYT, 5/11/65]. In the Yugoslav army paper, Defense Minister Malinovsky in February 1966 stated that the Soviet Union could bring down enemy missiles 'at great distances from the targets that are being defended'.

The construction of the Tallinn line upon the dismantling of the Leningrad system began in 1963. Construction began at sites originally used for anti-aircraft missiles and spread over a broad area, covering the Minuteman access routes to the north and later the Polaris access routes in the south. Despite these locations, the use of a mechanically steered radar for tracking and guidance, the distinctive construction signature of an anti-aircraft site with three launch sites, six launch positions, and one radar, and an assessment that the missile seemed designed for operations within the atmosphere (inconsistent with US notions that the Tallinn system seemed best located for an area defense which would require an exo-atmospheric missile) led McNamara to eventually conclude in 1967 that: 'The weight of the evidence at the moment tends to support the conclusion that the primary mission of the Tallinn system is air defense'. The upgraded Griffon (SA-5) seemed designed to hit targets at medium to high altitude between 12 to 20 miles. The US had already abandoned the high altitude penetrating B-70 bomber in favor of low altitude penetration tactics with the B-52s. The Soviet decision to deploy extensively a system for which the US analysts could find no threat had figured heavily in the conclusion that the SA-5 must possess an antimissile capability [F:90–95]. When the missile finally became operational in 1967, doubts about its capabilities began to decline. In his FY 1969 posture statement, McNamara concluded:

> Now, I can tell you that the majority of our intelligence community no longer believes that this so-called 'Tallinn' system [which is being deployed across the northwestern approaches to the Soviet Union and several other places] has any significant ABM capability. This system is apparently designed for use within the atmosphere, most likely against an aerodynamic rather than a ballistic missile threat [G:176].

The Western perception that the Griffon SA-5 system must deal with aero-dynamic threats failed to take into account the earlier US designs for an ABM, the Nike-Zeus. Soviet desire to develop a minimal capability against the warhead designs and tactics of the early 1960s can explain the extensive deployment of the SA-5, especially if the Soviets wished to have an infra-structure available for future technological breakthroughs. US intelligence analysis tends to emphasize the technical characteristics over the accom-panying infrastructure. Deployment of the SA-5 may seem stupid in the light of high beta RVs with penetration aids. The SA-5 would still possess limited capability against low-level threats and its infrastructure could provide the basis for a future area ABM system. The US had rejected the Nike-Zeus in favor of the Nike-X (which combined the Nike-Zeus missile with a phased array radar and a high acceleration interceptor, SPRINT). The Nike-Zeus missile had evolved out of the anticraft missile, Nike-Hercules. McNamara decided not to deploy the Nike-Zeus because it would have been obsolete. Nevertheless a description of the Nike-Zeus system resembles the SA-5 system:

> From the beginning, the scientists and engineers who manned DDR&E and ARPA questioned the basic feasibility of NIKE-ZEUS. First, they noted the difficulties currently inherent in defending populations. Because of limited interceptor range and acceleration, intercept would necessarily take place close to the interceptor launch site. Each system could protect only a very small area, a 'point', around the ABM. A separate system would be needed for each locus — say a city — to be protected. Either the entire network would be very costly, or some cities would go unprotected. Furthermore, an attacker could defeat the system by aiming the ICBM just outside the protected radius so that fallout would drift in (the 'upwind tactic') — requiring in turn an extensive system of fallout shelters. Second, they argued that the system's slow, mechanically steered radars made it vulnerable to saturation. Third, they noted that the ZEUS interceptors' low acceleration forced the system to fire its interceptors before incoming targets had penetrated the atmosphere very far, rendering the system unable to discriminate decoys [*Comm on Org of Gov for con of For Pol*, Vol. 4:164].

Administration claims that the Soviets did not deploy the SA-5 with missile defense in mind not only neglect the characteristics of the proposed US first-generation system but also the objectives the Soviets may have been pursuing by deploying the system. Soviet design practice often differs from the US. The US used the characteristics of their proposed second-generation system to suggest that the SA-5 possessed only an air defense mission. The US left open the issue of why the Soviets had deployed the system in the first place. The Soviets had claimed in the early 1960s that the system possessed antimissile capability.

The Soviets would see in the Tallinn debate excellent opportunities for deception. They had succeeded in deploying a system for which Western intelligence analysts could find no useful purpose. They had spread real doubts about their strategic intentions and had the opportunity (if they followed Western press accounts) to undermine the impression that the Tallinn system really had an antimissile capability. They had also succeeded (certainly something they had not intended) in stimulating US MIRV development. If the Soviets had intended the Tallinn to have an antimissile capability, they had created a situation where it would be extremely effective if a war should come because the US would discount its effectiveness in planning.

Those advocating a Tallinn ABM capability retreated in 1968 to its potential for a surge ABM capability through a rapid upgrade. To counter McNamara's statements, the Strategic Air Command and the office of the Director of Defense Research and Engineering argued:

> Rather than start from scratch with a new ABM system, which would be detectable and would involve long lead times, the Soviets might well forego quality in favor of a speedy and possible clandestine upgrade of Tallinn's existing radar and missile infrastructure. This, it was further argued would give them virtually overnight, an ABM network far more extensive than anything the United States would develop over a reasonable period of time [F:94; N:12].

Soviet claims about the effectiveness of their missile defense began to change just as part of the Tallinn system became operational in 1967. In February 1967, the head of the Frunze Military Academy, General Kurochkin said, 'Detecting missiles in time and destroying them in flight is no problem' [*NYT*, 2/21/67]. He went even further and claimed: 'If enemy missiles fly, they will not arrive in Moscow' [*NYT*, 2/23/67]. Two days later Marshal Grechko seemed to dispute Kurochkin's claims. Grechko, First Deputy Defense Minister, acknowledged that antimissile systems could not completely prevent enemy missiles from reaching their targets. The head of Soviet civil defense, Marshal Chuikov, claimed on television: 'Unfortunately, there are no means yet that would guarantee the complete security of our cities and the most important objectives from the blows of the enemy's weapons of mass destruction' [*NYT*, 2/23/67]. Obviously, Chuikov would find himself out of a job if Kurochkin's boasts proved correct. The Soviets now claimed that their defense would thwart most threats. Marshal Zakharov argued in February 1968: 'The country's anti-aircraft defense has undergone huge changes. It has obtained the means which guarantee the reliable destruction of any plane and many of the enemy's rockets.' The confusion over ABM and the Tallinn line stems in part from the Soviet inclusion of both ABM and air defense under the same organization, a fact illustrated by Zakharov's comment.

During the initial phases of SALT, the Soviets maintained a low profile. In February 1970, however, Marshal Grechko, now Minister of Defense, returned to earlier claims for Soviet ABM: 'Great changes have taken place also in the country's air defense forces. We possess weapons capable of reliably hitting enemy aircraft and missiles irrespective of height or speed of their flight, at great distances from the defended targets' [G:177]. Some Western analysts interpreted this claim as a bid by Grechko to gain resources for the ABM program in the negotiations over the upcoming five-year plan [G:177].

Extensive claims about the effectiveness of the Soviet ABM program in the early 1960s gave way to virtual silence and disclaimers as SALT approached. Only the Moscow ABM remained unambiguously an ABM system. Western analysts discounted the value of the Tallinn line for ABM, but still failed to explain its true mission.

THE MOBILE MISSILE DECEPTION, PART ONE

Concerned about the vulnerability of their missiles in the mid-1960s, the Soviets decided to deploy a mobile MRBM/ICBM system based on the SS-13 and the JS-3 heavy tank chassis. As in the current controversy over the SS-20 and the SS-16, the Soviets used the top two stages of the SS-13 as a basis for the SS-14, the mobile MRBM. Very little public information has appeared on the SS-15 which shares the same chassis as the SS-14. Claims about these systems began in the early 1960s, but never ranked with the claims made about the ABM system. The Soviets apparently never deployed extensively the SS-14 and SS-13 but they clearly served as the prototypes for the current SS-20 and SS-16 systems. The potential of a mobile missile never excited much attention in the West, in part because, despite claims of its existence, the Soviets never displayed an SS-13 with a transporter, erector, launcher (TEL).

The SS-13 and SS-14 first appeared in the May 1965 parade [*NYT*, 5/10/65]. *Tass* had very little to say about these missiles in May. The Soviets again displayed these missiles in November. The first deputy commander-in-chief of the Strategic Rocket Forces, General Tolubko, stressed the need to develop such systems because with current reconnaissance capabilities, stationary ICBM sites 'can hardly be concealed'. He went further to say, 'The presence of mobile roving intercontinental rocket complexes precludes the possibility of space and air reconnaissance. No one can know the areas of locality of such launching ramps, which increases the survival capacity of our strategic means' [*NYT*, 11/18/65:3:2]. Tolubko's need to stress the value of the mobile missile coincides with statements by Brezhnev and Malinovsky in 1965 disputing Western claims about US strategic superiority [see below]. If reconnaissance could not locate the mobile systems (especially the inter-continental SS-13 system which seems never to have reached operational status), then the Soviets obviously could have redressed the balance. The next year, Tolubko made very similar comments, again noting that the SRF possessed 'small-sized solid fuel missiles on self-propelled launching facilities, both of medium and intercontinental range' [*Tass*, 11/16/66].

An article appearing in the 10 July 1965 issue of *Red Star* noted:

> The launching of strategic rockets can be carried out from various installations — from the surface or underground, from stationary as well as mobile installations, including self-propelled installations which insure the maneuverability and invulnerability of the rocket troops.

At the annual Artillery and Rocket Day in November, the Soviet SRF leadership continued to make references to their mobile ICBM throughout the late 1960s. Tolubko in November 1967 in a *Tass* interview claimed:

> The power of the nuclear warhead has increased several times in [the last ten] years, while the weight of the head part of the rocket has considerably declined. This has made it possible to have both stationary underground launchers and mobile, small-size launching complexes with an international range of action. 'Such highly maneuverable rocket complexes are practically imperceptible to the enemy's space reconnaissance. It is impossible to strike an armed blow at them' [*Tass*, 11/17/67].

Tass noted the mobile missiles in the May 1968 parade as 'difficult for the enemy to hit'. Krylov in November 1968 noted, 'The Strategic Rocket Forces have at their disposal the most perfect missile systems, including intercontinental solid-fuel missiles with self-propelled launchers' [*FBIS*, 11/20/68]. In emphasizing recent advances, Marshal Zakharov noted in April 1969, 'A great number of new, and what is particularly important, mobile launching installations have been built for the Strategic Rocket Forces. These missiles are always ready for immediate action' [*FBIS*, 5/12/69].

The Soviets were clearly trying to convey the impression that they possessed an operational mobile ICBM, the deployment of which would go undetected by US reconnaissance. They emplaced the SS-13, not on a TEL, but in silos after it reached initial operational capability in 1969. The limited deployment of the SS-13 to 60 suggested that the Soviets did not view their first attempt as a success, a fact confirmed by their failure to deploy the SS-14 and SS-15. The Soviets last displayed the SS-14 in the November 1972 parade. On the other hand, the Soviets may have decided that deploying missiles in silos afforded enough protection with the US CEPs of the late 1960s and early 1970s and delayed deployment of a mobile system (with its logistical complications) until the SS-20. The claims about mobile missiles in the 1960s seemed designed to influence the Western perception of Soviet capabilities and to create the impression that the Soviets possessed greater capability than accorded them by the Western press. Tolubko even went so far as to cite attempts to conceal ICBM sites. In 1966 he described an ICBM site as possessing 'dependably concealed launching ramps [*sic*] with rockets'. During the Missile Gap period, Malinovsky had also made claims about camouflaging missile sites.

Soviet statements in the mid-1960s seemed designed to undermine the common impression that the Soviets possessed a dramatically inferior number of weapons. In early 1965, Sokolovsky claimed that the Soviet Union had reached parity with the US in atomic submarines [*NYT*, 2/18/65]. Whatever the veracity of this statement, Sokolovsky neglected to note the Soviet Union possessed no modern SSBN comparable to the Polaris submarines in the US inventory. Instead he said, 'The difference may be one or two. This does not alter the situation.' He characterized the Western comparisons between US and Soviet strategic arsenals as 'juggling' that did little to improve East-West relations.

Brezhnev also contested Western claims. In a speech to the graduates of the

Soviet military academies, Brezhnev warned:

> We hate to boast and we do not want to threaten anybody, but we must note that the figures and estimates attributed in the West to Soviet nuclear missile power do no credit at all to the information possessed by their compilers, particularly by the intelligence services of the imperialist states. Any attempt to take aggressive action against our country on the basis of this kind of evaluation of our military potential will prove fatal to its initiators [NYT, 7/4/65].

Brezhnev may have viewed the humiliation over the Cuban Missile Crisis and the clear inferiority of Soviet strategic weaponry as leading to the actions in Vietnam and the Dominican Republic. To compensate for this impression of inferiority, the Soviets displayed weapons and alluded to weapons that they still had in the development phase, such as the SS-14. Sokolovsky's earlier comments in 1965 obscuring the difference between ballistic missile, cruise missile, and attack nuclear submarines started the campaign punctuated by Brezhnev's speech. Brezhnev's comments clearly demonstrated his awareness of the relationship between deterrence and perceptions of nuclear strength. The display of weapons in 1965 indicated that the Soviets knew they needed tangible evidence of their recent developments.

THE GLOBAL MISSILE DECEPTION

The Soviets made more mileage out of their global than they did their mobile missile. Despite their attempts to portray their antimissile defense as impervious to US countermeasures, they described their global missile as capable of penetrating any defense. Although Khrushchev made the first claims about the global rocket in 1962, the Soviets did not display it until 1965 when Brezhnev feared the consequences of perceived Soviet strategic weakness.

Reacting to the Missile Gap fiasco, Khrushchev touted the 'global' missile for the first time in March 1962 [NYT, 3/17/62]. Claims about extreme accuracy generally accompanied any statement about the global rocket (for a discussion of the accuracy 'deception', see below). Khrushchev apparently viewed the deployment of 'radio location and other warning facilities' across Canada as prefatory to an antimissile system. (His views here may suggest something about the Tallinn deployments across northern Soviet Union):

> The United States military wanted to protect themselves by some barrier from the Soviet retaliatory blow. For this purpose they set up a system of radar and other facilities in order to intercept in flight rockets that go approximately across the North Pole, i.e. along the shortest line.

[The US never deployed the antimissile system based on the Nike-Zeus. The Soviets at this time were deploying something around Leningrad based on an air defense missile. Khrushchev may have interpreted US deployments in the same light as his own. If so, the SA-5 subsequently deployed may represent an attempt by Khrushchev to deploy an antimissile and not simply an anti-aircraft system]. To counter US ABM technology, Khrushchev had ordered his scientists to build the global missile, which he felt, because it avoided the US ABM system [!], was 'invulnerable to antimissile weapons':

> The new global rockets can fly around the world in any direction and strike a blow at any set target. The precision of the calculations is borne out, for instance, by the flights of the Vostok I and Vostok II spaceships.
>
> Global rockets can fly from the oceans or other directions where warning facilities cannot be installed. Given global rockets, the warning system in general has lost its importance.
>
> Global missiles cannot be spotted in due time to prepare any measures against them. In general the money spent in the United States to create antimissile systems is simply wasted ...

Why Khrushchev would worry about the US wasting its money on ABM would make sense only if he thought the US could field such a system. Soviet claims about the global missile contrast sharply with claims about the effectiveness of their own antimissile system. They had a missile invulnerable to countermeasures while no US missile could penetrate to its target in the Soviet Union.

In reacting to claims of US superiority, Khrushchev touted the invincibility of the global rocket. In the talk that contained the 'fly in space' claim in July 1962, Khrushchev argued: 'I am not boasting, but we actually have a global rocket that cannot be destroyed by any anti-rocket means and I know, if anybody knows, what anti-rocket means are because we do have them' [*NYT*, 7/17/62]. In December 1962 following the Cuban Missile Crisis fiasco, Marshal Biryuzov claimed that Soviet nuclear weapons could be 'delivered by our strategic rockets to any point on earth' [*NYT*, 12/11/62]. In February 1963, he asserted that the Soviet Union could 'at a command from earth ... launch rockets from satellites'. In November, Marshal Krylov, in an obvious reference to the global missile, contended that the latest Soviet tests demonstrated that they could hit targets with 'super-sniper accuracy' at a distance of over 8000 miles [*NYT*, 11/17/63].

In May 1965, the Soviets for the first time rolled out their orbital or global missile. *Tass* described the 110-foot missile as having unlimited range [*NYT*, 5/10/81]. *Aviation Week* speculated that the Soviets may have prepared the missile for show, noting that the 'metal-tube truss structure was questioned, particularly whether it could stand bending moments in pitchover' and the opinion of some that the missile may be 'an amalgamation of various stages' [*AWST*, 5/24/65]. When this missile, now identified as the SS-10, passed the reviewing stand Moscow radio said:

> Three-stage intercontinental missiles are passing by. Their design is improved. They are very reliable in use. Their servicing is fully automated. The parade of awesome battle might is being crowned by the gigantic orbital missiles. They are akin to the carrier rockets which put into space our remarkable spaceships like Voskhod 2. For these missiles there is no limit in range. The main property of missiles of this class is

their ability to hit enemy objectives literally from any direction, which make them virtually invulnerable to antimissile defense means [*Soviet Space Programs, 1966–1970*:335].

The SS-10 also appeared as an 'orbital rocket' in the May and November parades in 1966. In the November 1967 parade the SS-10 was relegated to intercontinental status: 'They were followed by three-stage intercontinental rockets firing [*sic*] new, highly efficient kinds of propellant. They need little time to be readied for firing and can be launched from silos and other launching ramps' [*SSP*, 66–70:337]. Brezhnev would later claim that the Soviet Union possessed intercontinental and orbital missiles 'sufficient to finish off once and for all any aggressor or group of aggressors [*NYT*, 7/4/65]. Closely following Brezhnev's speech, the 10 July 1965 issue of *Red Star* noted: 'Our rocket troops have a sufficient number of intercontinental, orbital, and other rockets to wipe any aggressor off the face of the earth.'

In November 1966, *Tass* ran an interview with Tolubko in which he claimed: 'Soviet global missiles have unlimited range and can hit a target literally from any direction.'

The November 1967 parade unveiled the SS-9 as the new orbital rocket. *Tass* noted: 'The last to appear were mammoth rockets each of which can deliver to target nuclear warheads of tremendous power. Not a single army has such warheads. These rockets can be used for intercontinental and orbital launchings' [*SSP*:337–8].

The May 1968 parade merely implied an orbital capability. When the SS-9 arrived in the square, *Tass* reported: 'The last to cross Red Square were the most powerful strategic missiles, whose range of flight is unlimited. They can strike blows on enemy objectives from any direction. The potential might of their warheads is unlimited' [*FBIS*, 5/1/68:B7]. References to 'orbital' missiles continued until the early 1970s, although the term orbital generally was converted into missiles of 'unlimited range'. Discussions of 'orbital' missiles generally contained references to their ability to penetrate effectively missile defenses. For example, the 1967 interview with Tolubko contained the following: 'There are no unreachable areas on the globe for the Soviet intercontinental missiles. Their use by no means depends upon natural or climatic conditions.' Krylov's address for Artillery and Rocket Day in November 1968 claimed:

> Strategic missiles, because of their unlimited operational range, are capable of hitting any target on the globe in the shortest time with their powerful nuclear warheads. This weapon is now practically invulnerable to existing antirocket defense systems.

In April 1969, Marshal Zakharov stated, 'Missiles of the global variety have an unlimited firing range'. In November 1969, Krylov seemed to retreat from earlier claims by stating, 'Our strategic missiles have practically unlimited range. They are capable of delivering powerful nuclear warheads in minimal time and with a high degree of accuracy to targets at any point of the globe' [*Pravda*, 11/19/69]. Marshal of the Artillery Kuleshov made a very similar claim, 'Modern missiles, which have an almost unlimited range and are capable of carrying nuclear warheads of colossal power and of hitting their targets with startling accuracy, are always on alert' [*TRUD*, 11/19/69].

Krylov in November 1970 did not repeat his earlier claims but instead emphasized the constant readiness of the missiles:

> Soviet strategic rockets are remarkable for their practically unlimited range and great accuracy and can carry thermonuclear warheads of tremendous power. They can be fired at any time of the year or day, irrespective of weather conditions and ensure exceptionally high degree of reliability in striking various targets at any distances.

In 1966, the Soviets began an active campaign to test the 'orbital' missile (known in US strategic vernacular as Fractional Orbital Bombardment Systems [FOBS]). They launched two unannounced flights in 1966, both of which left considerable debris in orbit. In 1967, they announced their flight test program (although they failed to specify mission) and continued the tests until 1970 [*SSP*: 334–338;523]. Soviet claims about FOBS eventually led to its development in the late 1960s and presumably to an operational capability. Although the Soviets may have exaggerated the accuracy of the missile and its invulnerability to missile defenses, the extent of their test program indicates that they seriously pursued a FOBS capability. Thus, their 'orbital' missile does not rate as a true strategic deception except insofar as they implied an operational capability when they had not advanced beyond the development stage. The use of the SS-10 in the military parades also suggests part of a campaign to tout Soviet military capabilities when the Western press was emphasizing Soviet strategic inferiority.

Although Soviet claims emphasized the ability of their orbital missiles to avoid those areas covered by US early warning radars, FOBS can defeat missile defenses by following a depressed trajectory. The FOBS would enter radar coverage later and closer to the target than a regular ICBM which would follow a minimum energy trajectory. A depressed trajectory would require more energy and thus lead to a smaller payload. Soviet interest in FOBS declined when it became clear that the US would not deploy its ABM.

THE 'ACCURACY DECEPTION', PART ONE

Controversy over the causes of the US systematic underestimation of the Soviet ICBM buildup in the late 1960s has led some authors to speculate that the Soviets also disguised the missions for their missiles, specifically that they systematically altered their flight tests to suggest lower accuracy. US analysts did underestimate Soviet commitment to an extensive buildup, in part because they failed to divine a purpose for the numbers of SS-11s the Soviets eventually deployed. In 1977, former Assistant Secretary of Defense for Intelligence, Albert C. Hall, noted:

> Since the USSR deploys more than 1,400 missiles, its nuclear arm has

almost inconceivable destructive ability. It is difficult to see why the Soviet Union requires a force of this magnitude, since less than one-fifth the force could destroy the economic structure of the US and there are no defenses to penetrate.

One must conclude that some fraction of the Soviet ballistic missile force is planned to attack the Minuteman force. Major changes now underway in the Soviet land-based force support this view . . . (quoted in Harris, p. 61).

This passage reveals a number of prejudices sufficient to explain US underestimation, even if the Soviets did not emphasize nuclear threat in their public targeting literature. First, it assumes that the Soviets would strike first with their missiles undamaged and their C3 system intact. A conservative Soviet planner would size his force against the targets he needed to cover should he lack warning sufficient to launch from under a US surprise attack. Second, it assumes that Soviet force sizing depends on some objective evaluation of the targeting requirements as dictated by strategic doctrine and the threat. An objective analyst would be hard pressed to relate US force structure to some 'rational' criteria. We should have as little reason to expect the rationality of Soviet deployments as we do our own. Third, that Soviet decisions to deploy 1,400 ICBMs occurred when the US had an active ABM program clearly pointed towards an operational status. The Soviet FOBS program made sense only in terms of the expected ABM deployment. Fourth, it neglects the sensitivity that the Soviets have displayed about the perception of strategic inferiority. The Soviet interest in SALT stems in part from their need to achieve publicly strategic parity. As Brezhnev warned in 1965, he did not wish the West to attack simply because it incorrectly viewed itself as strategically superior.

William Harris advances another argument, that the Soviets deceived the West regarding the accuracy of their missiles:

Nevertheless, during the 1960s, just as US intelligence analysts were growing confident that the Soviets overrepresented capabilities, and that we could catch them every time, just the opposite happened. With an understanding of the technical indicators and methods of US estimation of ballistic missile accuracy, the Soviets managed to underrepresent the accuracy of intercontinental ballistic missiles. The earlier bluffing upward corresponded to decisions not to invest in nuclear armed rockets early, while seeking silo-killing capabilities. US Defense Secretary Harold Brown has recently indicated that the Soviet SS-9 ICBM was always aimed at the launch control centers of the Minuteman missile complexes. Only systematic biasing of technical indicators would produce the apparently large errors in guidance and the actually quite limited errors needed to justify attack on so hardened a set of military targets [Harris:60].

Harris cites an article which directly relates the US assessments of low accuray and numerical underestimation to a Soviet strategic deception program.

There had appeared

> acute concern ... that ... the KGB may have succeeded over many years
> in systematically deceiving United States intelligence about Moscow's
> military capacities and intentions. Prior to the sacking of the key
> members of the CIA staff at the end of 1974 they were engaged [with the
> help of the CIA's Directorate of Science and Technology] in ... assess-
> ments of military intelligence culled from Soviet agents recruited by the
> FBI in New York ... The tentative conclusion reached was that much of
> the information from these suspect sources — for example, exaggerated
> accounts of the problems faced by the Russians in constructing missile
> guidance system[s] — was part of a strategic deception programme
> which was at least partly responsible for the CIA's notorious under-
> valuation of the Soviet defense effort in the mid-1970s [Harris:79–80].

Harris concludes that the Soviets may have introduced systematic error into
their flight test program. He argues that the time lags involved and the
predisposition of intelligence analysts to construe all error as random would
undermine any interpretation of part of the error as systematic. Of course, a
sufficiently large sample size would reveal, but not explain, systematic error.
Harris also believes that the Soviets may not have abandoned radio guidance
as quickly as the US. He interprets the Soviet experiments with Doppler
communications from satellites in the mid-1960s as indicative of a Doppler-
aided missile guidance program [H:72–75].

A Soviet strategic deception program in their flight tests of the mid-1960s
(for the third-generation missiles) and possibly for the mid-1970s (for the
fourth-generation, see below) seems at odds with their public statements
about targeting and the accuracy of their missiles. The Soviets continued to
claim 'super-sniper' accuracy for their orbital missiles and always listed
nuclear threat (and its accompanying command and control) at the top of
their target list. The Soviets also claimed to deploy a mobile ICBM in the mid-
1960s that reconnaissance could detect only with great difficulty. The Soviets
claimed in the mid-1960s that Western analysts were underestimating Soviet
capabilities. Thus, it would seem that the Soviets were trying to impress upon
the West that they had greater capabilities.

The little specific information on Soviet accuracy also conflicts with
Harris's thesis. An East German publication in 1967 generally touts the
overall superiority of the Soviet Strategic Rocket Force, but also stresses
accuracy improvements:

> ... the accuracy of the Soviet Rocket forces is extremely high. In the
> annual tests which the Soviet Union is conducting with its inter-
> continental rockets, generally covering a range of about 13,000 km, the
> deviation from the center of the target has been reduced since 1960 from
> 2,000 m down to 160 m. This kind of very near miss would not influence
> the accomplishment of the combat mission when a nuclear warhead in
> the megaton range is used [*Neues Deutschland,* 9/30/67].

A systematic Soviet program to disguise the accuracy of their third-generation missiles would conflict with the Soviet policy of deterrence which emphasizes defense and damage limitation. The Soviets value high accuracy because it increases their ability to fight and 'win' a nuclear war. Western thought considered high accuracy 'destabilizing' because it undermined the ability to launch an assured second strike. Such thought astounds the Soviet mind. To project an image of low accuracy would threaten deterrence from the Soviet perspective because an opponent need not fear inaccurate weapons.

III: Managing the Transition to Parity, 1968-1974

The tremendous expansion in Soviet strategic offensive programs in the mid- to late 1960s apparently excited very little interest in the US. Harris explained the lack of reaction by suggesting that the Soviets had deceived the West about the accuracy of their missiles and thus clouded their true counterforce mission. Others suggest that US doctrine pointed towards a sufficient number of missiles needed for deterrence and so long as the number of Soviet missiles did not threaten US second-strike capability, accuracy in estimates did not matter. The failure of the US intelligence to predict the Soviet build-up suggests a poor understanding of the missions that the Soviets expected their ICBMs to perform in war. Alternatively, the Soviets could have used strategic deception to fool US intelligence by disguising the magnitude of the build-up.

Material that Sullivan [*1980, in Godson*] has produced suggests that the Soviets did not attempt to disguise the magnitude of their build-up. Brezhnev had in 1965 voiced concern over US underestimates. The data on construction starts for silos in the mid- to late 1960s indicates ample evidence for predicting Soviet missile deployments (Sullivan does not reveal the source of the silo start data so any use of it must remain speculative). Perhaps Brezhnev thought that the Vietnam War drained enough US resources not to stimulate a US armament program, especially since the Soviets did not attempt to exploit their arrival at parity. In fact, the US responded by attempting to initiate arms control talks that would limit both offensive and defensive systems. To maintain strategic superiority, the US had decided to fractionate its warheads, a much less expensive proposition than building new missile launchers.

Although the Soviets had not initiated SALT, once it became clear that the US would continue with its ABM program, they seized upon SALT as a means to assure at least strategic parity and hopefully strategic superiority. The early phases of the talks would coincide with completion of the seven-year plan begun in 1963 after the Cuban Missile Crisis. Although giving lip-service to the goal of parity (and in that regard perpetrating a deception), the Soviets used SALT to gain a strategic advantage guaranteed by the movement from the third- to the fourth-generation missiles.

The Soviets realized that SALT I could only provide them a temporary breathing space unless they institutionalized the process. The tremendous expansion in US strategic programs in the early 1960s served as a warning that only an astute policy carried on over a number of years would delay a US response. Such a policy would require that the Soviet Union downplay any strategic advantage that the forces of modernization provided.

Blatant Soviet strategic deception during SALT itself would prove counter-productive. Rather the Soviets would agree only to do whatever necessary to assure strategic advantage and not limit their modernization programs. Blatant deception could easily backfire; 'sharp practice' that exploited US preconceptions would ease the way to Soviet advantage.

THE PURSUIT OF SUPERIORITY, SOVIET WRITINGS PRIOR TO SALT

Soviet military writings prior to SALT (and especially the 21st Party Congress held in 1971) provide the context for evaluating Soviet policy during SALT itself. These writings would reflect what objectives the Soviets would pursue in SALT. While some have argued that shifts in Soviet public statements after SALT reflect Soviet learning (or at least an appreciation) about the virtues of assured destruction, these shifts could just as easily represent lip-service to continue the gains of the SALT process itself.

Throughout the 1960s, the Soviets returned to the need to pursue superiority. Talensky argued in 1965: 'In our days there is no more dangerous illusion than the idea that thermonuclear war can still serve as an instrument of politics, that it is possible to achieve political aims by using nuclear weapons and still survive . . . ' [G:115]. Garthoff argues that critics disavowed Talensky's view because they thought it undermined the argument for weapons procurement not because they found it theoretically unpalatable. However, the passage by Talensky may simply reflect his desire to undercut Western urges towards nuclear war. In 1965, Brezhnev had argued that Western perceptions of their strategic superiority should not lead them to initiate nuclear war. Talensky could be arguing that the West should not try to pursue political objectives through the use of nuclear weapons.

In the 1960s, the Soviets viewed superiority as necessary (but not sufficient) to deter Western aggression. Writing in the restricted circulation General Staff journal, *Military Thought,* in 1964, a Capt. Kulakov argues that 'depriving the enemy of superiority in military technology does not mean depriving him of the capability of starting a new war'. Although Kulakov argues that the 'military potential of the state, its ability to wage war and win victory is now determined by its capability of using [nuclear weapons] in combination with highly effective rocket means of delivery', he cites the need for greater conventional forces:

> . . . in a war against a strong enemy, with extensive territory enabling him to use space and time for the organization of active and passive defense, the maneuver of forces and the mobilization of reserves — a single attack with strategic rocket-nuclear weapons is not enough for a complete victory over such an enemy.

Kulakov is simply acknowledging the tradition of the 'long war' in Soviet military thought, that if socialism fails to achieve its strategic objectives in the initial period of the war (generally comprised of the initial massive nuclear exchanges) then it must continue to fight. His article also carries a warning for the West that reliance on nuclear weapons alone will not suffice (although he is actually quarreling with the conventional cutbacks under Khrushchev).

Writing in the public journal, *Kommunist,* Bondarenko continued Kulakov's theme in 1966. He argued that 'under contemporary conditions, the significance of strictly military factors — alongside moral political factors — and especially of military-technological superiority over the enemy is greater'. Bondarenko defines superiority in the context of war, noting that 'military-technological superiority of one side over the other is not absolute, its truth can actually be tested only in direct armed conflict'. He defines superiority as follows:

> military-technological superiority consists in a relation between the quantity and quality of military equipment and weapons, the degree of training of the troops for action with it, and the effectiveness of the organization structure of the army, which gives one side superiority over an actual or potential enemy and make it possible for this side to achieve victory over the enemy.

Bondarenko also makes a revealing comment about the need for techno-logical surprise which explains in part the appearance of the 'mobile ICBM' and the global missile in the parades of the 1960s:

> Achievement of quantitative and qualitative superiority over an adversary usually requires lengthy production efforts. At the same time creation of a basically new weapon, secretly nurtured in scientific research offices and design collectives, can abruptly change the relation between forces in a short period of time.
>
> An important factor, especially under present conditions, is the suddenness of the appearance of this or that new type of weapon. Suddenness in this realm not only affects the morale of an adversary but also deprives him for a long time of the possibility of applying defensive means against the new weapon.

Bondarenko cites orbital rockets and the success that the Soviet Union has achieved in 'creating, for the first time in the world, small size intercontinental solid fuel rockets launched from cross-country caterpillar vehicles' as examples of Soviet superiority.

In a December 1967 issue of *Red Star,* Rear Adm Andreyev explained to the troops the meaning of military superiority. He notes: 'The superiority in forces which is so necessary to win victory still does not mean victory itself: It merely creates the opportunity to win it.' Andreyev notes that the introduc-tion of nuclear weapons has qualitatively changed the nature of warfare:

> Because the main tasks in a possible rocket-nuclear war will be performed by strategic missiles, attack, as well as defense, implemented to various degrees, will acquire a principally new character.
>
> The question of the deployment and covering of troops is now posed in a completely different manner. This is only logical: Superiority over the enemy is not only achieved by destroying his forces, but also by saving one's own forces.

Discussions such as Andreyev's indicate that little controversy surrounded the notion that superiority increased the probability of success in war. Andreyev's article clearly indicates that the Soviets intend to fight on after the initial nuclear strikes until they achieve their objectives.

The Soviets also acknowledged that inferior forces could, if properly applied, defeat the enemy. Such reasoning reflects the Soviet strategic disadvantage relative to the US. Grudinin in mid-1968 does not argue that smaller forces will suffice to launch a retaliatory blow. Rather, he emphasizes:

> A concentration of superior forces at the decisive moment in selected directions at present presupposes primarily the creation of superiority in rocket and nuclear weapons, in morale, in combat skill and the physical readiness of the personnel, in military arts and in the capability of using the forces and the means available to a commander with maximum effectiveness in a minimum time. Nuclear weapons and the modern delivery systems create the possibility of defeating a more numerous weapon in a short period of time. But it must not be excluded that under the designated conditions it is also possible to be defeated by a relatively small-sized enemy. In other words, the role of the subjective factor in turning an unfavorable situation into a favorable one by skillful use of new weapons has risen [sic] as never before. The correct and prompt use of these weapons — not only on a strategic but also on the operational and tactical scale — is the main problem in military art.

Thus, Grudinin resolves the issue of simple quantitative and technological superiority. Until the Soviets gain such a superiority, they need to rely on their troops and their strategy. This strategy involves in part correct choice about the procurement of weapon systems. For example, Bondarenko, in the article cited earlier argues that the Soviets purposely bypassed procuring an intercontinental bomber fleet:

> In our time the strategy of military-technological construction can become a very important element which — if there is correct evaluation of the prospects of the development of military equipment — makes it possible not to follow up all known samples [sic] blindly, but rather to concentrate attention and focus on the more promising types of weapons, skipping some intermediate transitional stages. [The Central Committee has] made it possible for our country, by concentrating efforts on the creation of basically new means of delivery: rockets, to surpass the United States which at that time concentrated its efforts on the development of intercontinental bombers as the only [according to their view at the time] means of delivering nuclear charges.

Even after the debate had begun in Moscow over involvement in the Strategic Arms Limitation Talks, Soviet military leaders continued to stress the need to defeat the enemy should a nuclear war occur. The commentary of the head and deputy head of the Strategic Rocket Forces on the annual Artillery and Rocket Day (19 November) provide an indicator of the trends in Soviet attitudes towards the possibility of victory in nuclear war. In his address in 1968, the SRF commander, Marshal Krylov stated: 'Missile Forces servicemen see their sacred duty in maintaining every launcher in ever-ready, year-round preparedness for inflicting a resolute defeat on imperialist aggressors.' In a 19 November 1969 *Pravda* interview, Krylov styled the Strategic Rocket Forces as 'the main, decisive force for restraining the aggressor and inflicting defeat on him should he unleash a nuclear missile war'. The phrase 'restrain' in this passage represents the Russian equivalent of the American term 'deter' and occasionally appears in *FBIS* translations as 'contain'. When referring to the US deterrent the Soviets generally use the word 'scare' or 'frighten'. The Strategic Rocket Force Political Director, Col. Gen. Yegorov used a similar formula in the 18 November 1969 issue of *Red Star*: 'The strategic missile forces' combat and technical characteristics have made them one of the main means of restraining the aggressor and, in the eventuality of war, of decisively defeating him.'

The formula apparently began to change in 1970. The SRF chief of staff, Col. Gen. Shevtsov did portray the SRF as 'the main force capable not only of restraining an aggressor, but also of inflicting defeat on him, jointly with the armed forces, should a nuclear missile war break out' [*Soviet Russia*, 19 November 1970]. Marshal Krylov toned down his earlier comments and viewed the SRF as simply 'the main striking force in the nuclear war, should the aggressors dare unleash it' and that the SRF should always be prepared 'to inflict a crushing blow at the aggressor'.

The shift continued in 1971. In his 19 November 1971 *Pravda* interview, Marshal Krylov argued that the SRF had become 'a reliable means of deterring the aggressor and maintaining peace', that they were always prepared to 'bring down retaliatory blows against the aggressor'. The article by the SRF deputy commander, Col. Gen. Grigoryev, in the 19 November 1971 issue of *Red Star* did not even mention the need to deal an aggressor 'a crushing rebuff'.

In a radio talk on 18 November 1972, Shevtsov repeated his 1970 comment that the SRF had become 'the main strike force of our army, the main factor in the containment [deterrence] of the aggressor and his crushing defeat in the event of war'. None of the written material cited in *FBIS* for the Rocket and Artillery Day contained references even to dealing the aggressor a 'crushing rebuff'. Tolubko had replaced Krylov as SRF commander and his 19 November 1972 *Pravda* interview simply identified the SRF as the 'army's main strike force and the main means of deterring an aggressor'. The deputy SRF commander, Col. Gen. Grigoryev, did cite the ability of the SRF to 'inflict massive retaliatory nuclear strike on the aggressor's most important regions and military targets at any point on the globe'.

With the advent of SALT, the Soviet military had shifted from emphasizing the need to defeat an aggressor to simply dealing him a 'crushing rebuff'. Bellicose statements had virtually disappeared. During the period when the Soviets found themselves accused of strategic weakness they had made their most aggressive statements. As deployment continued on their third generation missiles and SALT codified strategic 'parity', the Soviets moved from victory to retaliation.

SALT AND SOVIET DECEPTION

Soviet strategic policy under Brezhnev continued the strategic deceptions begun by Khrushchev. The Soviets claimed and touted capabilities such as the mobile ICBM that they had not deployed to compensate for their apparent weakness. As they began to overtake the US in numbers of ballistic missile launchers deployed, the Soviets exploited the opportuity provided them by the SALT process. With SALT, they could achieve the appearance of parity and defuse the pressures that the US would begin to feel towards strategic modernization. SALT would allow the Soviets to modernize without a dramatic US response. The Soviets had learned from Khrushchev's early failures. Bellicose statements when the US felt itself weak would only precipitate US force modernization. The adoption of a public stance for parity, while proceeding with modernization, would allow the Soviets to achieve strategic superiority.

Many of the claims that the Soviets engaged in strategic deception during SALT stem from what individuals have identified as violations of the agreement. Others have argued that the Soviets simply engaged in 'sharp practice', that one should expect a burglar to rob an unlocked room. SALT provided the Soviets with a grand opportunity, but the US initiated the negotiation process and insisted on tying the offensive limitation to ABM treaty. The US insisted on including unilateral declarations, which could only lead to problems later (simply because the Soviets did not accede to the unilateral statements did not mean that they disagreed with them per se; they could have objected to their specific nature). If the Soviets actually lied in SALT, then they either thought that they would not have the lie discovered (that is, they underestimated the capabilities of US technical national means) or they realized that their lie would be discovered in time but that they could successfully gloss over it. Soviet 'violations' could represent clear areas of ambiguity from their perspective. Anything not specifically prohibited may be permitted.

David Sullivan, among others, identifies a number of SALT violations. Some of these violations make more sense in the light of deceptions conducted by the Soviets in the 1960s. Others make sense in the light of what the Soviets did not do, especially their decision not to deploy a MIRV except with the test of the fourth-generation missiles. But all of them make sense in the light of Soviet public statements, in the shift from superiority and victory to parity. As Soviet capabilities to achieve victory in nuclear war increased, their claims about the prospects of victory disappear. The Soviets clearly wished to defuse US modernization.

Cyrus Vance included a number of possible violations in his presentation to Congress:

1) Launch control facilities (special purpose silos); 2) Concealment measures; 3) Modern large ballistic missiles (SS-19 issue); 4) Possible testing of an air defense system (SA-5) in an ABM mode; 5) Soviet reporting of dismantling of excess ABM launchers; 6) Soviet ABM radar

on Kamchatka Peninsula; 7) Soviet dismantling or destruction of replaced ICBM launchers; and 8) Concealment at test range.

Vance also raised some other issues which he indicated did not represent SALT violations largely because the US had not detected these activities:

1) 'Blinding' of US satellites; 2) Mobile ABM; 3) ABM testing of Air Defense Missiles; 4) Mobile ICBMs; 5) Denial of test information; and 6) ASAT.

Vance does not list the specific concealment measures that the Soviets have taken. He does indicate that the Soviets had engaged in concealment practices before the SALT agreements and that these practices increased substantially during 1974. After 1975, the US concluded that 'there no longer appeared to be an expanding pattern of concealment activities'. The wording of the SALT agreement does not prohibit concealment measures if they represented 'current construction, assembly, conversion, or overhaul practice'. The list of concealment measures cited in the press include [*Foreign Report*, 3/5/81; Laird, 12/77; Garn, Sum/79]:

1) disruptive painting; 2) tonal blending; 3) dummy roads and launch sites; 4) satellite warning system; 5) missile covers; 6) submarine tunnels; 7) submarine covers; 8) dummy submarines; 9) night tests (SS-16); 10) covered rail sidings; and 11) covered submarine hulls.

Foreign Report indicates that most of these practices began before 1972 and are thus covered under the current practices provisions of the SALT agreement. The satellite warning system ('to stop electronic emissions . . . from missiles and early warning radars . . . when western intelligence satellites' come in range) does not really fit in this group. Most of these activities seem designed to hide Soviet actions or to make the US think that the Soviets are doing something when they are not. Two activities would lead the US to overestimate Soviet capabilities or lead to different tactics: the dummy SAM launch sites and the dummy submarines. The appearance of the dummy submarines seems particularly interesting in the light of claims that the Soviets lied about the number of SSBNs they had deployed in 1972.

The nature of these alleged violations must also be considered in the light of claims by some that the Soviets purposely engaged in questionable activity to test the capability of our national means. The apparent compromises by Kampiles and Boyce of US intelligence assets would lend support to this theory, advanced by, among others, a former head of the Defense Intelligence Agency, Lt. Gen. Daniel Graham.

David Sullivan contends that the Soviets actively misled the US in three major areas of the SALT negotiations. First, the Soviets led the US team to believe that they would not deploy a follow-on missile to the SS-11 that significantly exceeded it in volume. Secondly, the Soviets lied about the number of SSBNs they had operational or under construction so that they could delay the dismantling of their second-generation ICBMs. Sullivan claims that the Soviets delayed testing of the SS-N-8 missile so that they could continue the charade that they needed more SLBMs because of geographical asymmetries. Thirdly, that Brezhnev agreed not to deploy a mobile ICBM. Each of Sullivan's claims must be considered in the light of Soviet objectives and tactics in SALT.

SOVIET OBJECTIVES AND TACTICS IN SALT

Four days after the US voted to deploy an ABM, the Soviets agreed to participate in SALT. After languishing during the last days of the Johnson administration, SALT began in earnest in 1969. The Soviets initially wanted to limit the talks to defensive systems only, and failing that, to conclude the offensive agreement only after the defensive agreement. The Soviets were not particularly interested in limiting offensive weapons in part because the US had already unilaterally limited itself. Thus, any offensive limitation would apply unequally to the Soviets. Nevertheless, the Soviets did feel the economic burden of strategic forces. In his account of the first session to President Nixon, the US negotiator, Ambassador Gerard Smith, commented that the head of the Soviet delegation, Semenov, in his opening remarks:

> spoke of nuclear war as a disaster for both sides — of the decrease in security as the number of weapons increases — of the costly results of rapid obsolescence of weapons — of the dangers of grave miscalculations — of the unauthorized use of weapons — and of hostilities resulting from third power provocation [Smith:84].

Smith's initial view of Soviet objectives in December 1969 seemed confirmed by subsequent events:

> My hunch at this early stage of the talks is that the Soviet purposes are a mix of at least three possible main ingredients: a) To see if an arrangement can be negotiated that would improve their prospects, or stabilize the strategic balance at lower cost; b) To 'cover' their ICBM/SLBM buildup and hopefully to defer, if not defeat, a US reaction; c) To advance their general arms control image as well as their specific non-proliferation interests by appearing to meet the obligations of Article VI (NPT) [Smith:106].

The US had during the first Helsinki session (November–December 1969) tabled a statement of 'Illustrative Elements' that indicated the kind of SALT agreement that the US and Soviet Union might conclude. The Soviets countered with their 'Basic Provisions for Limiting Strategic Armaments' during the Vienna session (April–August 1970):

> Although Semenov called it a plan for concrete measures it was simple and in general terms. It called for limitations on strategic offensive armaments, defined as those capable of striking targets within the territory of the other side, regardless of where those armaments were deployed. Forward-based delivery systems in a geographic position to strike such targets should be destroyed or moved out of range. An

unspecified aggregate total would be established for land-based ICBM launchers, ballistic missile launchers on nuclear submarines, and strategic bombers. Replacement of units of one type by those of another would be permitted. The production [but not testing] of multiple warheads of any kind and their installation in missiles would be banned. Limitations would be placed on ABM launchers and certain associated radars. Verification would be by national means only. No on-site inspection [Smith:123–4].

The Soviet proposal contained no specifics. It represented merely one in a long series of attempts to gain an agreement in principle before hammering out the details. As many who have dealt with the Soviets have noticed they have a tendency to accept the favorable points and ignore the unfavorable, requiring later that all the unfavorable points be renegotiated [Rowny:5]. The JCS representative to SALT II also lists, 'take the raisins out of the cake', the 'red herring technique', complete reversal of position, and eleventh hour tactics in the face of an agreed deadline. A reading of Smith's book reveals that the Soviets clearly used those tactics during SALT I. The use of such tactics across negotiations suggests that what often may appear haphazard and inadvertent, may result from design. The Soviets may have planned to isolate Kissinger and delay agreement on major substantive points until the final phases of SALT I in May 1972.

MODERN LARGE BALLISTIC MISSILES (SS-19)

The missiles that the Soviets began to test in mid-1973 as follow-ons to the SS-11 significantly exceeded its volume. The SS-19 has a throwweight of 7,525 pounds, the SS-17, 6,000 pounds, the SS-11, 2,500 pounds and the SS-9, 12,500 pounds [Collins:446]. The SS-19 thus has a throwweight roughly halfway between an SS-11 and an SS-9. The understanding in the agreement pertaining to ICBM modernization reads: The Parties understand that in the process of modernization and replacement the dimensions of land-based ICBM silo launchers will not be significantly increased. Smith made a unilateral interpretation of 'significantly increased' as meaning not greater than 10 to 15 per cent in the dimensions of the silo launcher. Semenov apparently 'replied that this statement corresponded to the Soviet understanding' [Smith:510]. The Agreement itself states in Article II: 'The Parties undertake not to convert land-based launchers for light ICBMs ... into land-based launchers for heavy ICBMs ...'

The US wished to limit the number of heavy missiles deployed from the beginning of the talks. In April 1970, the US defined any missile having a volume greater than 70 cubic meters (roughly the size of the SS-11) as a Modern Large Ballistic Missile (MLBM). In August 1970 the US proposed that any silo modified in an externally observable way should count under the MLBM ceiling. The July 1971 draft agreement fell on fallow ground because the Soviet negotiator argued that an agreement between Nixon and Kosygin on 20 May 1971 (worked out by Kissinger and Dobrynin) did not preclude the 'modernization and replacement' of offensive weapons [Smith:233]. Thus, Semenov's surprise may have been more real than feigned.

As the May 1972 summit approached, the Soviet position on MLBMs softened. On 3 December 1971, the Soviets agreed that the freeze on launchers included both heavy and light missiles and that they would agree to a provision that neither side could convert light launchers to heavies. They did not define a heavy missile and argued that the importance of the issue would lead both sides to respect the accord [Smith:333]. Discussions about MLBMs failed to reach an agreement in the spring of 1972.

In late May 1972, the Soviets tabled a statement on silo upgrades:

> The Parties understand that in the process of modernization and replacement there will be no substantial increase, observable with the aid of national technical means of verification, in the external dimensions of land-based ICBM silo launchers currently in their possession [Smith: 388-9].

The Soviets argued that this statement together with a commitment not to convert light launchers into heavies eliminated the need to define light and heavy missiles.

The Soviets indicated that they did not want to foreclose the options available to the design bureaus in developing new missiles. A Soviet indicated that they had developed one or two missiles beyond the design phase to replace the SS-11. He indicated that they did not intend 'to approach the halfway mark between the volume of their current light missiles and heavy missiles' [Smith:390]. The Helsinki round ended without any agreement on the definition of a heavy missile.

The heavy missile issue became quite confusing during the Moscow round. In the second session on 23 May, the Soviets apparently told Nixon that they would not increase the volume of their silos or missiles [Smith:412] and that they were prepared to drop the word 'significant' from the proposed interpretive statement. Smith reported to Kissinger that the change in the Soviet position conflicted with intelligence information that showed the Soviet follow-on missiles as larger. On 24 May Smith received word that the Soviets were considering a statement that defined 'significant' as 10 to 15 per cent to pertain to the missile volume [Smith:415]. Smith objected to this interpretation because it would preclude the replacement of Minuteman I misiles with Minuteman III. By the evening of the 24th, the Politburo apparently discovered [?] that they could not deploy their follow-on missiles with the 10 to 15 per cent limitation on the increase in missile volume. The Soviets then agreed to adopt a resolution that called for no increase in silo dimensions, but for some reason the US in Moscow decided to retain the term 'significant' as it reads in the final statement.

The give and take on the heavy missile issue may suggest a coordinated Soviet deception campaign. The Soviets had initially rejected any constraints on modernization of their missile force. To accommodate the US concern over the proliferation of heavy missiles they agreed to language which said that they would not replace light with heavy missiles and elsewhere defined constraints on missile modernization. They refused to define a heavy missile. As was clear to the participants at the time, the Soviets were searching for a formula which would allow them to deploy their fourth-generation missiles and to reach an agreement with the US on ABM. The Soviets did engage in dissimulation by arguing that both sides understood what a heavy missile was and that neither side would take actions to threaten the agreement. The Soviets made several statements about follow-on missiles that clearly suggested that they would not significantly exceed the size of the SS-11. To Smith and the SALT negotiators, they said that the follow-on missile would not approach the half-way point. At Moscow, they told Nixon that they did not intend to increase the size, not only of the silos, but also of the missiles. When Kissinger raised the issue regarding the promise to Nixon about no increases in Soviet missile volume on 25 May, 'Gromyko said that Kissinger had misunderstood' [Smith:431]. These statements, especially those directed at Nixon and Kissinger in Moscow, seem clearly designed to assuage fears about Soviet modernization. We cannot determine whether these statements reflect ignorance about the true size of the follow-on missile or deception. Kemp[79] cites a report by Beecher that Brezhnev himself may have had little command of the technical characteristics of the SS-19:

> ... one source noted that in May 1972, in the hours immediately preceding agreement on the SALT I pact in Moscow, a conversation was intercepted in which Soviet Party Chairman Brezhnev check[ed] with a top weapons expert to get an assurance that an about-to-be concluded formula covering permissible silo expansion would allow the Soviets to deploy a bigger new missile then under development. That intercept provided the first solid information that the SS-19 as it is now known, was destined to replace some of the relatively small SS-11 missiles, which comprise the bulk of the Soviet ICBM force. The SS-19 has three to four times the throwweight of the older missile.

Newhouse also reports that Ogarkov, the Soviet military representative to SALT and now Chief of Staff, had chided the US negotiators for revealing state secrets to the civilian members of the Soviet SALT team. Smith comments that he found the Soviet SALT team lacking in technical expertise. The case for deception on the heavy missile at SALT must rest on who said what to whom when, on whether claims regarding the follow-on missiles could have been taken as authoritative and not simply as uninformed or fragmentary opinion.

SLBM CEILINGS

However ambiguous regarding deception about heavy missiles, Soviet tactics on the SLBM suggest coordinated deception, especially in the light of the revelation that the Soviets have deployed dummy submarines (especially if the dummy submarines resemble Yankees or appear in slips where the Yankees would normally dock). Although the US intended to include SLBMs in SALT from the beginning, the Soviets wished to exclude them, in part because they possessed no clear advantage in the numbers of these systems as they did in ICBMs. The Soviets found quite congenial Kissinger's comment that the US would not insist on including SLBMs in an offensive weapons agreement. Kissinger's comments in February 1971, like those on modernization in the 20 May accord, differ significantly with the objectives being pursued by the negotiators at SALT. The Soviets delayed discussing the inclusion of SLBMs until the Moscow talks. Brezhnev himself had given Kissinger the first Soviet position paper on SLBMs.

The Soviets argued that geography and politics conferred strategic advantages on the US that the Soviets would need to compensate with greater numbers. The US and its allies could possess 50 modern submarines with up to 800 launchers (including 41 US SSBNs) while the Soviets would possess 62 modern submarines with not more than 950 launchers. The Soviets stressed that the issue of the forward basing of US submarines should form part of subsequent negotiations. Smith argues that he did not know the source of this proposal, especially the figures of 62 SSBNs and 950 launchers. The current US intelligence estimate projected for 1977 a high of 62 SSBNs with about 950 launchers. The Soviet offer conflicted with US guidance to include a freeze on further SSBN construction.

Having once secured a commitment by the Soviets to include SLBMs, the US next tried to relate additional SLBM launchers to the replacement of older heavy ICBM launchers (SS-7 and SS-8). The US also wished to include the older Golf and Hotel class boats under the SLBM launcher limit. The Soviets countered with a proposal to defer dismantling of older ICBMs and to exclude the Golf and Hotel class boats. The US position rested on the procedures for replacing older systems for modern SLBMs. The Soviets eventually countered with the following draft:

> The Soviet Union agrees that for the period of effectiveness of the interim 'freeze' agreement the USA have 41 modern submarines with a total of 656 ballistic missile launchers on them. The Soviet Union during the same period will have a total number of not more than 950 ballistic missiles on modern submarines. In the Soviet Union this number of launchers will be deployed on modern submarines which are operational or under construction as of the date of the signature of the Interim Agreement, as well as on submarines which will be constructed additionally. In the Soviet Union commissioning of additional launchers on submarines, over and above 48 modern submarines operational or under construction, will be carried out in replacement of ICBM launchers of old types constructed before 1964 [Smith:392].

The Soviet proposal would not allow the US to replace its 54 Titan II missiles with modern submarines, but more importantly it implies that the Soviets had 48 SSBNs operational or under construction when US technical means later determined that they possessed only 42 [Smith:393]. The Soviets contended that the 48 figure had come from US sources. They claimed that the US had agreed to allow them five or six more submarines 'as an offset'. Kissinger had apparently replied that the 950 launchers contained the offset and that he was not the source of the 48 figure. Semenov argued that, 'while replacement would begin with the forty-ninth submarine, the proposal did not constitute a claim that the USSR had 48 modern submarines in operation and under construction at that time' [Smith:399].

On the evening before the signing of the agreements, Gromyko proposed a formula for SLBMs that Nixon and Kissinger accepted. The Hotels but not the Golfs would be included in the 740 figure at which replacement would begin. To Kissinger's claim that the Soviet leadership had agreed that replacement would start immediately, Smirnov argued that the US had been given an offset of five or six submarines. Replacement would begin with the deployment of the seven hundred and fortieth launcher [Smith:431]. The Soviets even claimed a right to build additional SSBNs if the French or British increased their fleets.

Smith thought the technical nature of the Nixon negotiations during the Moscow summit inappropriate:

> ... it seemed out of keeping for President Nixon to negotiate about what constituted a significant increase in the dimensions of a concrete silo, what was the appropriate cutoff point between a light and heavy ballistic missile, or when and what kind of missile launcher must be decommissioned if replaced by a new launcher. These were the main subjects of concern at Moscow. It is hard to avoid a conclusion that there was some pretense about the nature of these Moscow negotiations. They were tense. They lasted well into the night. But they concerned secondary, and not central issues. Kissinger was to say later that most of the Moscow phase was spent on 'esoteric aspects of replacement provisions and not the substance of the agreement'.

Smith's claim that the Moscow negotiations concerned only secondary matters is true only in a strict sense. The major issues of contention regarding SALT surround those last-minute negotiations. The Soviets had delayed any discussion of the heavy missile and the SLBM issues until the last minute. They knew, because of their experience with Kissinger over the 20 May 1971 accord, that they could get a better deal out of Kissinger than they could out of the SALT negotiating team. They also knew that Nixon would not return home empty-handed. On the evening of 23 May, the Tuesday before the Friday on which they would sign the agreements, the Soviet leadership had provided Nixon with private assurances of no increase in silo or missile volume, that the Golf and Hotel submarines would soon be scrapped, and that replacement would begin immediately rather than after 48 submarines were deployed [Smith:412]. Two days later, the day before the signing, Gromyko told Kissinger that Nixon had misunderstood.

Considered alone, the heavy missile issue could have resulted from ignorance. The treatment of SLBMs at SALT clearly suggests deception. The figure 48 represents the only number that the Soviets provided during the negotiating process for estimates of their current capabilities. All other numbers had come from the US. In fact, the interim agreement contains no statement of the deployments on either side.

The allegation that the Soviets deployed dummy submarines should figure heavily in any estimate of whether the Soviets exploited the SALT process to conduct strategic deception. The only clear Soviet lie occurs when they claimed that they possessed 48 modern submarines operational or under construction when the US could only establish evidence for 42. (Collin lists only 33 SSBNs deployed in 1972, 26 Yankees and 7 Hotels. The Soviets did not reach the 740 figure on modern SLBMs deployed until late 1975) [Collin:449]. A dummy submarine constitutes prima facie evidence of deception, intended to convey the impression of greater numbers or to suggest deployments different than those which actually occur. Soviet covers over submarine construction yards aid in this deception. Unfortunately, little has appeared in the public press about the appearance of these dummy submarines and about reasonable Soviet expectations about the effectiveness of US technical means. If the dummy does not resemble a Yankee but the dummy appears in Yankee slips, then the Soviets may not know how well US technical means work. The Soviets have a strategic rationale for displaying the dummy submarine from 1967, when the Yankees first became operational until 1975 when they deployed over 740 modern SLBMs. If the dummy submarine appeared after 1975, then the Soviets would need to dismantle additional older ICBMs to maintain the facade of greater SLBM strength. For the dummy submarine to figure in a SALT deception, it must have appeared prior to May 1972. If it did, the 48 figure may derive from Soviet perceptions of what they thought we could discern about their number of modern SSBNs from national technical means.

The Soviets did not agree on a definition of 'under construction'. Although the 48 figure may have resulted from a broadened sense of boats under construction, such an argument makes too many excuses for Soviet behavior. Rather, the negotiating record suggests that even the Soviets thought the 48 figure a pretense granted them for including SSBNs.

Sullivan also argues that the Soviets engaged in a deception regarding the geographical asymmetries facing the US and the Soviet Union over the deployment of SSBNs. He argues that the Soviets delayed testing of the SS-N-8 missile until after the May 1972 accords because its 4,800 nm range would weaken the justification for the three to two Soviet preponderance in modern submarines. The Soviets had initially wished to restrict submarine patrols, but immediate US rejection of that proposal leaves us without any idea as to the specific content of the proposal [Smith:102]. The Soviets would have known in 1969 that they had the SS-N-8 under development, so perhaps their proposal does represent a negotiating deception. However, the Soviets continued to argue that SLBM limitations should appear in negotiations after the initial agreement, a fact that the US SALT team had come to accept by April 1972. Thus, the appearance of the Brezhnev SLBM paper in April 1972, barely a month before the summit, came as a surprise. The Soviets had appeared to make a great concession; they would include SLBMs. They justified the three to two disparity by appealing to the strategic 'disbalance' in the location of submarine bases [Smith:371]. The surprise 'concession', the timing of the Brezhnev proposal, and Soviet knowledge that they had already readied for testing the SS-N-8 missile designed to compensate for geo-graphical asymmetries suggests that the Soviets did indeed orchestrate the SLBM issue for maximum effect. The Soviet handling of the SLBM issue more convincingly points towards strategic deception than the heavy missile issue. The Smith account of the negotiating history suggests that the US would have accepted a SALT I without SLBMs.

MOBILE ICBMs, PART II

According to Sullivan, the Soviets promised Nixon that they would not deploy a mobile ICBM:

> Nixon and Brezhnev recognized the complexity of the problem. After lengthy debate, they promised one another that they would not build land-based mobile ICBMs. But Brezhnev refused to write this promise into the interim agreement. Nixon stressed that the United States would state its own understanding of the prohibition in a separate declaration that would be submitted to Congress; and he warned that if the US caught Russia cheating on this issue, it would immediately abrogate the entire SALT agreement. Brezhnev said that he understood and agreed.

This passage from Kalb and Kalb's book on Kissinger seems odd in light of the fact that the Soviets had claimed a mobile ICBM capability for the SS-13 in the mid-1960s. The Soviets actually deployed the SS-13 in silos when it reached initial operating capability in 1969, but they continued to display the SS-14 on its launcher in the November parades until 1972. Smith devotes little space to the issue of mobile ICBMs, except to note that the SALT team pressed for their ban throughout negotiations after a false start with the Illustrative Elements which included a ban on mobile M/IRBMs but not ICBMs. Even by convoluted standards of the language embedded in the US unilateral statement on mobile ICBMs, the Soviet Union has honored the agreement:

> In connection with the important subject of land-mobile ICBM launchers, in the interest of concluding the Interim Agreement the US Delegation now withdraws its proposal that Article I or an agreed statement explicitly prohibit the deployment of mobile land-based ICBM launchers. I have been instructed to inform you that, while agreeing to defer the question of limitation of operational land-mobile ICBM launchers to the subsequent negotiations on more complete limitations on strategic offensive arms, the US would consider the deployment of operational land mobile ICBM launchers during the period of the Interim agreement as inconsistent with the objectives of that Agreement [Smith:513].

The Soviets may have engaged in strategic deception regarding mobile ICBMs, but this has occurred separately from the SALT process. During SALT I, the Soviets did not mislead the US regarding mobile ICBMs.

BREZHNEV'S IGNORANCE AND STRATEGIC DECEPTION

Sullivan's contentions about strategic deception and the SALT rest very strongly on private assurances that Brezhnev made to Nixon on the first day of the Moscow summit. In these sessions, Brezhnev negotiated directly with Nixon (accompanied by Kissinger and later Hal Sonnenfeldt). Brezhnev did not have any experts with him. The later repudiation of some of Brezhnev's position provides some evidence that he was out of his element. After these sessions, Brezhnev did not again appear without technical assistance. To ensure no further mistakes, the Soviets decided to introduce the man responsible for overseeing the Soviet build-up, Deputy Premier L. V. Smirnov, to the talks on 25 May [Kissinger:1233]:

> ... Smirnov knew everything about weapons and little about diplomacy, while of Gromyko ... exactly the opposite was true. His skill was diplomacy; his briefing on weapon systems had obviously been rudimentary. He could put forward the official Soviet position but not negotiate it; this task was left to Smirnov and me. Gromyko found himself in the unusual position of making soothing noises whenever matters between me and Smirnov threatened to get out of control.
>
> To begin with, Gromyko was in a frame of mind dour even by his standards. For on him fell the painful duty of withdrawing almost everything put forward by Brezhnev during his meeting with Nixon the previous day. He handled it masterfully by passing around papers that summed up the alleged state of play on various issues — all of them at variance with Brezhnev's position.

Thus, the Soviets had indulged Brezhnev's desire for direct negotiations and then the next day repudiated everything he had said. The Soviets needed Smirnov involved to ensure that no last-minute concession would restrain Soviet strategic modernization. They would not repeat the Brezhnev fiasco. In fact, despite his penchant for high-level contacts, Kissinger had not met Smirnov before.

IV: Preventing the US Response: Parity from 1974

SALT provided an opportunity for Soviets to gain through negotiation what they would find difficult to achieve simply through the dynamics of strategic modernization. By freezing offensive levels of ICBMs and allowing the Soviet build-up in SSBNs to continue, SALT guaranteed eventual Soviet superiority as they MIRVed their fourth-generation missiles. Whether the Soviet build-up would have been even greater, as some have claimed, without SALT matters little. SALT constrained a US response. From the Soviet perspective, the uncertainties of an American political process that could catapult a virtual and inexperienced unknown like Jimmy Carter to the presidency provided little comfort that the US would not respond. (Although the comparison seems insulting to the US, the transformation in German political life from Hitler's legitimate accession to power in 1933 to his attack on Poland in 1939 still serves as a lesson to the Soviets.)

The centrality of SALT to the Soviet pursuit of strategic advantage suggests that they did not intend any deception, per se, in the initial negotiations. The Soviet SALT negotiators and even Gromyko and Brezhnev seemed uninformed about the details of the Soviet strategic modernization program. Ignorance, of course, aids deception. The German Foreign Ministry in the early 1930s remained uninformed about the extent of German rearmament and thus could negotiate in good faith with Britain and France. The heavy missile episode suggests sharp practice; the mobile missile claim, ignorance. Deception seems to surround the SSBN negotiations. The delay in testing the SS-N-8 seems good practice to buttress the geographic asymmetry claims (which the Soviets still make). The 48 figure alone seems mysterious, but Soviet practice to that point had been to use US numbers. In any case, the Soviets would not agree to a definition of 'under construction' which they could construe to mean any component of the submarine. The claim of the 48 SSBNs would not undermine the agreement later and in fact would facilitate Soviet compliance by delaying the dismantling of Soviet second-generation ICBMs.

The controversy over the SS-17 and SS-19 may have caught the Soviets unawares. To smooth the SALT process they would need to reiterate Soviet commitment in the interim period while the forces of modernization granted Soviet strategic advantage. The earlier Soviet statements would have to change. As the Soviets displayed that they did not share the spirit of SALT trumpeted in the American press, as they pushed the boundaries of the agreement to test the limits of US tolerance, Brezhnev found that he had a real public relations problem in 1974. He solved that problem by reversing earlier Soviet statements and establishing parity as the goal of Soviet policy. The continuing Soviet build-up, at all levels, seemed incongruous. But Brezhnev had learned from the mistakes of Khrushchev. Soothing words would delay the US response and the SALT process itself would continue to strengthen elements within the US government against modernization.

SOVIET SALT OBJECTIVES AND STRATEGIC DECEPTION

The Soviets secured a SALT agreement on offensive arms that did not impinge upon their modernization program and codified Soviet numerical advantage. They achieved their negotiating coups largely through eleventh hour tactics and by isolating an individual predisposed to the agreement per se (Kissinger may have also believed that he knew enough to negotiate about the technical characteristics of strategic weapon systems). By delaying agreement on critical details until the Moscow summit, the Soviets successfully managed to gain the ABM limitation with little effect on their offensive programs.

In the light of the negotiating record, it would seem difficult to refute reports that appeared in late 1973:

> According to intelligence reports recently received here, Leonid I. Brezhnev, the Soviet Communist party leader, has emphasized to East

European leaders that the movement toward improving relations with the West is a tactical policy change to permit the Soviet bloc to establish its superiority in the next 12 to 15 years [*NYT,* 9/17/73:2].

At the end of this period, in about the mid-1980s, the strength of the Soviet bloc will have increased to the point at which the Soviet Union, instead of relying on accords, could establish an independent position in its dealings with the West.

In the light of the current looming window of vulnerability, Brezhnev seems at least partially to have succeeded.

Sullivan, among others, argues that the Soviets clearly intended to engage in strategic deception in SALT. He fails to explain how they intended to succeed in this deception. The deployment of the SS-19 and the SS-N-8 would become evident rather quickly. To defuse US reaction over claimed SALT violations when it did occur, the Soviets first continued the SALT process and secondly launched a public relations campaign designed to convince the US that they pursued parity (see below). The intended ambiguity of the agreement (no numbers) was designed to allow the Soviets maximum flexibility. The Soviets also knew that they would have a staunch defender in Henry Kissinger who would be loathe to admit that the Soviets had deceived him into codifying eventual Soviet superiority in the SALT I agreements. He had already shown himself susceptible to manipulation through his back-channel negotiations culminating in the 20 May 1971 accord.

INTELLIGENCE AND SALT

A number of the alleged violations regarding the ABM treaty suggests that the Soviets were using SALT to test the capabilities of US national technical means. The apparent use of SA-5 radars to track Soviet ballistic missile tests and the Soviet notification that they had dismantled excess ABM test launchers at Sary Shagan when in fact they had not, may have been tests of US intelligence capabilities. The US had argued that it would not conclude a treaty which it could not verify. The openness of US society facilitated Soviet verification of US compliance. The US could verify only through national technical means. Although the US has cloaked its intelligence capabilities in considerable secrecy, the reports on compliance within the Standing Consultative Commission (SCC) set up by the SALT agreements would provide the Soviets with a grand opportunity to test the limits of US capabilities. The failure of the Soviets to dismantle fully excess ABM launchers at the Sary Shagan range suggests an attempt to discern US intelligence capabilities:

> On July 3, the agreed procedures worked out in the SCC for dismantling excess ABM test launchers entered into force. After the detailed procedures entered into effect, the USSR provided notification in the SCC that the excess ABM launchers at the Soviet test range had been dismantled in accordance with the provisions of the agreed procedures. Our own information was that several of the launchers had not, in fact, been dismantled in complete accordance with these detailed procedures.

This small episode seems inconsequential and in fact it may be. But why would the Soviets cheat on such a small thing?

THE ABM DECEPTION, PART TWO

Vance revealed: 'During 1973 and 1974, US observation of Soviet tests of ballistic missiles led us to believe that a radar associated with the SA-5 surface-to-air missile system had been used to track strategic missiles during flight'. The Soviets soon stopped this activity suggesting that they had been attempting to discover yet again what the limits of US technical means were, especially since this 'observation' would require means other than photographic. A discussion during the SALT negotiations substantiates the view that the Soviets were testing US national technical means:

> A Soviet delegate remarked informally that he understood that the United States had once thought this Soviet SAM system [SA-5] was an unsuccessful ABM system which had been converted to anti-aircraft purposes after its inadequacy had been discovered. Though the US was wrong initially, he asserted, it had now concluded correctly that the system had originally been deployed for anti-aircraft purposes. This showed that the purposes of a system could be determined by national means. When his American counterpart commented that it had taken some years to determine whether this system was for ABM defense, the Soviet official said that the necessary sensors to pick up electronic emissions did not exist when this system was built [Smith:314].

The Soviet comment seems startling in the light of subsequent US detection of the Soviet use of the SA-5 radars to track re-entry vehicles into their ABM test range.

The SA-5 system resembles a first-generation ABM system. The Soviets had initially claimed an ABM role for the SA-5. The Soviets' decision to exploit the missile-tracking capabilities of the SA-5 radars suggest an intent to operate the system against incoming ballistic missiles. The failure at SALT to recognize that the SA-5 already was an ABM system, albeit a primitive one, stems from US technological snobbery. The ABM treaty loses much of its meaning if the Soviets intended all along to use the SA-5 as part of their ABM system. Whatever the true role of the SA-5, the Soviets lied either in the early sixties or during SALT.

Other reports have appeared that the Soviets have used 'non-ABM' equipment in an ABM role. In the article cited above, Safire writes:

> Soviet deception managers must know our surveillance capacity, but occasionally we get a break: a careless Russian radar operator made it possible for us to discover that enormous radar facilities supposedly to be used only for 'early warning' were really battle-management ABM radar, an egregious treaty violation.

If we assume that Safire has a good piece of information, then the Soviets have internetted their radars and their interceptors, so that the early warning radar can be used to track the incoming missile for the interceptor. Others have mentioned that the Soviets have deployed a number of large phased-array radars 'similar in size [400 feet high and 600–700 feet wide] to the Soviet Hen House radar, which is an ABM radar' [Kemp:22]. If these radars are those referred to by Safire, then US problems increase. This leaves open the question of whether the Soviets have internetted their SA-5 system with their early warning radars and thus circumvented some of the current inadequacies with their mechanical radars. According to Garn [27], General Holloway, then CINCSAC, told Congress in 1971 that 'with predicted intercept data from remote ABM radars [the SA-5] could defend large areas of the Soviet Union from attack'.

During SALT, the US presented the Soviet delegation with a list of ABM test ranges that did not include the Kamchatka impact area. The Soviets made no response, even though they had constructed an older type ABM radar at Kamchatka. In October 1975, the Soviets installed a new ABM radar at Kamchatka. When the US raised this matter, the Soviets replied that the radar instrumentation complex on Kamchatka peninsula had qualified it as a current ABM test range under Article IV of the ABM treaty. The Soviet Union now agrees that Sary Shagan and Kamchatka are the only ABM test ranges. By failing to identify the Kamchatka range as an ABM test range in 1972, the Soviets revealed their unwillingness to share information. They may have also revealed that they thought they could achieve a free ride on whatever 'older type' ABM radar appeared at Kamchatka.

Vance has discredited claims that the Soviets are working on a mobile ABM. Article V of the treaty prohibits either side from developing, testing, or deploying 'ABM systems or components which are sea-based, air-based, space-based, or mobile land-based'. Vance states that the new Soviet ABM system 'can be installed more rapidly than previous ABM systems, but they are clearly not mobile in the sense of being able to be moved about readily or hidden'. Vance estimates that the Soviets can ready a single operational site in about six months but that a nationwide system would take years. Apparently the Soviets have developed new radars, one of which they can emplace on prepared concrete foundations. This system seems to fall under the 'movable' category in the same sense that a house on its foundations is movable.

The bulk of the evidence suggests that the Soviets are developing a 'surge' ABM capability. Soviet notions regarding the likelihood of nuclear conflict presuppose that a period of tensions would precede nuclear war. If the Soviets viewed a nuclear war as a likely occurrence, they would feel no need to honor the ABM treaty. Moreover, the deployment of even a partially effective nationwide ABM system may deter a US attack.

MOBILE ICBM DECEPTION, PART TWO

Just as the Soviets seem to be developing a 'surge' ABM, they also seem to be developing a 'surge' mobile ICBM capability. The Soviets cloaked their tests of the SS-16 in great secrecy, apparently conducting a night test in 1973. The Soviets had already touted the value of mobile ICBMs in the 1960s but presumably decided not to deploy them because of problems with the SS-13 system. The continued and large deployment of the SS-20 suggests that the Soviets have solved the SS-13/SS-14 problems. The Soviets can upgrade the SS-20 to an SS-16:

> The SS-20 comprises the first two stages of the three-stage SS-16. By upgrading SS-20 deployment to the SS-16, the Soviets would increase their mobile ICBM capability relatively quickly. This could be accomplished by the addition of a third stage to the two SS-20 stages. Such action could significantly increase the number of ICBMs in Soviet intercontinental forces [Garn].

The Soviet emphasis on modularity may have led them to build the SS-16 third stage as part of another system. If so, then they could mate those missiles with the SS-20. The Soviets could simply build and stockpile these third stages until tensions would mount and they felt it necessary to deploy a mobile ICBM. Violation of the SALT agreement would matter little if the Soviets strongly thought that nuclear war would occur.

COPING WITH US REACTION: THE SOVIET PURSUIT OF PARITY

Awareness of Soviet duplicity began to build after they started tests of their fourth-generation missiles in 1973. By 1975, a number of articles had appeared on Soviet SALT violations. To counter US perceptions about their motives, the Soviets launched a propaganda campaign, beginning in about 1974 that stressed the peacefulness of the Soviet objectives and the horrors of nuclear war. Although some have interpreted this shift in Soviet statements as reflecting an acceptance of the US position on mutual assured deterrence, it seems odd that the Soviets would actively pursue superiority when clearly at a strategic disadvantage relative to the West while they would adopt parity when they had achieved the basis for superiority. Rather, it seems more likely that the Soviets have changed their public position to defuse the US reaction.

An *FBIS* special analysis published in May 1979 argues that the shift in Soviet statements represents an accommodation of Soviet thinking to the reality of nuclear weapons:

> The results of the 1972 and 1973 US-Soviet summits — the agreements on principle of mutual relations, limiting strategic arms, and the prevention of nuclear war — appear to have opened the way to a new push by those advocating a more radical adjustment of Soviet security policy to the reality of nuclear weapons. Evidence of debate on these subjects appeared in the wake of the 1973 summit in Washington. Although the full outline and implications of the debate were obscure at the time, it centered on whether a change in the Soviet Union's traditional approach to military power was appropriate given the emerging strategic balance and the development of detente in relations with the West.
>
> In retrospect, it is apparent that the revisionists in this debate won a

significant victory. Beginning in 1974, President Brezhnev introduced new concepts and accompanying vocabulary into Soviet strategic discourse, signaling a clear break with the notion that security derives directly from military power. Brezhnev began by describing the world's strategic arsenals as excessively large and already redundant and arguing there was a greater risk in accumulating arms than reducing. He completed the process of adjustment, beginning in 1977, by embracing the concept of military parity with the West and suggesting that the pursuit of anything more was pointless.

The new security posture introduced by President Brezhnev, while in the first instance a recognition of the realities of military balance, was not brought about without controversy; there was evidence of resistance to the idea that security could be enhanced by arms control arrangements that restricted the core elements of Soviet military power. They thus represent a cardinal victory for proponents of change in the USSR who have argued, since early in the nuclear era, that the mutual vulnerability introduced by nuclear weapons required a departure from traditional doctrine on war and peace. The changes establish a more hospitable domestic environment for joint efforts to restrain the strategic arms competition than existed during SALT I or even the early stages of SALT II. They also challenge the traditional dominance of military professionals in the sphere of defense policy by clarifying that the primary goal of strategy in the missile age is to prevent war, not to win it.

While this passage accurately tracks shifts in Soviet statements, it fails to place them in context. The Soviet attitudes towards parity have become more favorable because they have succeeded in preventing a US response. Some Soviets have in fact styled SALT I as a victory for the socialist people. Soviet statements about the advantages of military-technical superiority (while certainly more valid as we move into the 1980s) would hardly coincide with successful negotiations with the West. The Soviet use of arms control to achieve strategic superiority required that they shift their public emphasis on the need to win a nuclear war, a shift that began to appear in the late 1960s as evidenced by the statements of the SRF commander on annual Artillery and Rocket Day.

At the 24th Party Congress, Brezhnev stated that the Soviets would seek 'the security of parties considered equally' and renounce efforts to seek unilateral advantage. The inconsistent guidance provided by the leadership led to a debate between Georgiy Arbatov and Aleksandr Bovin, both of the Institute of the USA and Canada, and a number of military writers. Bovin argued in the 11 July 1973 edition of *Izvestiya* that neither side stood to gain by the use of nuclear weapons:

> At the basis of the agreements [between the USSR and the United States] lies sober calculation, understanding of the catastrophic nature of a global thermonuclear conflict, awareness that under conditions of a nuclear missile balance further growth of nuclear arsenals loses political ·

meaning and does not increase, but diminishes, the security of the parties.

Bovin found himself under attack by name. But in a 7 February 1974 *Red Star* article, it became clear that the debate was caused by insufficient guidance. Rear Admiral Shelyag disparaged Bovin's argument, characterizing it as over-simplistic:

> If arguments about the death of civilization and about no victors in nuclear war are to be presented in an over-simplified manner, they are based on mathematical calculations. The authors of these arguments divide the quantity of accumulated nuclear potential in the world by the number of people living on earth. As a result it emerges that all mankind really could be destroyed. This is an over-simplified one-sided approach to such a complex socio-historical phenomenon as war.

The Arbatov-Bovin view that nuclear war would see no winners conflicted with what Shelyag knew to be current guidance:

> Our understanding of the consequences of a possible world war are defined in the CPSU program [approved by the 22d CPSU Congress in 1961]: 'In the event the imperialists nevertheless dare to unleash a new world war, the peoples will no longer be able to tolerate a system which plunges them into devastating wars. They will sweep imperialism away and bury it.'

Shelyag believed that current doctrine argued that the Soviet Union will emerge victorious from a nuclear war no matter how it started. Imperialism would lose. Such ideas led inevitably to arguments for superiority and such notions would threaten Soviet interests in pursuing detente with the West.

To end the debate, Brezhnev opted for the Arbatov-Bovin view in a speech on 21 July 1974:

> For centuries mankind, in striving to ensure its security, has been guided by the formula: If you want peace, be ready for war. In our nuclear age this formula conceals particular danger. Man dies only once. However, in recent years a quantity of weapons has already been amassed sufficient to destroy everything living on earth several times. Clearly understanding this, we have put it and continue to put it another way: If you want peace, conduct a policy of peace and fight for that policy. This has been, is, and will continue to be the maxim of our socialist foreign policy.

Brezhnev's last comments on the strategic situation had appeared in 1965 when he warned that the West should not launch a strike because they had failed to correctly assess Soviet strength. At that time, the Soviets significantly increased the number of strategic weapons that they displayed in their parades (see above). From 1971, the Soviets had reduced their military parades from twice to once a year. The Soviets displayed strategic missiles for the last time in the 1974 parade. Brezhnev's comments made themselves felt in his displays of military might.

In his remarks at Tula on 18 January 1977, Brezhnev explicitly renounced superiority as a goal of Soviet policy: 'The Soviet Union's defense potential must be sufficient to deter anyone from taking a risk to violate our peaceful life. Not a course of superiority in armament, but a course of reducing them, at lessening military confrontation — such is our policy.' Significantly, Brezhnev's views had finally made an impression on those who had been arguing forcefully that the Soviet Union should pursue superiority, that the Soviet Union can fight and win a nuclear war. Col. Ye. Rybkin, a veteran of the debates in the mid-1960s and in 1973-4 argued in the lead article of the January 1977 issue of the *Military-Historical Journal*:

> The objective necessity of ending the arms race is apparent. In first place because the quantity of nuclear weapons has reached a level whereby further increase will in practice make no change. 'In recent years', noted L. I. Brezhnev in July 1974, 'a quantity of arms has already been amassed sufficient to destroy everything living on earth several times'. In the second place, because 'nuclear parity', as it is called, has been established between the USSR and the United States; that is a definite balance of power, which was officially recognized at the Soviet-American talks in 1972-74 with a mutual agreement not to disturb this balance.

Apparently, Brezhnev had listened to the counsel of Arbatov and Bovin on how to achieve his strategic objectives through arms control and open disavowal of the pursuit of superiority. When Arbatov and Bovin made their claims in the press, they met with resistance because official Soviet policy had not yet changed. After Brezhnev's speeches in 1974 and 1977, official policy became quite clear and even those who had argued forcefully for military-technological superiority now joined the chorus for parity. The Soviet principle of democratic centralism had made itself felt.

Other publications have changed. Dmitri Simes has tracked the changes in General Il'in's book, *The Moral Factor in Modern Wars*. In the second edition which appeared in 1969, Il'in stressed on the first page the need for 'strengthening Soviet Army and Navy readiness to wage a victorious war against any aggression'. This sentence failed to appear in the third edition published in 1979. While in the second edition, Il'in argued that 'the Soviet Union is doing everything to ensure military technological superiority of our armed forces over the imperialist armies', in the third edition, he states: 'The Soviet people do everything to ensure a high level of technological equipment for the Soviet armed forces in the spirit of current requirements'.

Other Soviet leaders also adopted the new line. In February 1977, Defense Minister Ustinov, writing in *Kommunist,* argued that the US could not achieve military superiority over the Soviet Union: 'our country's economy, science and technology are now at such a high level that we are capable, within the shortest period, of matching any type of weapon that the enemies of peace create' [*NYT,* 2/18/77:3:1].

In an interview in May 1978, Brezhnev argued:

As for the Soviet Union, it believes that an approximate equality and parity is sufficient for defensive needs. We do not set ourselves the goal of achieving military superiority. We know also that this very concept becomes pointless in the presence of today's huge arsenals of already stockpiled nuclear weapons and means for their delivery.

Recently, as SALT II foundered, the Soviets have begun to speak of victory in nuclear war, although they continue to emphasize that the Soviet Union does not seek superiority. In his discussion of military strategy in the *Soviet Military Encyclopedia* in September 1979, the chief of the Soviet General Staff, Marshal Ogarkov does not disavow the possibility that the socialist countries will seek victory should a nuclear war occur:

Soviet military strategy is determined by the policy of the CPSU and the Soviet state, which combines the struggle for peace with preparedness for decisively repelling aggression and reliably protecting the independence and socialist achievements of the Soviet people and the peoples of other friendly socialist nations. Soviet military doctrine as a whole has a particularly defensive focus and does not provide for any sort of preemptive strikes or premeditated attack. Its main task is that of developing methods of repelling an attack by an aggressor and of defeating the aggressor by conducting decisive operations. Unlike the military strategy of the imperialist states, which openly espouses the arms race and the establishment of military-technical superiority, Soviet military strategy is based on the need to provide the Soviet Armed Forces with everything necessary to defend the country and defeat an aggressor and to maintain the armed forces at a level insuring homeland's security. Soviet military strategy takes into account the capability of the USSR and the other socialist countries to prevent a probable enemy from achieving military-technical superiority. At the same time it does not pursue the goal of achieving military-technical superiority over other countries. '... While building up our armed forces, we in no way go beyond what is actually necessary for our security and the security of our socialist friends. We threaten no one and impose our will upon no one' [L. I. Brezhnev].

Except for the comment about military-technical superiority, Ogarkov does not deviate significantly from the statements contained in the Sokolovsky edited volume on military strategy. In other words, victory remains the objective should war start, but the Soviet Union will not pursue, at least publicly, superiority to achieve that objective. Ogarkov is clearly playing games with the concept. Unlike Western writers, he details the campaign after the initial massive nuclear exchanges. Thus, he has not embraced the notion that no side can achieve victory in a nuclear war.

Even in the face of Reagan administration claims that the US needs to catch up on the Soviet Union, Soviet leaders have argued that the US and the Soviet Union remain equal. In a *Pravda* article that appeared on 24 July 1981, Defense Minister Ustinov argues:

The United States has no need to upgrade its arms, since it does not lag behind the USSR. Something else is involved: The military-strategic equality which has become established between our countries is not to the liking of the bellicose leaders in the present administration because it hinders the aggressive intentions in the world arena and restricts its expansionist actions. That is why the principle of equality is being sacrificed for a stake on superiority.

Ustinov warns the West with a quote from Brezhnev:

'One could, however, hope', Comrade L. I. Brezhnev said at the 26th Party Congress, 'that those who determine the policy of America today will be able to see things in a more realistic way. The military-strategic balance which exists between the United States and the USSR, between the Warsaw Treaty and NATO, objectively serves to preserve peace on our planet. We have never tried and are not trying to achieve military supremacy over the other side. This is not our policy. But we will not allow the creation of such supremacy over ourselves. Such attempts, as well as talks with us from a position of strength, are absolutely hopeless.'

Conclusion

The Soviets have engaged in systematic strategic deception since 1955. When they were weak, the Soviets touted their capability: under Khrushchev to achieve general political objectives; under Brezhnev, to forestall further US adventurism. The Soviets used their military parades and public statements to convince the West that they had an extensive ABM capability, that they alone possessed the means to thwart an ABM with the orbital missile, and that they had deployed systems, such as the mobile ICBM, unlocated by US reconnaissance systems. They argued in their doctrine that they had achieved and were continually pursuing military-technical superiority. The Soviets seized on SALT as a means to limit US ABM development. They exploited US preoccupation with an offensive limitation to use eleventh hour and isolation tactics to conclude an agreement that they realized would eventually guarantee them strategic superiority. To further defuse US reaction as word appeared of Soviet violations and 'sharp practice' in the early 1970s, Brezhnev took the counsel of Arbatov and Bovin of the Institute of the USA and Canada, and began advocating parity and disparaging superiority. The Soviets had learned from their experience under Khrushchev, that bragging when the US felt weak would precipitate massive US rearmament. A low profile would institutionalize eventual Soviet superiority, much as Brezhnev had argued in 1973.

REFERENCES

Mnemonic:

A   Allison, Graham, *Essence of Decision* (Boston, Mass.: Little Brown, 1971).

G   Greenwood, Ted, *Making the MIRV* (Cambridge, Mass.: Ballinger, 1975).

F   Freedman, Lawrence, *US Intelligence and the Soviet Strategic Threat* (Boulder, Co.: Westview, 1977).

H&R   Horelick, Arnold, and Myron Rush, *Strategic Power and Soviet Foreign Policy* (Chicago, Illinois: University of Chicago, 1965).

Anderson, Raymond H., 'Russians Concede Missile Net Flaw', *The New York Times,* 23 February 1967.

'Another Cuban Missile Crisis', *Foreign Report,* 1668, 19 February 1981.

Aspin, Les, 'Debate over US Strategic Forecasts: A Mixed Record', *Strategic Review* VII, Summer 1980.

Baldwin, Hanson W., 'Antimissile Defenses', *The New York Times,* 5 April 1963.

Baldwin, Hanson W., 'Missile Interception', *The New York Times,* 24 July 1964.

Beecher, William, 'Laird Says Soviets Renew ABM Work', *The New York Times,* 28 April 1971.

Beecher, William, 'Soviet's Antimissile Steps Spur Study of US Needs: Nike-X Project Weighed', *The New York Times,* 8 December 1966.

Bittman, Ladislav, *The Deception Game* (New York: Ballantine, 1972).

Bogdanov, Radomir, and Lev Semeiko, 'Soviet Military Might: A Soviet View', *Fortune,* 26 February 1979.

Commission on the Organization of the Government for the Conduct of Foreign Policy, Appendix K: Adequacy of Current Organization: Defense and Arms Control (Washington, D.C.: GPO, June 1975).

Douglas, Joseph, 'Soviet Disinformation', *Strategic Review,* Winter 1981.

Erickson, John, ' "The Fly in Outer Space": The Soviet Union and the Antiballistic Missile', *The World Today,* 23 March 1967.

Ermath, Fritz, 'Contrasts in American and Soviet Strategic Thought', *International Security* 3(2), Fall 1978.

'Excerpts from Premier Khrushchev's Address at Peace Congress in Moscow', *The New York Times,* 11 July 1962.

Finney, John W., 'Brezhnev Said to Assure East Europe That Accords With West Are a Tactic', *The New York Times,* 17 September 1973.

Finney, John W., 'Soviet Fires Record Bomb of 30–50 Megaton Range; Claims Anti-Missile Gain', *The New York Times,* 24 October 1961.

Finney, John W., 'US to Test at High Altitude in Search for Missile Defense', *The New York Times,* 3 March 1962.

Frankel, Max, 'US Rebuffs Khrushchev on Berlin Bid and Testing', *The New York Times,* 11 July 1962.

Garn, Jake, 'The Suppression of Information Concerning Soviet SALT Violations by the US Government', *Policy Review* 9, Summer 1979.

Garthoff, Raymond, 'Mutual Deterrence and Strategic Arms Limitation in Soviet Policy', *International Security* 3(1), Summer 1978.

Grose, Peter, 'Soviet Says Missile Power Exceeds West's Estimates', *The New York Times,* 4 July 1965.

Harris, William R., 'Counterintelligence Jurisdiction and the Double-Cross System by National Technical Means', in Roy Godson (ed.), *Intelligence Requirements for the 1980s: Counterintelligence* (Washington, D.C.: National Strategy Information Center, 1980).

'Is Russia Violating Arms Pacts?' *Foreign Report,* 1677, 30 April 1981.

Katz, Amrom, H., *Verification and SALT,* The Heritage Foundation, 1979.

Kemp, Jack, 'The SS-19 and the New Soviet ICBM's vis-a-vis SALT II', Congressional Record, 2 August 1979, pp. E4076–7.

Kissinger, Henry, *White House Years* (Boston, Mass.: Little Brown, 1979).

Laird, Melvin, 'Arms Control: The Russians are Cheating!' *The Reader's Digest,* December 1977.

Lee, William T., 'Debate over US Strategic Forecasts: A Poor Record', *Strategic Review* VII, : Summer, 1980.

Lee, William T., *Understanding the Soviet Military Threat* (New York: National Information Strategy Center, 1977).

'Malinovsky Lauds New Missile Might', *The New York Times,* 23 April 1966.

Middleton, Drew, 'Deception Alleged in First Arms Talks', *The New York Times,* 9 April 1979.

Mihalka, Michael, *German Strategic Deception in the 1930s* (The Rand Corporation, N-1557-NA: Santa Monica, CA, July 1980).

Miko, Francis T., 'Soviet Strategic Objectives and SALT II: American Perceptions', Congressional Research Service, Report No. 78-119-F, May 25, 1978.

'Military Parades', *Soviet Military Review,* No. 10/80.

Ogarkov, N. V., 'Military Strategy', *Soviet Military Encyclopedia,* Vol. 7, 1979.

President Brezhnev and the Soviet Union's Changing Security Policy, *Foreign Broadcast Information Service* 25 May 1979, FB 79-10009.

Ross, Dennis, 'Rethinking Soviet Strategic Policy: Inputs and Implications', *Journal of Strategic Studies* 1(2), May 1978.

Rowny, Edward L., 'The Soviets Are Still Russians', *Survey,* 25(2), Spring 1980.

'Russians Say Antimissile System Will Protect Them From Attack', *The New York Times,* 21 February 1967.

Safire, William, 'Deception Managers', *The New York Times,* 6 August 1981.

Semple, Robert B., 'McNamara Hints Soviet Deploys Antimissile Net', *The New York Times,* 11 November 1966.

Shabad, Theodore, 'Khrushchev Says Missile Can "Hit a Fly" in Space', *The New York Times,* 17 July 1962.

Shabad, Theodore, "Russian Reports Solving Rocket Defense Problem', *The New York Times,* 24 October 1971.

Shabad, Theodore, 'Sokolovsky Says Soviet Matches US Fleet of Atom Submarines', *The New York Times,* 18 February 1965.

Sienkiewicz, Stanley, 'Salt and Soviet Nuclear Doctrine', *International Security.*

Simes, Dmitri K., 'Deterrence and Coercion in Soviet Policy', *International Security,* Winter 1980–81.

Slocombe, Walter, 'A SALT Debate: Hard but Fair Bargaining', *Strategic Review* VII(4), Fall 1979.

Smith, Gerard, *Doubletalk* (Garden City, NY: Doubleday, 1980).

'Soviet Aide Tells of Mobile Rockets', *The New York Times,* 18 November 1965.

'Soviet Firm Shows Missiles in Action', *The New York Times,* 11 May 1965.

'Soviet Missile Parade Features Anti-ICBM, Wheeled Carriers', *Aviation Week and Space Technology* 81, 16 November 1964, pp. 26–27.

'Soviet Pronounces its Missiles Finest', *The New York Times,* 17 November 1963.

'Soviet Statements on the Consequences of Nuclear War', *FBIS Trends* 17, August 1977.

'Soviets Brandish Medium, Long Range Missiles', *Aviation Week and Space Technology* 82, 24 May 1965.

Sullivan, David S., 'A SALT Debate: Continued Soviet Deception', *Strategic Review* VII(4), Fall 1979.

Sullivan, David S., 'Evaluating US Intelligence Estimates', in Roy Godson (ed.), *Intelligence Requirements for the 1980s: Analysis and Estimates* (Washington, D.C.: National Strategy Information Center, 1980).

Sullivan, David S., 'The Legacy of SALT I: Soviet Deception and US Retreat', *Strategic Review* VII, Winter 1979.

Szulc, Tad, 'Soviet Tests Laid to Defense Goal', *The New York Times*, 6 September 1961.

Tannee, Henry, 'Moscow Parades 110-Foot Missiles', *The New York Times*, 10 May 1965.

Tanner, Henry, 'Soviet Parades "Antimissile Missiles" on 46th Anniverary of Revolution', *The New York Times*, 8 November 1963.

Topping, Seymour, 'Khrushchev Cautions US, "Global" Rockets Render Warning Systems Useless', 17 March 1962.

Topping, Seymour, 'Soviet Claim of Rocket Superiority', *The New York Times*, 11 December 1962.

Twining, General Nathan, 'Report from Moscow', *Air Force Magazine*, August 1956.

Vance, Cyrus, 'Compliance With the SALT I Agreements', Congressional Record, S2553–6, 28 February 1978.

Wilson, George, 'Senate May Force New Anti-Missile Policy', *Aviation Week and Space Technology*, 84, 2 May 1966.

Wolfe, Thomas, *Soviet Power and Europe, 1945–1970* (Baltimore: Johns Hopkins, 1970).

Military Deception, Strategic Surprise, and Conventional Deterrence: A Political Analysis of Egypt and Israel, 1971-73

Janice Gross Stein

'The Egyptian and Syrian attack on Yom Kippur came as a surprise, though it was not unexpected' (Moshe Dayan, *Story of My Life*, New York: William and Morrow, 1976: 380).

'... I never practice ethical deception; strategic and tactical deception I can accept, but ethical deception never' (Anwar el-Sadat, *In Search of Identity*, New York: Harper & Row, 1977: 309–10).

Deception and Surprise

Military deception and strategic surprise are both prominent in military history. Although deception is not the only cause of surprise, the two are often intimately related. When deception succeeds, surprise results and, generally, it is a defender who is surprised by a challenger's deception. Deception is designed to create false expectations or, at the very least, uncertainty in a defender's calculations about the likelihood, timing, place, and type of military attack. A challenger may attempt to persuade an opponent that an imminent attack is unlikely, or that military action will be limited rather than general, or that an attack is likely in one rather than another location and, consequently, encourage a defender to disperse its forces to protect multiple objectives. In all these cases, challengers choose to deceive because they greatly improve their military position against a defender.

The attractiveness of a strategy of deception to a challenger is obvious. Deception is a force multiplier and military leaders know this only too well. Indeed, the greater the disparity of forces in favour of a defender, the more important a stratagem of deception becomes to a challenger. Military action that catches a defender's forces unaware may disrupt existing defense plans, interfere with mobilization and movement of additional forces to the battlefield, and destroy lines of communication, at least in the early phases of battle. These initial phases can be critical to the outcome: if a challenger is seeking a quick decisive military victory, if the strategy is blitzkrieg, a defender may not have enough time after a surprise attack to recover and reorganize. Even if the attack is limited in scope or the military strategy is one of attrition, an unanticipated attack can so affect the balance of capabilities that the prewar ratio of forces becomes obsolete. In the ensuing 'fog of war', a challenger becomes less vulnerable to retaliation by a defender's forces. And while a strategy of deception promises substantial advantage, it entails few immediate costs.[1]

The advantages of deception are so obvious that the capacity to deceive becomes a decided military asset, an asset, moreover, that is easily acquired. The requirements of a successful strategy of deception are not overly demanding. In their planning, challengers must be able to organize and coordinate their strategy in secrecy; generally, military bureaucracies emphasize organizational skills and a modicum of security. And as we shall see, total security is not a prerequisite to successful deception. Second, military and civilian leaders must design a plausible 'lie' that reinforces the expectations and preferences of a defender. Neither of these two requirements would strain the ingenuity of most contemporary military establishments and, indeed, have not done so in the past. It is not surprising that when deception is tried, it almost always succeeds.[2] Defenders are surprised even in the face of serious breaches of an opponent's security, elaborate intelligence collection systems built around sophisticated instruments, and warnings of impending action. Under the circumstances, one would expect a challenger bent on military action to try to reap the benefits deception brings. The frequency of deception in military history is easily understood. Understanding the pervasiveness of strategic surprise requires a little more elaboration.

Analysts look to a series of interrelated factors which make intelligible the high incidence of surprise in military history. A failure to anticipate a military attack has been traced to the dilemmas of the international environment, to the organizational setting in which intelligence information is handled, and to the nature of the intelligence task itself and the attendant characteristics of warning.[3] Each of these three factors contributes to the painful disjunction between past and present which defines military surprise. A brief restatement of the principal premise of each explanation makes abundantly clear why leaders are so often surprised when an opponent attacks.

Military historians suggest that, in the contemporary international system, the difficulty of distinguishing between offense and defense contributes significantly to the incidence of surprise. Much of conventional military technology is multi-purpose and, to the extent that it is, it can be used both for offense and defense. The anti-aircraft missile, for example, traditionally would be considered a defensive weapon but it also provides essential coverage for an army advancing in open space and vulnerable to strikes of opposing aircraft. Similarly, equipment which increases the mobility of infantry might well be classified as offensive, but mobility is central to much defense planning.[4] Analysts encounter similar difficulty in differentiating between offensive and defensive formations, at least until hours before an attack begins. Alerts, mobilizations, activation of passive defense, redeployment, can all be undertaken to defend against an anticipated attack as well as to prepare for military action.

A number of implications flow from this blurring of the distinction between offense and defense. Most important, deception becomes easier to execute and surprise becomes more likely. Military planners can deploy equipment and personnel in formations that legitimately are open to different interpretations. Defenders consequently encounter considerable difficulty in assessing the intentions of their opponents from tactical indicators. The military evidence before their eyes does not speak for itself; it is often ambiguous. When the offense and defense blur, the advantage goes to the challenger and the disadvantage to the defender.

Second, analysts look to the institutional framework of intelligence collection and analysis to account for military surprise. Adequate information is no longer a problem for most intelligence agencies, at least those in the industrialized world. Experts generally have access to highly reliable signal and electronic intelligence which is rapidly transmitted to national centers for analysis. If anything, analysts are swamped by data and cannot survey and digest all the evidence at their disposal. Recently, for example, NATO headquarters reduced its critical indicator list from 500 to 100 items to increase it efficiency in processing information and transmission of warning.[5] The obstacle to better performance lies rather in the analysis and interpretation of evidence and, here, the consensus among those who have studied the incidence of strategic surprise is pessimistic: institutional tinkering is unlikely to help.

Pluralist intelligence communities, which divide authority and apportion tasks, as in the United States, fare little better in their predictions than do intelligence agencies with exclusive responsibility for evaluation. Indeed, overlapping bureaucratic jurisdictions, hierarchy and specialization, and elaborate procedures characteristic of all complex organizations often compound the difficulties of intelligence analysis.[6] Not only the bureaucratization of the intelligence task but also its politicization complicate analysis. In pluralist communities, agencies with independent ambitions and interests compete for access to evidence and the attention of leaders. Yet, where intelligence evaluation is the responsibility of a single agency, the assumptions and expectations of senior officials structure and at times dominate the thinking of their subordinates. Restructuring the intelligence community promises marginal improvement at best — there is no 'organizational fix' for the contingency of military deception and the ensuing strategic surprise.[7]

The unmasking of deception is complicated still further by the inherent difficulties of the intelligence task and the characteristics of warning. We have already noted the ambiguity of much of the evidence intelligence analysts receive and the consequent difficulty of inferring an attack from evidence of military capabilities. Even experienced analysts of good judgment differ in their interpretation of this so-called 'hard' evidence. The conventional wisdom of attending to an adversary's capabilities provides little practical guidance to analysts responsible for warning of attack. If analysts were to follow this maxim and base their estimates of the likelihood of attack exclusively on military capabilities, warnings would be frequent, frustrating, and ultimately futile. Because so many would prove false, political leaders would quickly discount the significance of warning from their intelligence advisors; by warning too frequently, intelligence agencies reduce their own credibility. Strategic warnings, like much else in political life, are not cost-free and the scarce capital of an intelligence community must be expended with care.

If they are to warn effectively, analysts must estimate not only the capabilities but also the intentions of an opponent. To do so, they must consider the significance of diplomatic, political, and economic as well as military data. Even assessments of military intentions depend at least in part on an evaluation of the international and domestic political and economic factors which shape a challenger's decision on whether or not to use force. Assessment of the impact of these factors is no easy matter. There is enormous debate, even among social scientists with wide access to historical evidence, on the effect of all these factors on the incidence of war. It is not at all surprising that analysts confront this evidence equipped with inadequate, poorly formulated, and at times contradictory arguments. Evaluation of the significance of this kind of 'soft' evidence, in comparison to the 'hard' evidence of military capabilities, is even more open to conflicting — yet plausible — interpretation. Not only is the evidence ambiguous, but experts can legitimately disagree on the arguments which underlie the interpretation of the evidence. By its very nature, assessment of the intentions of an opponent is laced with uncertainty and ambiguity. Only hindsight brings clarity and certainty.

In addition to ambiguous evidence and problematic argument, experts encounter a third difficulty, one which arises directly from the nature of the task at hand. If they are to warn of a military attack, intelligence analysts must predict the likelihood of a single event and do so, moreover, with no baseline probability data. Fortunately, military attacks do not occur with such frequency that 'objective' probabilities can be validly estimated. Yet estimation of likelihood under these conditions, a task beyond the capability of the most sophisticated mathematicians, is routinely expected of intelligence experts. Moreover, they are expected to predict the probability of a single event which breaks sharply from the recent past, using evidence precisely from that past. It is little wonder, then, that intelligence 'fails' at what is almost an impossible task. What is surprising is that experts sometimes do succeed.

One further complication bedevils intelligence professionals — the difficulty in determining whether or not their predictions are accurate. Failures are easy to establish. Experts predict a low likelihood of military attack, an adversary strikes, the error is obvious, and the consequences are often catastrophic. When they warn of imminent action and an opponent does attack, then accuracy seems apparent. Even here, however, analysts cannot be sure of the premises of their prediction. An adversary may choose to use military force for reasons quite different than those suggested by intelligence advisors. If the estimate is 'right' for the 'wrong' reasons, analysts may be seriously misled in their estimates in the future.

Experts can have even less confidence in the accuracy of their predictions when they consider an attack unlikely and an opponent does not strike. A challenger may have planned military action but cancelled the scheduled attack for reasons unsuspected by the intelligence community. An inference that the challenger planned no attack would, of course, be in considerable error. Or, suspicious that a defender has guessed and is prepared, a challenger may postpone military action temporarily. The Japanese strike force on its way toward Pearl Harbour, for example, was under orders to abort action if it became clear that the United States had anticipated the attack. With hindsight, a low estimate of the likelihood of attack would have been incorrect, but a warning, followed by appropriate defensive action, would have cancelled the planned strike. The outcome could not validate the accuracy of the estimate. It is extraordinarily difficult to warn accurately and to know that one has warned accurately. Working with ambiguous evidence, poorly articulated theory, and limited opportunity for validation through feedback, the world of the intelligence analyst is a scientist's nightmare.

This brief review of environmental, organizational, and functional analyses of strategic surprise dramatizes their convergent conclusions: when a challenger sets out to deceive, surprise is usually the result. It is the norm rather than the exception. This rather pessimistic conclusion suggests the need to expand the focus of the study of deception and surprise beyond their international and institutional context to the substance of the concerns that animate civilian and military leaders. Beyond the rather obvious assertion that deception brings significant military advantage and is easy to achieve, we must know something about why and when challengers choose to use force. The central question for analysis becomes neither 'why deception?' nor 'why surprise?' but rather 'why military challenge?'.

This is the critical policy question for a defender as well. Insofar as a defender can understand why its opponent resorts to force, it can reduce its vulnerability to deception and surprise. There are, of course, important limits built into an assessment of the intentions of an adversary; a significant element of uncertainty always remains. Nevertheless, by asking what factors leaders are likely to consider in making their decision to go to war, and what factors they are likely to consider especially important, a defender can hedge against some of the most egregious errors of omission which contribute significantly to the incidence of surprise. A broad focus on the content of a challenger's calculus at least provides the appropriate categories for analysis.

Wars are not fought to deceive. When they are planned, as all attacks built around a strategy of deception must be, they are fought for a set of purposes which transcend military objectives and it is analysis of these purposes which must form the core of a study of military deception and strategic surprise. If policy prescription is to move beyond recommendations of procedural reform and institutional tinkering, it must deal with the substance as well as the processes of political and military decisions.

Studies of conventional deterrence provide a rich source of explanations of why leaders deliberately choose or refrain from military action and it is to this literature that we now turn to develop a list of explanations and to structure our consideration of a challenger's calculus. Five principal explanations of the collapse of deterrence are particularly relevant to our central concern of why challengers choose to use force. We briefly review and then assess the validity of these explanations by looking at the calculations of Egypt's leaders from

1971 to 1973, calculations which culminated in the successful deception of October 1973. The optic then switches to intelligence estimation and warning in Israel during the same period. Through this comparative analysis, we can discover which factors Egypt's leaders considered and which of these same factors Israel's leaders ignored. At the same time, we can assess the relevance of the other three explanations of surprise and evaluate their importance. In so doing, the paper can speak not only to the practices that may help a defender guard against deception but also to those policies that can reduce a challenger's incentive to use military force.

Conventional Deterrence: Explanations of the Planned Use of Force

In the three years that followed the termination of the War of Attrition in August 1970, Egypt's leaders seriously considered a surprise military attack against Israel at least four times. After President Sadat proclaimed a 'year of decision' in July 1971, he planned an air strike against Israel's military installations in Sinai preparatory to a landing of paratroopers, for the month of December. The President subsequently explained that he postponed the use of force because of inadequate military shipments from the USSR and the transfer of military equipment to India after the outbreak of the Indo-Pakistani War on 3 December.[8] Again the following year, Sadat ordered the Egyptian General Staff to prepare an attack across the Canal, to follow shortly after the American presidential elections, but cancelled the attack in mid-November after dismissing his senior military commanders for refusing to follow his orders.[9] In early 1973, Egyptian officers planned a surprise military attack for limited military objectives, in coordination with Syria, for the month of May. And again, the attack was postponed, this time because of the impending Soviet-American summit, inadequate arms deliveries from the Soviet Union, and Israel's military preparations.[10] In the summer of 1973, Egypt and Syria jointly planned a surprise attack across the ceasefire line and on 6 October, the two launched a coordinated military attack, surprising Israel's leaders and catching their armed forces unprepared.

Four times, then, Egypt planned military action and all four times deception was an integral part of the strategic plan. Only once, however, did Egyptian armed forces actually attack and when they did, deception succeeded. Why did Egypt cancel its planned military action three times? How did the calculus of Egyptian leaders differ the fourth time? What factors were critical in the decision to use force? Using as evidence one or more components of a challenger's calculus, at least five major approaches to conventional deterrence attempt to explain a challenger's decision to use military force.

The first of these explanations focuses on a challenger's assessment of the balance of interests and gives considerable weight to leaders' estimates of the importance of their own interests in comparison to those of a defender. If leaders consider their opponent's interests to be greater than their own, they will consider the defender's resolve to be high and, very likely, will forego military action.[11] Other variants of the interest explanation attach less importance to a comparative assessment and give greater weight to a challenger's evaluation either of its own interests or those of its adversary. Some argue that a challenger will not use force if it considers a defender's interests to be large and obvious while others insist that even a credible commitment by a defender, based on visible interests, is insufficient to deter military action.[12]

When we look at the calculations of Egypt's leaders from 1971 to 1973, we find little support for any variant of an interest explanation. In all four cases, Egypt considered its interests to be of overwhelming importance — the President defined the issue as 'to be or not to be' in November of 1972 — yet three times Egypt did not attack. Nor were the defender's credibility and reputation for resolve in question in any of the four cases: Egypt's leaders had no doubt that Israel would respond vigorously to a military attack. Finally, we find no evidence that Egypt's leaders paid any attention to asymmetries of interest nor did they use finely tuned calculations of relative interest to estimate Israel's likely response. On the contrary, calculations of interest were general rather than specific and differed little whether Egypt's leaders chose to proceed or to refrain from military action. Because they did vary so little, calculations of interest cannot be an important component in an explanation of a challenger's decision to use force.

A second explanation, one which has received somewhat less attention than it deserves, suggests that a challenger may abstain from a use of force if its leaders see a plausible alternative to military action. If, on the other hand, leaders consider that no option but military action can bring about the minimum change they require, then military attack becomes likely.[13] Consideration of this component of a challenger's calculus is particularly important if explanations of the use of force are to become broader, less technical, and more explicitly political.

In examining the calculations of Egypt's leaders, we do notice a relationship between a narrowing of the bargaining range and the use of force. In February of 1971, in a speech to the Egyptian National Assembly, President Sadat offered to sign a peace agreement with Israel in return for a full withdrawal to the borders of 4 June 1967.[14] The President was explicit in rejecting normalization of relations but expressed his interest in a diplomatic resolution of the conflict. Shortly before, Israel's Minister of Defense had proposed an interim agreement along the Canal, a proposal received with some initial interest by President Sadat and, for the next several months, the American Secretary of State worked on the details of a partial agreement. Although the two sides were unable to agree on terms, throughout most of 1971, Egypt's leaders did see some alternative to a use of force and actively pursued diplomatic options even while they prepared for military action.

They were considerably less optimistic by the end of 1972. Diplomatic negotiations were stalemated and President Sadat spoke repeatedly of the necessity to use force. Even then, however, after the expulsion of Soviet military personnel in July of 1972, the President offered to resume a dialogue with the United States. In his autobiography, President Sadat displayed his familiarity with the nuances of American politics. Acknowledging that he expected little movement during a presidential election year, he did not rule out some progress immediately following the election in early November.[15] That autumn, secret negotiations through a 'back channel' began between Henry Kissinger, then national security advisor to President Nixon, and Hafez Ismail, security advisor to President Sadat.[16]

At least in the first two cases when Egypt did not resort to military force, its leaders could see some hope of diplomatic progress. Scope for bargaining, though not large and constantly diminishing, nevertheless did exist. By 1973, even this residual hope of diplomatic progress had disappeared. In his May Day speech, President Sadat acknowledged that negotiations with the United States had failed to produce results and concluded that Egypt would not receive help from any quarter unless it took military action to break the deadlock.[17] Over time, there appears to be an inverse relationship between identification of a plausible diplomatic alternative and a use of force. At least in these four cases, this component of a challenger's calculus was a valid index of impending military action.

A third explanation of the use of force, a challenger's estimate of the probability of military success, has received a great deal of attention. Theories of conventional deterrence argue that unless challengers consider the balance of military capabilities to be favourable, they will estimate that the cost of military action will exceed its benefits and be dissuaded from action. Not only assessments of the general balance, but also estimates of changing trends in the balance may shape a decision whether or not to use force. If leaders consider trends to be negative, they may feel a growing sense of urgency to act. Japanese leaders in 1941, for example, made exactly this kind of calculation. Some analysts suggest, however, that more important than either quantitative analyses or estimates of the trend in the military balance is a challenger's evaluation of the prospects of its military strategy. When leaders think they can achieve a rapid military victory, they are likely to choose force, but when they see no alternative to a long costly war of attrition, or a limited victory which may nevertheless degenerate into attrition and stalemate, they are likely to refrain from military action.[18]

A careful inspection of the Egyptian evaluation of military capabilities in these four cases suggests a more complicated relationship between assessment of the military balance and a use of force. In 1971, Egyptian military leaders argued strongly that Egypt was incapable of a general attack across the Canal. The General Staff emphasized the lack of bridge-building equipment and aircraft that could strike at air bases deep within Israel-held territory. Again and again, senior Egyptian officers demanded improved offensive capability in the air as well as the capability to strike at Israel's population centers to deter renewed strategic bombing of Egyptian civilians.[19] These demands, forcefully reiterated by the General Staff as preconditions to military action, would become well known to Israel's Military Intelligence.

Little had changed a year later. Senior commanders in the Egyptian army strongly opposed President Sadat's directive, issued in mid-July, to prepare for attack in mid-November of 1972. At an acrimonious meeting of the Armed Forces Supreme Council on 24 October, the Commander of the Third Army, General Wasel, the Commander-in-Chief, General Sadek, and the Vice-

Minister of war, General Hassan, all opposed military action and argued that even a limited operation without adequate offensive capability in the air could turn into a disastrous defeat.[20] Two days later, President Sadat dismissed the principal dissenters and confirmed as Chief of Staff General Shazly, a proponent of attack for limited military objectives. General Ahmed Ismail became the new Minister of War.

By May of 1973, the pessimistic evaluation of the military balance had changed significantly not only in response to accelerated arms deliveries from the Soviet Union, but also to a reorientation of Egypt's military strategy. Under Generals Shazly and Ismail, the General Staff was planning a canal-crossing and a ground offensive that would not exceed the range of a dense anti-aircraft system. The absence of effective offensive capability in the air became considerably less important in the context of the new strategy. By the summer of 1973, after Soviet delivery of the long-promised SCUD missiles and intensified joint planning with Syria, Sadat estimated that Egypt had reached the zenith of its military capability. Moreover, Egypt was unlikely to achieve military parity with Israel in the future; it was unlikely to receive additional military aid of sufficient scope. This, the President concluded, was Egypt's best chance.[21]

Egyptian military calculations over this time period shed some light on the changing impact of an unfavourable assessment of the military balance. When military leaders first began serious consideration of a use of force, their negative assessments dissuaded them from military action. A determined president, however, replaced these military leaders and challenged their successors to develop a military strategy to compensate for strategic weakness. A new set of senior officers planned force deployments, adapted military technology, and built deception into a strategy designed to confound the advantages of their opponent. Deception was an essential component of the strategy, a component designed to compensate, at least in the first forty-eight hours, for an acknowledged inferiority in military capability.[22] By multiplying its military advantage through surprise, Egypt could meet its limited military objectives even from an inferior military position. The advantages of deception become especially important when leaders recognize military weakness.

Contrary to prevailing arguments, military officers did not persist in their traditional insistence on a decisive general victory but adapted military strategy to suit their president's political purposes. And, in this adaptation, an unfavorable assessment of trends in the military balance was more important than a negative assessment of the balance itself. The Egyptian experience suggests that an unfavourable estimate of the military balance was not a barrier to the use of force but an obstacle to be overcome. A careful reading of the trend of Egyptian military calculations over time demonstrates the frailty of superior military capabilities as a durable deterrent to a use of force.

A fourth explanation of the use of force looks to the attitudes of allies and military suppliers. Particularly in a penetrated security system, where the principal protagonists are chronically short of resources and depend largely on the superpowers to equip their armies, anticipation of patron support or opposition may be critical to a decision to proceed with military action. Attention to a superpower's attitude will be especially careful when superpower-client relationships are symmetrical and polarized, as they were in the Middle East until 1973. At least, this is an argument frequently made by those who hold the superpowers responsible for the action of their smaller allies.

Examination of the calculations of Egyptian leaders suggests at best a modest relationship between their assessments of a likely Soviet response and the use of force. Both military and civilian analysts reported in 1971 that the Soviet Union repeatedly urged Egypt to give serious consideration to diplomacy, at least until it could increase its inadequate capabilities.[23] The next year, Mohamed Heikal wrote a series of provocative pieces in *Al-Ahram*, arguing that the Soviet Union benefited from the continuing stalemate of 'no-war, no peace'.[24] After the Nixon-Brezhnev summit in the spring, President Sadat expressed his alarm at the direction of detente: the two superpowers ' . . . had agreed on no war in the Middle East. There was to be nothing but surrender'.[25] By the spring of 1973, the President was only mildly more optimistic. He acknowledged the increase in arms deliveries but reiterated his charge that the two superpowers had agreed to freeze the situation in the Middle East in their quest for detente.[26] And only days before the start of the October War, when Egypt and Syria were fully committed to the use of military force, Sadat again asked for clarification of Soviet attitudes to military action by Egypt.[27] At best, the President was uncertain.

The evidence is inconclusive. When Egypt refrained from military action, its leaders anticipated opposition from the Soviet Union, but when they chose to go to war, they did not expect Soviet support. We find little evidence, moreover, to substantiate the popular argument that the Soviet Union encouraged and incited Egypt to military action. A challenger's expectation of its patron's likely response does not seem to be critical to a decision to use force.

The last explanation of a planned use of force focuses on a challenger's comparative calculation of loss. In a reformulation of the central tenet of classical deterrence theory, leaders are expected to assess the losses of action and inaction — rather than estimate the losses and gains of military action. Losses are not defined exclusively in military terms, but encompass economic, political, and diplomatic consequences as well. Leaders are expected to compare 'alternative risks' and choose the least damaging option. In 1914, for example, German leaders expected their military position to deteriorate, their allies to divide, and their adversaries to coalesce with the passage of time; the estimated consequences of inaction were far more negative than those of a use of force.[28] Here the minimization of loss, rather than the maximization of gain, shapes a decision to attack.

Both when they chose war and when they refrained from action, Egyptian leaders paid a great deal of attention to the losses of inaction. As early as 1971, after learning from his Minister of Finance that the treasury was virtually bankrupt, the President concluded that only a reversal of the defeat of 1967 would restore confidence in Egypt's economy. Sadat was also pessimistic about the political and diplomatic consequences of inaction; he argued that time was running out as Egypt came face-to-face with 'lasting facts'.[29] One year later, the sense of urgency was greater. The President warned that if the stalemate were not broken, there would be serious domestic disturbances and the influential Heikal wrote of the 'fossilization of the situation in the Middle East'.[30] In the spring of 1973, Sadat spoke again of the 'explosive' consequences of continued inaction, the intolerable impact on domestic morale, and the alarming deterioration of Egypt's position in the Arab world.[31] That summer, shortly before the October War, he used even more graphic language: Egypt was the 'laughing stock' of the Arab world and its economy had 'fallen below zero'; continued inaction was intolerable.[32] Throughout the period between 1971 and 1973, then, assessment of the risks of inaction were large and prominent in Egyptian calculations.

Precisely because an emphasis on the risks of inaction was prominent both when Egyptian leaders chose war and when they refrained from military action, it is a necessary but insufficient component in an explanation of the decision to use force in October of 1973. To assess the validity of an explanation built around a 'calculus of alternative risks', we must examine leaders' consideration of the losses of action as well as those of inaction. If the explanation is valid, the losses of inaction should outweigh those of military action when leaders choose to use force while the risks of military action should appear to be greater when they abstain.

Here the evidence provides considerable support for the argument. In the first two cases, as we have seen, military leaders predicted calamity should Egypt attack; indeed, in 1971 and in 1972, the estimated losses of both attack and delay were so grave that the choice must have been extraordinarily difficult. And even in May of 1973, Sadat spoke of substantial losses from military action: inadequate opportunity for consultation with Syria, deficiencies in delivery of equipment that had been promised by the Soviet Union, military readiness in Israel and the reduced probability of successful deception — all these dimmed the prospects of military action. The President also expressed reluctance to disrupt the Nixon-Brezhnev summit, a consequence which would follow inevitably from an Egyptian military attack.[33] By the end of the summer, however, Sadat could identify few losses from military action: the summit was over, extensive consultation had taken place between senior Egyptian and Syrian officers, the long-awaited SCUDs had arrived from the Soviet Union, military aid had peaked, and the prospect of deception was good. Even the losses were now less than those consequent to inaction. The President subsequently recalled the Soviet estimate that an attack would probably entail the loss of 40 per cent of Egyptian aircraft and a high level of military casualties, losses that were not considered insupportable.[34] The choice was easy.

This examination of five components of the calculus of Egyptian leaders speaks to the failure of Israel's deterrent strategy and, in so doing, addresses both Egypt's choice of deception and Israel's vulnerability to surprise. A summary of the findings should make clear the relationship between deterrence, deception, and surprise.

First, no single component of Egyptian calculations provides a complete or even an adequate explanation of the collapse of deterrence and, consequently, no single indicator can or should be relied upon to predict the likelihood of attack. *Ab initio,* a single-variable prediction should be suspect; indeed, reliance by intelligence analysts on a single indicator is likely to increase the probability of surprise. Second, our evidence suggests that two kinds of indicators are not terribly helpful in estimating the likelihood of attack. A high Egyptian valuation of the interests at stake was in and of itself an insufficient stimulus to a use of force and estimates of patron opposition were inadequate deterrents to military action. The first explains too little while the second explains too much. Because these estimates remained constant both when leaders chose to challenge and when they refrained from action, monitoring of these estimates would be of little help in protecting against surprise attack.

More useful as an indicator were Egyptian estimates of plausible alternatives to military force. The evidence suggests a steady, if inverse, relationship between these estimates and a use of force. Over time, Egyptian leaders grew increasingly pessimistic about diplomatic initiatives to break the logjam. We can make no judgment here about why Egypt identified less and less room for bargaining as time progressed; a narrower estimate of the bargaining range may be a function of either a challenger's or a defender's specification of minimum requirements. What is relevant is that Egypt's leaders lost hope of diplomatic progress. When they did so and found themselves simultaneously in a position of military inferiority, deception and a surprise attack became increasingly attractive. Intelligence analysts responsible for warning should be alerted by prolonged stalemate and by pessimistic evaluations of the prospects of diplomacy.

Also relevant were the challenger's estimates of the military balance and the prospects of battlefield success, but here interpretation must be cautious. Estimates of military defeat did constrain Egypt's leaders from going to war, but these unfavorable estimates of the military balance were only a temporary deterrent to military action. Indeed, over time these unfavorable estimates served as a spur rather than as a barrier as Egyptian officers designed a military strategy to compensate for acknowledged military weakness. Deception may be especially likely if challengers consider the military balance unfavorable: strongly motivated to attack but recognizing the military odds, leaders hope to compensate, at least in part, through surprise.

Finally, Egyptian leaders openly expressed an acute sense of the losses of inaction and perpetuation of the status quo. And far from becoming resigned to an unpleasant reality, their assessment of its economic, political, and diplomatic costs grew; their estimates of the losses of inaction intensified over time. Reluctant to concede on the processes of bargaining or the substance of the issues, President Sadat concentrated not on reducing the costs of inaction, but rather on reducing the expected losses of action. Given the ingenuity of the military mind and the flexibility of modern multi-purpose conventional technology, design of a strategy that would meet minimum constraints was only a matter of time. Officials responsible for assessing the likelihood of attack should probably give special weight to a challenger's repeated expression of the intolerable consequences of inaction; again, these can serve as a preliminary warning and as an incentive to consider the possibility that an adversary is engaged in deception. Especially when a defender is confident of its capacity to defeat an attack, when it is confident of its military superiority, a challenger may be spurred to deceive and a defender will be vulnerable to surprise.

Given the advantage of the challenger who chooses to deceive and the vulnerability of the defender to deception, encomiums must go to those analysts who somehow manage to warn in time. A focus on these components of a challenger's calculations, components that were critical in determining Egypt's decision to use force — and to deceive — cannot assure improved estimation and accurate warning, but it can improve the odds. It cannot assure accuracy because challengers may express pessimism about the prospects of diplomacy, chagrin about the consequences of inaction, and gloom about their military prospects, and yet take no action or choose to delay. This is indeed what happened in May of 1973.

Attention to these components of a challenger's calculus can, however, perform one essential function. It can alert intelligence experts to the possible failure of deterrence, to its 'buckling', and consequently to deception.[35] Once analysts introduce the competing assumption of deception into their analysis, they can challenge other assumptions and consider the best fit with the tactical evidence. Experts need help, however, if they are to know when to give serious consideration to the possibility of deception, when to challenge an assumption that deterrence is succeeding, that an adversary will not attack. It is especially difficult to challenge the premise of successful deterrence when tactical evidence can be plausibly interpreted through other explanations. Ideally analysts need a systematic and differentiated list of conditions which promote the breakdown of deterrence and deception; they need policy-relevant theory. Unfortunately, no such list presently exists. In the absence of a set of specified conditions, acknowledgement by an opponent of military inferiority, an acknowledgement followed by estimates of severe losses consequent to inaction and expressions of frustration, of 'no way out', should sound at least a preliminary alarm. If these estimates persist over time, no matter what other evidence is available, experts should become progressively more skeptical and actively consider, as one of several hypotheses, an explanation of deception. A focus on these components of a challenger's calculus should help intelligence experts to restructure their analysis of the likelihood of attack, hopefully in time.

Armed with *ex post facto* wisdom, wisdom that is dangerous to a balanced evaluation of past performance, we turn our attention to Israel's estimates of Egyptian intentions during this period.[36] Did intelligence analysts pay attention to these components of Egyptian calculations? What indicators of attack did they use? Did they seriously consider the possibility of deception? How important were errors of omission? What explains these errors? How significant were other factors in explaining the surprise of October 1973?

Israel's Estimates of Egypt's Intentions: Deterrence and Surprise

Although Israel has several intelligence units, it is Military Intelligence, housed within the Israel Defense Forces, that is principally responsible for assessment of the likelihood of Arab attack.[37] Although its formal mandate is restricted to the assessment of military capabilities, because of its special competence in assessing military data, it is considered uniquely capable of amalgamating evidence on capabilities and intentions to produce an integrated intelligence estimate. For the last several years, Military Intelligence has dominated the processes of estimation and warning.

At least four times between December 1971 and October 1973, Military Intelligence considered the likelihood of an Egyptian attack. Unfortunately, we have little valid information about the details of the intelligence estimates presented at the end of 1971 and 1972. No official records are yet available and, in contradistinction to their extensive discussion of the estimates presented in 1973, the principals have said little about analyses proferred in earlier years. We do know that Military Intelligence considered the possibility of an attack in December of 1971: Egyptian reserves and civilian vehicles were mobilized, field forces were engaged in maneuvers, general formations of armor had advanced toward the Canal, bridging equipment had been brought forward, and civil defense procedures had been activated. Egypt's President, addressing the troops on 21 November, was explicit: 'The time for battle has come ... The next time we shall meet in Sinai.'[38] Apparently, however, Military Intelligence did not consider an attack likely, since the Chief of Staff, at that time General Bar-Lev, did no more than put the army on alert, reinforce selected units at the front line, and delay his scheduled retirement for a short time. For a civilian army which relies on mobilization of its civilian reserves, the response was modest.

Again at the end of 1972, a second large Egyptian mobilization took place, differing only in detail from the preparations of the previous year. Earlier that summer, however, President Sadat had expelled Soviet military personnel; in so doing, at least in the estimation of many of Israel's leaders, he had seriously constrained Egypt's military option. Still, a report was received from a 'highly reliable source' that an attack was imminent. At the same time, Israel was receiving a detailed flow of information reporting the skepticism of the Egyptian General Staff about its capability to wage war. Particularly important was the Egyptian estimate of its inadequate capability to strike at Israel's airfields and to deter strikes by Israel's aircraft against its civilian population. After reviewing the conflicting evidence, Military Intelligence estimated the probability of attack as 'low'.[39] In a restrained response, the Chief of Staff, now General David Elazar, alerted the army and postponed plans to shorten conscript service.

By the spring and early summer of 1973, some of Israel's most senior officers, although not Military Intelligence, were alarmed. Again Egyptian military preparations were extensive and the secret transfer of 16 Mirage fighters from Libya to Egypt was known to intelligence officers.[40] In an interview on 9 April, President Sadat spoke of his satisfaction with the pace of arms shipments from the Soviet Union and warned once more of the coming battle.[41] And during the third week of April, Israel again received a report from a 'reliable source' which set a definite date for the impending attack.[42]

General Ze'ira, then head of Military Intelligence, reviewed the evidence on 13 April and again for meetings of the General Staff on 16 April, 9 May, 14 May, and 21 May. Intelligence continued to receive a stream of reports reiterating the emphasis within the Egyptian military on adequate capability in the air as a precondition to attack. These reports, which did not reach Military Intelligence directly but came through another intelligence channel, were circulated to senior civilian as well as military leaders. Drawing on this evidence, General Ze'ira concluded that no fundamental change in Egypt's evaluation of its own capabilities had occurred; deterrence still held. He suggested rather that by increasing tension, President Sadat was trying to improve the Arab bargaining position in the private talks scheduled between Egypt and the United States and at the Nixon-Brezhnev summit to take place in June. Consequently, alarm in Israel would invite American pressure and, in so doing, accomplish Egyptian purposes.[43] Questioned subsequently at a closed meeting of the Foreign Affairs and Defense Committee of Israel's parliament, Ze'ira explained that although Sadat found it difficult to tolerate the status quo, all other available alternatives were worse.[44]

The Head of the *Mossad,* or Central Intelligence Collection Agency, was skeptical of the analysis of Military Intelligence and at one of the General Staff meetings, challenged the assumptions which were at the basis of the estimate. General Zamir suggested that Sadat's preconditions for war had been met: an invading army could operate on the east bank of the Suez Canal under the protection of the missile umbrella and the anti-aircraft system could defend Egypt's heartland against strategic bombing.[45]

The Chief of Staff was also concerned. Alluding to the fruitless exchange betwen Hafez Ismail and Henry Kissinger and to Egyptian frustration over the continuing deadlock, Elazar suggested that Egypt's President might be tempted to launch a limited military attack to force negotiations. Although the risks of action were greater than its prospects, Sadat might chance military action rather than suffer the consequences of continued stalemate. Alternatively, it was very possible, as Military Intelligence suggested, that Egypt was seeking to manipulate military tension for political purposes; Sadat would go to the brink and then retreat. By military logic, Egypt should be deterred but, the Chief of Staff concluded, he was not persuaded that Egypt would not attack.[46] The Minister of Defense shared this concern but was also chary of needlessly alarming the United States and, consequently, inviting unwelcome pressure. Accordingly, precautionary measures, falling far short of preparation for war, were put into effect: the date of previously scheduled military exercises was advanced, the army was put on extended alert, major improvements to infrastructure and defense were undertaken, and a very small number of reservists — largely technicians — were mobilized.[47]

On the last day of September, the Director of Military Intelligence once again summoned his staff to consider evidence of large troop concentrations, this time on both the Egyptian and Syrian borders. In the north, reinforcement of front-line armour and artillery followed an air battle with Israel on 13 September, a battle in which Syria had lost 13 planes. Intelligence experts consequently anticipated some military activity in preparation for a reprisal. Alternatively, it was possible that Syria was preparing for a reprisal by Israel for the hijacking of a train carrying Soviet Jews to Vienna. The Egyptian army was deployed in battle formation, but it had been so deployed several times before. These manoeuvres were larger in size but, again, they had been increasing every year for the past several years and, this time, civil defense procedures had not been activated. However, in the early hours of the morning of 1 October, a report arrived alleging that that day, or at the latest on 6 October, Egypt and Syria would launch a full-scale attack.[48]

After lengthy deliberations lasting throughout most of the night, General Ze'ira reported his conclusions at a meeting of the General Staff the next morning. The Egyptian army had begun a large-scale multi-branch exercise which was due to end on 8 October; this information had come from several reliable sources.[49] The high level of alert was routine in an army on such large manoeuvers. Alternatively, the alert might be designed to deter military action by Israel against Syria — Egypt viewed the air battle earlier that month as a premeditated attack against Syria and was attempting to prevent any further military action. The alert could be defensive or deterrent. The Director of Military Intelligence concluded that the probability of attack was low.

Military activity intensified and on 3 October, at the request of the Minister of Defense, the Prime Minister convened a meeting of her closest civilian and military advisors. The Minister of Defense was especially concerned by the forward deployment of anti-aircraft missiles by Syria, a deployment inconsistent with the explanation of a miscalculated Syrian estimate of an impending reprisal by Israel. The Director of Military Intelligence was ill and was represented by the Head of Intelligence Research, Aryeh Shalev. The Head of the *Mossad* did not attend the informal meeting.

Shalev reported some unusual Syrian military activity — forward deployment of part of the air force, artillery, and a bridging battalion, reinforcement and forward movement of the air defense system, and the appearance near the border of special briefing units. Nevertheless, the general deployment could still be considerd defensive. Furthermore, Israel had reliable information from abroad indicating that although Syria would like to attack, it would not do so without Egypt.[50]

Turning his attention to Egypt, Shalev reported some unusual deployment of artillery but, on the other hand, civil defense procedures had not been activated, critical changes in the disposition of aircraft had not been made, and army officers had been given permission to make a pilgrimage to Mecca after 8 October, the day the exercise was scheduled to end. In short, the tactical evidence was not consistent. Shalev was scrupulous in telling those assembled that both armies were so deployed ' ... that they were able at any moment to launch an attack ...'.[51] Nevertheless, he concluded, '... the possibility of an Egyptian-Syrian war does not seem likely to me, since there has been no change in their assessment of the state of forces in Sinai so that they could go to war'.[52] To estimate the likelihood of attack, Military Intelligence gave special importance to the flow of documentary evidence on Egypt's negative evaluation of its relative military capabilities. More important than evidence of capability to attack was evidence of estimates by the Egyptian military of its inadequate capability.

The Chief of Staff shared the intelligence assessment that Egypt and Syria were technically capable of attack with little advance warning and the estimate that a coordinated attack was nevertheless unlikely at this moment. He concluded, however, by reiterating his expectation that he would be given adequate warning of an attack. Indeed, most war-gaming had been premised on a warning period of two to six days and a warning of only twenty-four hours was considered catastrophic. Yet this assumption of certain warning was inconsistent with Elazar's assessment that Egypt and Syria could attack with little notice. As a precaution, the Chief of Staff authorized a transfer of additional armour and artillery to the more vulnerable northern border.

Late in the evening of 4 October, photographs from a special air reconnaissance mission revealed considerable strengthening of Egyptian forces along the Canal and the forward movement of bridging equipment toward three different sectors of the front.[53] The Director of Military Intelligence received other disquieting information that same evening: units of the Soviet fleet stationed near Alexandria and Port Said had begun to move out and Antanov-22 aircraft had arrived in Cairo and Damascus to withdraw the families of Soviet advisors. Military Intelligence considered at least three explanations of the withdrawal. First, the Soviet Union knew of an impending attack and, anticipating the military consequences of a counter-attack by Israel, was withdrawing its personnel. Such an interpretation was alarming in its implications. Alternatively, if Soviet-Syrian relations had deteriorated badly, as some speculated, Syria might have requested all Soviet advisors to leave, but this would not explain why Soviet personnel were being withdrawn simultaneously fom Egypt.[54] Third, it was possible that the Soviet Union had accepted Syrian allegations, broadcast repeatedly in the last several days, that Israel was about to attack.[55] Again, however, if this were so, Moscow would have asked Washington to warn Israel against attack and no such warning had been received. Uncommitted yet to any explanation, the Director of Military Intelligence considered the withdrawal so disquieting that he immediately informed the Chief of Staff. Within moments Elazar decided to alert the air force and mobilize its support personnel.

Throughout that night and the following morning, senior intelligence, military, and civilian leaders debated the significance of the Soviet withdrawal. General Ze'ira preferred the first of the three interpretations, even though it was inconsistent with his estimate that Egypt and Syria would not attack, that they were deterred. The other two explanations, as he pointed out, were inconsistent with the evidence; they were flawed. Yet, General Ze'ira did not pursue his reasoning to its logical conclusion. Rather, in a series of briefings to military and civilian leaders the next morning, he presented all three interpretations, two with their attendant qualifications, but accepted none, explaining that he did not know why Soviet personnel were being withdrawn and was awaiting further information. Here a critical opportunity to revise the estimate of a low probability of attack was missed.[56]

General Ze'ira also reported that the pace of military activity on both borders had quickened. In what appeared to be an offensive deployment, Syria had moved two squadrons of Sukhoi bombers to front-line air bases and Egypt had sent additional tanks and artillery forward. After reviewing all the evidence, the Director of Military Intelligence estimated that the probability of attack was still low. Nevertheless, his confidence in the success of deterrence began to waver and Ze'ira concluded by informing his colleagues that he anticipated confirmation of Egyptian intent from a 'reliable' source within a few hours.[57] The Chief of Staff added that he too expected additional evidence if Egypt and Syria intended to attack. Because of the growing uncertainty, however, Elazar recommended a full-scale alert at the highest level.

The warning came early that next morning of 6 October. A report from a 'highly reliable source' informed General Ze'ira that Egypt and Syria would attack that day at sunset. Although warning had finally come, it was not the first time this kind of warning had come from this source.[58] Nevertheless, most of Israel's leaders now considered war highly probable if not certain. In a series of emergency meetings, they ordered a large-scale mobilization of reserves to meet the expected attack. Only a few hours after mobilization had begun and four hours earlier than anticipated, Egypt and Syria attacked in full force across the ceasefire lines, surprising Israel's forces and catching them unprepared.

Deterrence, Deception, and Surprise: A Reprise

Equipped with evidence of Egyptian civilian and military thinking, evidence that became available long after these estimates were made, and using the unfair advantage of hindsight, we can do at least a preliminary evaluation of the performance of Military Intelligence. Two assessments were accurate more or less for the reasons given — those of 1971 and 1972 — one estimate was 'right' but for the 'wrong' reasons — that of May 1973 — and one was inaccurate, culminating in the surprise of October 1973. Given the well-documented obstacles to the estimation of the intentions of an opponent, it is not at all unusual that intelligence experts should be 'right' for the 'right' reasons only half the time. Earlier we suggested that at least four factors may account for surprise: the organizational context of intelligence assessment; the difficulty in distinguishing between offense and defense in the current international environment; the nature of the intelligence task and the characteristics of warning; and the components of a challenger's calculus that are considered by intelligence analysts. How important were each of these factors in complicating the assessment of the likelihood of an Egyptian attack? How much did each contribute to flawed estimates and strategic surprise?

Analysts commonly look to the institutional framework of intelligence collection and analysis as the proximate cause of military surprise. This explanation has received a great deal of attention and, indeed, was offered by the official commission of inquiry appointed in Israel after the October War.[59] The Agranat Commission strongly recommended the creation of a pluralist intelligence community and the reactivation of the moribund research unit within the foreign ministry which could provide competing assessments of political intention. Other *ex post facto* analyses have referred to the pervasiveness of 'group think' which inhibited independent evaluation and still others have argued a directly contradictory thesis of a 'disturbed hierarchy' which bedeviled relationships among Military Intelligence, the General Staff, and the Cabinet.[60] The former suggests homogeneous group dynamics which inhibit independent thinking while the latter looks to the personalities and styles of senior leaders as the principal cause of the intelligence failure in October 1973.

Discounting the often blinding biases of hindsight, it is difficult to make a convincing case for any of these explanations. Most easily disposed of is the argument that a monolithic intelligence agency was the principal cause of surprise. In October 1973, the American intelligence community, composed of multiple civilian and military institutions, fared no better in its estimates than did its counterpart in Israel. American leaders received almost no advance warning of the impending attack. Even more damaging to the argument, in the early days of October, the Head of the *Mossad* expressed his skepticism of the estimate of a low probability of war to the Prime Minister, who in turn asked him to convey his doubts to the Minister of Defense.[61] It appears that the two most senior members of the Cabinet did hear competing estimates from at least two intelligence services. Finally, as we have seen, the documentary evidence of Egyptian military thinking, evidence which was so crucial to the estimate of a low probability of attack, did not come through the channels of Military Intelligence but through a different network and was circulated directly both to civilian and military principals.

For many of the same reasons, it is difficult to accept an explanation of 'group think', a group syndrome born out of the need to protect group solidarity and characterized by immunity to criticism and excessive risk-taking.[62] Only four months earlier, in May of 1973, with the same men and women in office, the group did not think alike. The Chief of Staff and the Minister of Defense were both skeptical of the low estimate of attack and General Zamir, the Head of the *Mossad,* disputed the assessment at a meeting of the General Staff. The same group of decision-makers who disagreed substantially amongst themselves were not likely to fall victim to the vicissitudes of 'group think' within a few short months. Although Israel's senior military and political leaders did think alike that October, we must look elsewhere for the explanation.

Perhaps the personalities and styles of 'heroic' leaders contributed to excessive risk-taking and distorted judgments. In testimony before the Foreign Affairs and Defense Committee of Israel's parliament in May of 1973, General Ze'ira explained that his obligation was to provide the Chief of Staff with evaluations that were as clear and sharp as possible. Of course, he continued, a sharp evaluation, if it were in error, would translate into a clear and sharp mistake, but that was a risk, he concluded, which the Head of Military Intelligence must take.[63] A predisposition toward certainty rather than ambiguity, clarity rather than nuance, may indeed mask the considerable risks inherent in the estimation of the likelihood of military attack. And, as we noted, there were lacunae in General Ze'ira's assessment of the significance of the Soviet withdrawal, even within the parameters of his analysis. Here too, however, the explanation cannot carry the burden of the evidence. Moshe Dayan, then Minister of Defense, was generally considered to be skeptical, pragmatic, and nuanced in his thinking. Yet he too, with access to some of the critically important raw intelligence data, with military expertise, and with a personality profile considerably different from that of the Director of Military Intelligence, doubted until the very last minute that Egypt would attack.

The roots of the surprise go deeper than the interaction among individual personalities or the dynamics within groups. While it is tempting to fault an individual, or a group, or an institutional structure, such an approach often obscures more than it reveals. It avoids the hard questions. Moving beyond the specifics of an individual or an organization, analysts look to the characteristics of military technology and of the warning process itself to explain surprise.

The difficulty in distinguishing between offense and defense, a complicating factor in the estimation of an adversary's intentions, was very much a part of Israel's security environment throughout this period. As early as the spring of 1970, when the Soviet Union assisted Egypt in emplacing a system of missiles during the last phase of the War of Attrition, Israel's military planners began to consider the offensive impact of the 'defensive' anti-aircraft missile.[64] Military Intelligence was also fully aware of the adaptation by Egypt's army of Soviet military doctrine, a doctrine which made possible a rapid shift from a defensive to an offensive deployment. The close proximity of a large standing Egyptian army to the ceasefire line further complicated the distinction betwen offensive and defensive preparation. The Egyptian army was often at a high state of alert and mobilization of support personnel was frequent: from January to October 1973, for example, some twenty mobilizations took place. Throughout this period, there were very few military actions that unambiguously indicated offensive intent and those that did — the forward basing of bombers — could be implemented within a matter of hours. Military Intelligence was quite correct in its insistence that intention could not be inferred from capabilities alone. But precisely because difficulty in distinguishing between offense and defense was constant throughout this period, this difficulty alone cannot fully explain the flawed estimates of May and October 1973. While it is an important contributing factor, it is an insufficient explanation of strategic surprise.

Equally relevant are the difficulties inherent in the intelligence task and the warning process. We have just noted the difficulty of inferring attack from capabilities. Senior military and intelligence officers were scrupulous in arguing that Egypt had the capability to attack; indeed, they did so even when evidence available to them suggested that Egyptian officers themselves doubted this capacity. From this capability, however, they could draw only limited inferences. Perforce, they turned to the far more difficult task of searching for evidence of Egyptian intentions which could serve as a basis for estimating the likelihood of attack. Evidence of this kind is very hard to come by and even more difficult to validate.

Israel's Military Intelligence did have access to documentary evidence of Egyptian intentions, documents which they considered to be valid. And, as we have seen, the Egyptian military command did doubt its capability to mount a general attack during 1971 and 1972; deterrence did succeed during these two years. In response to a limited military strategy designed by a new set of Egyptian officers, this evaluation began to change in early 1973, but the flow of documentary evidence did not. Egyptian officials have suggested subsequently that Egypt knew that Israel knew of Egyptian military doubts and that, consequently, Egypt continued to provide information, or dis-information, which emphasized Egyptian skepticism of its own capability long after the change in military strategy made this skepticism far less relevant.[65] A campaign of disinformation would be consistent with the priority accorded deception in Egypt's military strategy. And, as Whaley finds in his classic study of military deception, there is little defense against disinformation which reinforces existing preconceptions.[66]

It was impossible, of course, for intelligence officials in Israel to distinguish *a priori* between disinformation and valid information. Their only recourse was to multiple sources of evidence which, hopefully, would produce convergent conclusions. As is clear from the record, Military Intelligence did draw on several sources of evidence to assess Egyptian intentions, but the thrust of the information was contradictory rather than convergent. From the field, for example, intelligence officers received a warning in December 1972 and several warnings again in May of 1973 that an attack was imminent. In each case, these warnings contradicted documentary evidence of Egyptian reluctance to risk war. And at the time, the warnings quickly appeared to be false although we now know that President Sadat did seriously consider and then postpone military attack. Ironically, these warnings may well have been 'wrong' for the 'right' reasons. Yet the 'cry-wolf' syndrome operated here: with each successive warning, the prediction of an impending attack became less credible.[67]

The 'cry-wolf' syndrome is an occupational hazard in intelligence analysis. Endemic to processes of estimation and warning, its consequences become more difficult to discount over time. To validate the warnings they had received, intelligence officers relied on the accuracy of the forecasts. As we argued earlier, however, the accuracy of intelligence warnings is a poor basis for their validation. Built into the intelligence process is an inverse relationship between the inaccuracy of a series of warnings and success over time. To the extent that a warning is judged to be 'false' at one moment in time, it is more likely that a subsequent warning that is 'true', coming from the same source, will be treated as 'false'. The General Staff in Israel confronted this dilemma writ large: it had no basis for evaluating past estimates by Military Intelligence that the probability of an attack was low. Just as experts unjustifiably concluded that past warnings from the field were 'false', with as little basis senior military and civilian leaders concluded that past estimates of Military Intelligence were 'true'. It is this more than anything else which explains why members of Israel's decision-making group thought alike. This kind of judgment is one that both intelligence experts and policy-makers must resist making; they must recognize that they cannot determine the validity of a specific warning by its immediate outcome.

Senior intelligence, military, and civilian leaders all refused to come to grips with the limits inherent in the warning process, limits that grew more severe over time and provide a convincing explanation of the failure to anticipate the attack of October 1973. It is crucially important to recognize how severe these limits are. Notwithstanding the criticism of official — and scholarly — inquiries, all drawing on after the fact evidence, analysts could not estimate the likelihood of attack exclusively from 'hard', 'tactical' evidence of capabilities.[68] Yet even with multiple sources of evidence on Egyptian intent, some of it of the highest quality, President Sadat's intentions were ambiguous and open to different interpretations. In May of 1973, General Ze'ira suggested that Egypt was engaging in brinksmanship to force American pressure while General Elazar suspected that frustration with the lack of diplomatic progress might lead Egypt to risk war. Both interpretations were plausible, some evidence was consistent with each, and the deployment of military capabilities could not discriminate between the two. Given the ambiguity, it is hardly surprising that Military Intelligence relied on a steady stream of documentary evidence to formulate its estimate of Egyptian intentions. Assessment of intentions, vital to the prediction of military attack, is the most difficult, uncertain, and risky component of intelligence estimates. To estimate the likelihood of military attack, an intelligence expert has recourse to 'hard' evidence of military capability, from which limited inference can be drawn, to 'soft' evidence of intentions from which inferences must be drawn, and to past experience, which is a poor guide to the future.

We began by suggesting that the outlook for reducing vulnerability to deception and surprise attack is not bright. The principal obstacle to accurate and timely warning lies not in individuals or groups, or even institutions, but rather in the limits of the intelligence process. To underestimate these limits and excoriate particular individuals or groups is to create dangerously unrealistic expectations among those who depend on warning to mobilize forces for defense. Recognition of the limits of warning, however, dictates an initial set of three recommendations, directed as much to defense planners as to intelligence analysts.

First and most important, adequate warning of attack can be devoutly hoped for but never assumed. Rather than plan on 'certain' warning, military officers must build the contingency of surprise into their defense planning. General Elazar violated precisely this precept in 1973. In discussions with his commanders and senior officers, he reiterated his expectation of a warning of at least forty-eight hours should Egypt move to attack. Given the obstacles to warning, the difficulty in assessing an adversary's intentions, the ambiguity of much of the evidence, the inherent uncertainties, such an expectation is simply not justified. A promise of warning should neither be given by intelligence experts nor be believed by commanding officers. Rather, as Betts concludes from his examination of surprise attacks, leaders must plan for survival despite surprise.[69] To do so, they must often sacrifice future defensive capability to present defense readiness. That choice is never easy.

Second, defense planners as well as intelligence experts must recognize that warnings cannot be validated, except long after the fact. Consequently, the premises of past warnings that appear inadequate should not be discounted and the reasoning which generated predictions that do match outcomes should not be inflated. Civilian as well as military leaders must be as wary of the 'cry sheep' as of the 'cry wolf' syndrome. Given the problematic basis of most politico-military prognoses, arguments must be reevaluated on their merits each time they are made.

Third, military commanders must recognize that intelligence experts deal with ambiguous evidence open to multiple interpretations. They must resist the fallacy of misplaced concreteness. Rather, in discussions with intelligence advisors, they must insist on the presentation of alternative explanations which might plausibly explain the evidence. Those who depend on intelligence estimates can challenge experts to disprove alternative explanations as well as to document and defend the interpretation they offer.[70] Recognition of the inherent uncertainties will encourge healthy skepticism both among those who 'consume' as well as among those who 'produce' intelligence forecasts. Once military and civilian leaders acknowledge uncertainty, they will have to confront the difficult choice between reducing the risk of unintended war by avoiding provocative military action or avoiding surprise by early deployment of defensive forces. That choice too is not easy.

A seond set of recommendations derives directly from our examination of the calculations of Egyptian leaders who considered whether or not to attack. Drawing on the factors Egyptian leaders considered important and matching Israel's estimates to these calculations, we pinpointed the obvious errors of omission in the process of intelligence estimation. These errors suggest categories for inclusion in subsequent assessments and a structure for analysis which may provide a more complete basis for estimating the likelihood of surprise attack.

Three components in the calculations of Egyptian leaders were particularly important in shaping their decision whether or not to use force. Their assessment that the military balance precluded attack was a strong but temporary deterrent to action. Israel's intelligence gave overwhelming priority to this component of Egyptian calculations. Indeed, drawing on direct evidence of Egyptian thinking, they virtually excluded all other factors from their analysis. Herein lay a major error, an error which provokes a fourth recommendation. The complexity of a decision to go to war suggests that any single factor analysis, no matter how well corroborated by evidence, should be suspect. A calculation of military inferiority, as we have seen, may be at best a temporary deterrent, an obstacle to be overcome, if other factors favour military action. A fifth conclusion, then, is that an analysis based exclusively on a challenger's calculation of relative capabilities should become especially suspect as time goes on. It does not provide an adequate basis for assessing either the likelihood of attack or deception.

Intelligence experts can look to at least two other closely related factors to broaden the analytic basis of their assessments. Especially important in the calculations of Egyptian leaders were their estimates of the plausible alternatives to military force and their assessments of the costs of inaction in comparison to those consequent to military attack. Both these calculations emphasize not military factors but rather the political, diplomatic, and economic consequences which colour consideration of a military option. Over this period, Egyptian estimates of the domestic and international losses of inaction grew substantially and, as they grew, they reshaped the comparison of the two options of military action or inaction. Closely related was the increasing pessimism in Egyptian estimates of the alternatives to military action. In shaping a decision whether or not to use force, consideration of the prospects and consequences of inaction was as important as evaluation of the consequences of a military option.

Military Intelligence, however, paid all too little attention to Egyptian estimates of the costs of inaction, costs alluded to publicly by Egypt's leaders. Ironically, both the Chief of Staff and the Minister of Defense, at different times, spoke of Egyptian frustration, of the diplomatic impasse which intensified in the latter part of this period, and of the political and economic pressures operating on Egypt's President. When they did consider these factors in April and May of 1973, they were skeptical of the intelligence estimate of a low probability of attack. This was not the case for General Ze'ira who, when asked to evaluate Sadat's calculus of alternative risks, testified that although the President found the consequences of inaction severe, he considered the alternative to be worse. For other senior civilian and military leaders, however, a broader and more explicitly political perspective dramatically altered their estimates of the likelihood of attack, even though they had documentary evidence of Egyptian calculations of military inferiority. Consideration of Egyptian leaders' comparison of risks shifted the prognosis of war.

A sixth recommendation is immediately obvious. When intelligence analysts begin to uncover these kinds of estimates, estimates of severe losses of inaction and repeated expressions of frustration with the available alternatives to a use of force, they should immediately begin to give serious consideration to the likelihood of attack and deception. They should do so moreover, even if they have solid evidence that opposing leaders consider their capabilities inferior and discount a military option. At the very least, incoming information should be evaluated against the two competing hypotheses — successful deterrence and deception — to determine which better explains the broadest range of evidence. Such a comparative look at the evidence should reduce reliance on a single factor and generate uncertainty rather than certainty. More concretely, explicit consideration of the possibility of deception should do much to alert analysts and policy-makers to its probability.

Leaders generally do not choose to go to war for military objectives but for far broader economic, diplomatic, and political purposes. Israel's Military Intelligence in 1973 cannot be excoriated for its evaluation of military capabilities — analysts were scrupulous in underlining Egypt's capability to attack — nor even for its estimate of Egyptian assessments of their military inferiority as a constraint to action — solid evidence pointed in this direction. They can be faulted, however, for the overwhelming attention paid to Egyptian military calculations and to the consequent discounting of Egyptian consideration of political, economic, and diplomatic factors. To decrease vulnerability to deception and surprise attack, an opponent's calculation of these consequences of inaction must be explicitly built into estimates of the probability of military action. Analysis of the collapse of deterrence, deception, and surprise cannot be encapsulated within a narrowly focused military perspective; their causes are far too complex and their consequences far too important.

NOTES

1. When a conflict is ongoing and one party successfully deceives the other, the victim is likely to mobilize quickly in future at the earliest indication of preparation for attack in order to avoid the consequences of surprise. Successful deception thereby creates an incentive to pre-empt in the future. The costs of deception are long-term, while its benefits are immediate. This cost-benefit structure no doubt explains part of the attractiveness of deception to military and civilian leaders.

2. Whaley, in the classic study of military deception, finds that deception succeeded in 91 per cent of the cases in which it was tried, an astonishingly high rate. Moreover, in 68 per cent of these cases, deception succeeded despite breaches of security and explicit warnings. See Barton Whaley, *Stratagem, Deception, and Surprise in War* (Cambridge, Mass.: MIT Center for International Studies, 1969).

3. A fourth explanation of surprise, an important one which is omitted from this study, looks to cognitive biases as the principal cause of error. The psychological literature is considerable and an examination of the validity of this approach requires a meticulous detailing of the estimation process to document biases. The impact of motivated and unmotivated biases on surprise is treated in a forthcoming paper.

4. For a discussion of the importance of offense and defense in different periods of military history and the difficulties of distinguishing between them in the contemporary international system, see George Quester, *Offense and Defense in the International System* (New York: John Wiley, 1977).

5. Richard K. Betts, *Surprise Attack: Lessons for Defense Planning* (Washington, D.C.: Brookings Institution, forthcoming), Chapter 7.

6. Harold Wilensky, *Organizational Intelligence* (New York: Basic Books, 1967).

7. See, for example, Steve Chan, 'The Intelligence of Stupidity: Understanding Failures in Strategic Warning', *American Political Science Review* 73, 171–80, and Richard K. Betts, 'Analysis, War, and Decision', *World Politics* XXXI, Oct. 1978, 1, 61–89.

8. Anwar el-Sadat, Speech, 23 Jan., in BBC/SWB/ME, 25 Jan. 1972; Speech to Egyptian publishers and editors, 25 July 1972, published by Arnaud de Borchgrave in *Newsweek*, 7 Aug. 1972; and Interview by Arnaud de Borchgrave, *Newsweek*, 9 April 1973.

9. Mohamed Heikal, *The Road to Ramadan* (New York: Quadrangle Books, 1975), 180–82; Anwar el-Sadat, *In Search of Identity* (New York: Harper & Row, 1977), 234–237; and Saad el-Shazly, *The Crossing of the Suez* (San Francisco: American Mideast Research, 1980), 174–181.

10. Anwar el-Sadat, Interview, *Ahbar al Yom*, 3 Aug. 1974; Speech, *Middle East News Agency* (MENA), 22 Sept. 1974; Interview, *MENA*, 8 Oct. 1974; cf. *In Search of Identity*, op. cit., 242–243. See also Ahmed Ismail, Interview, *Al-Hawadess*, 16 Aug. 1974.

11. Glenn Snyder and Paul Diesing, *Conflict Among Nations* (Princeton: Princeton University Press, 1977), 186, and Stephen Maxwell, 'Rationality in Deterrence', *Adelphi Papers* 50 (London: Institute for Strategic Studies, 1968), 10.

12. Patrick M. Morgan, *Deterrence: A Conceptual Analysis* (Beverly Hills, Calif.: Sage Library of Social Science, 1977), 106; and Alexander L. George and Richard Smoke, *Deterrence in American Foreign Policy* (New York: Columbia University Press, 1974), 526.
13. George and Smoke, op. cit., 531.
14. Anwar el-Sadat, Speech to the People's Assembly, 4 Feb. 1971, Radio Cairo and *In Search of Identity*, op. cit., 279–280.
15. Anwar el-Sadat, *In Search of Identity*, op. cit., 229.
16. Henry Kissinger, *The White House Years* (Boston: Little, Brown, & Co., 1979), 1293, and Sadat, ibid., 232–233.
17. Anwar el-Sadat, May Day Speech, 1 May 1973, *MENA*, 3 May 1973.
18. John Mearsheimer, *The Theory and Practice of Conventional Deterrence*, unpublished doctoral dissertation, Cornell University, Ithaca, New York, 1980, and Richard Rosecrance, 'Deterrence and Vulnerability in the Pre-Nuclear Era', *Adelphi Papers*, 160 (London Institute for Strategic Studies, 1980), 14–30.
19. Anwar el-Sadat, *In Search of Identity*, op. cit., 219–221.
20. Anwar-el-Sadat, ibid., 234–237, and Lt.-Gen. Saad el-Shazly, *The Crossing of the Suez* (San Francisco: American Mideast Research, 1980), 173–175. Sadat dates this meeting as 28 Oct.
21. Cited by Mohamed Heikal, *The Road to Ramadan*, op. cit., 20.
22. Maj.-Gen. Hassan el-Badri, Maj.-Gen. Taha el-Magdoub, and Maj.-Gen. Mohammed Dia el-Din Zohdy, *The Ramadan War, 1973* (Dunn Loring, Virginia: T.N. Dupuy Associates, Inc., 1978), 20.
23. Mohamed Heikal, *The Road to Ramadan*, op. cit., 117, 155–156; Saad el-Shazly, op. cit., 125–126; and Anwar el-Sadat, Speech to the Congress of the ASU, 24 July 1971, Radio Cairo Domestic Service, 25 July.
24. Mohamed Heikal, 'Soviet Aims and Egypt', *Al-Ahram*, 30 June 1972.
25. Mohamed Heikal, *The Road to Ramadan*, op. cit., 174, citing a briefing by Sadat of a small group of editors in Cairo in July 1972; see also Anwar el-Sadat, *In Search of Identity*, op. cit., 229.
26. Anwar el-Sadat, Interview by Arnaud de Borchgrave, 9 April 1973, *Newsweek* and May Day Speech, 1 May 1973, *MENA*, 3 May 1973.
27. Anwar el-Sadat, *In Search of Identity*, op. cit., 246. The evidence suggests some inconsistency in President Sadat's estimate of the likely Soviet response to a use of force by Egypt. Heikal reports that Sadat, commenting on the stepped up flow of Soviet arms, observed that it seemed as though the Soviet Union wanted '. . . to push me into battle'. See Mohamed Heikal, *The Sphinx and the Commissar: The Rise and Fall of Soviet Influence in the Middle East* (New York: Harper & Row, 1978). In an interview given after the war, however, the President insisted that the Soviet Union had continued to urge Egypt to forego a military solution; its attitude remained unchanged. See Sadat, Interview, *MENA*, 3 April 1974.
28. Richard Rosecrance, op. cit., 25.
29. Anwar el-Sadat, Speech, 16 Sept. 1971, Radio Cairo Domestic Service, 18 Sept. 1971.
30. Mohamed Heikal, *The Road to Ramadan*, op. cit., 181.
31. Anwar el-Sadat, May Day Speech, 1 May 1973, *MENA*, 3 May 1973.
32. Anwar el-Sadat, *In Search of Identity*, op. cit., 214.
33. Anwar el-Sadat, Interview, *Ahbar al Yom*, 3 August 1974; Speech, *MENA*, 22 Sept. 1974; and Interview, *MENA*, 8 Oct. 1974.
34. Anwar el-Sadat, *In Search of Identity*, op. cit., 249.
35. Richard K. Betts, *Surprise Attack: Lessons in Defense Planning*, op. cit.
36. For an excellent discussion of the pitfalls of *ex post facto* reconstruction, see Chan, op. cit.
37. The other two agencies are the *Mossad*, or the Central Intelligence Collection Agency, responsible directly to the prime minister, and the Center for Research and Strategic Planning, a small research unit within the Ministry for Foreign Affairs, responsible for medium and long-range forecasting.

38. Anwar el-Sadat, Speech to Egyptian Soldiers, 21 Nov. 1971, BBC Summary of World Broadcasts/Middle East/3845/ A 6–7, 22 Nov. 1971.

39. Hanoch Bartov, *Dado — 48 Years and 20 Days* (Tel Aviv: Ma'ariv Book Guild, 1978), Hebrew, English translation forthcoming, 192. Bartov's prize-winning biography of General David Elazar draws extensively on official documentation and heretofore inaccessible private papers of the Chief of Staff to reconstruct the critical deliberations among intelligence officers and military leaders.

40. Ibid., 190.

41. Anwar el-Sadat, Interview by Arnaud de Borchgrave, *Newsweek,* 9 April 1973. Sadat told de Borchgrave: '... everything in this country is now being mobilized in earnest for the resumption of battle — which is now inevitable ... the Russians are providing us now with everything that is possible for them to supply and I am now quite satisfied'. On 24 Mar. 1973, Abdal Quddus, editor of *Ahbar al-Yom,* reported that Egypt was '... importing arms from the Soviet Union ... and is no longer concerned with the types of weapons ...' (*FBIS,* Middle East, 26 Mar. 1973).

42. See Moshe Dayan, *The Story of My Life* (London: Weidenfeld and Nicolson, 1976), 381 and Bartov, op. cit., 190. Bartov reports the expected date of attack as 15 May.

43. Bartov, op. cit., 192.

44. Ibid., 217–218.

45. Ibid., 197–198.

46. Ibid., 194–195.

47. Ibid., 224, 226, and Interview, member of Military Intelligence. The official recalls that only 2 per cent of reserve forces were mobilized.

48. Bartov, op. cit., 243.

49. Interview, member of Military Intelligence.

50. Interview, member of Military Intelligence. The official suggested that Military Intelligence drew on the CIA for this estimate.

51. Cited by Dayan, op. cit., 395.

52. *Agranat Report, A Partial Report by the Commission of Inquiry to the Government of Israel* (State of Israel: Government Press Office, April 2, 1974), 9.

53. Ibid., 19.

54. One possible explanation of a Soviet-Syrian rift was the failure of the Soviet Union to come to the assistance of Syria during the 13 September air battle with Israel. However, Intelligence discounted this explanation since the air battle took place outside the range of SAM missiles then in place. Interview, member of Military Intelligence. However, no prominent Soviet leader had attended a ceremony inaugurating the Euphrates Dam, Moscow's principal development project in Syria. Unlike 1972, however, there had been no slowdown of Soviet arms shipments nor reduction of effort in the strengthening of Syria's air defense system.

55. Damascus Radio had charged that Israel was about to initiate a major military action. The Syrian newspaper, *Al-Thawra,* also alleged that Israel was preparing for military adventure and insisted that a comparison of the declarations of Israel's leaders issued in early October and before the June 1967 war demonstrated the similarity of Israel's tactics in preparing for aggression. See *Al-Thawra,* 4 Oct. 1973.

56. The error can best be explained by psychological rather than logical processes. Cognitive psychologists suggest that when people are confronted with evidence inconsistent with their beliefs, they at first seek to deny or downgrade the quality of the evidence. When they can no longer do so, they acknowledge their inability to explain the inconsistency, but still do not change their beliefs.

57. Agranat Report, op. cit., 7. Military Intelligence, it appears, gave less weight to evidence from agents in the field than to official documents obtained secretly. This may have been because the agent expected to deliver confirmatory intelligence on Egyptian intent had been 'wrong' in forecasting an attack in December 1972 and in May 1973.

58. Elazar said: 'Saturday, at 04.00 hours, the telephone rang and told me that Egypt and Syria will attack at 18.00 hours. This had happened several times. We were given a precise hour of attack, but the attack did not occur' (Interview with author). The Prime Minister was even more explicit: 'No one in this country realizes how many times during the past year we received information from the same source that war would break out on this or that day, without war breaking out' (Golda Meir, Interview, *The Jerusalem Post Weekly*, 11 Dec. 1973). Dayan also confirmed the receipt of several such warnings in the past: 'We had received similar messages in the past, and later, when no attack followed, came the explanation that President Sadat had changed his mind at the last moment' (Moshe Dayan, op. cit., 375).

59. Agranat Report, op. cit., 24.

60. Bartov, op. cit., 252 and 257, and Alouph Hareven, 'Disturbed Hierarchies: Israeli Intelligence in 1954 and 1973', *The Jerusalem Quarterly*, 9, Fall 1978, 3–19.

61. Bartov, op. cit., 255.

62. See Irving L. Janis, *Victims of Groupthink: A Psychological Study of Foreign Policy Decisions and Fiascoes* (Boston: Houghton Mifflin, 1972).

63. Cited by Hareven, op. cit., 15.

64. See Ezer Weizman, *On Eagles' Wings* (Jerusalem: Steimatzky's Agency Ltd., 1976) and Yitzhak Rabin, *The Rabin Memoirs* (Boston: Little, Brown, and Co., 1979).

65. See Mohamed Heikal, *The Road to Ramadan* (New York: Quadrangle Books, 1975), 17, and interview with member of the Office of the President of Egypt, 1980.

66. Whaley, op. cit. He finds that 79 per cent of the cases of successful deception exploited the preconceptions of the defender.

67. It is interesting to note that senior officers of Military Intellligence did not behave quite as cognitive psychologists would expect. When warnings from one source proved to be 'inaccurate', experts should have discounted the significance of future warnings and reduced the credibility of that source. Because of the high credibility of that source, intelligence analysts did not discredit the source, although they did discount the significance of each subsequent warning. This issue is treated more fully in a forthcoming paper on cognitive biases and intelligence estimation.

68. Two exceptions in the scholarly literature on the Yom Kippur War are Michael Handel, 'Perception, Deception, and Surprise: the Case of the Yom Kippur War', *Jerusalem Papers on Peace Problems 19*, Jerusalem, 1976, and Avraham Shlaim, 'Failures in National Intelligence Estimates: The Case of the Yom Kippur War', *World Politics* 28, No. 3, April 1976, 348–380.

69. Richard K. Betts, forthcoming manuscript on *Surprise Attack: Lessons for Defence Planning* (Washington, D.C.: Brookings Institution, 1981).

70. Richards C. Heuer Jr., 'Improving Intelligence Analysis: Some Insights on Data, Concepts, and Management in the Intelligence Community', *The Bureaucrat*, Winter 1979–1980, 1–11.

Intelligence and Deception

Michael I. Handel

> The ultimate goal of stratagem is to make the enemy quite certain, very decisive and wrong.[1]

> If surprise is indeed the most important 'Key to Victory', then stratagem is the Key to surprise.[2]

> Ming: Lay on many deceptive operations, Be seen in the west and march out of the east; lure him in the north and strike him in the south. Drive him crazy and bewilder him so that he disperses his forces in confusion.[3]

> The Taking of Ai[4]
> *(see schematic plan opposite)*

Deception can be found in any human activity which involves competition over scarce resources or any other desired benefits that are limited in supply. Whenever and wherever a situation exists — in business, economic life, politics on all levels, love — through which an advantage can be gained by cheating, there will always be individuals or groups who will resort to it. Although in civilian affairs, cheating, deception, or fraud are usually punishable by law or by informal sanctions (such as the loss of credibility or reputation in certain circles) this not the case in war nor, to a lesser extent in international politics, which have their own norms and morality (i.e. raison d'etat). Deception in international politics (not to be discussed in this article) and more frequently in war is rewarded by greater achievements and success. While extremely helpful in war, deception has frequently failed, or failed to achieve its intended objectives, and on occasions has even proved to be counterproductive. Despite this word of caution, deception must be seen as an accepted and integral part of any rational conduct of war. In the words of Sun Tzu, 'All warfare is based on deception'.[5]

Deception in war must be considered a *rational* and necessary type of activity because it acts as a force multiplier, that is it magnifies the strength or power of the successful deceiver.[6] Forgoing the use of deception in war undermines one's own strength. Therefore when all other elements of strength in war are roughly equal, deception will further amplify the available strength of a state — or allow it to use its force more economically — by achieving a quicker victory at a lower cost and with fewer casualties. In the case of unequal opponents, deception (and surprise) can help the weaker side compensate for its numerical or other inadequacies. For that reason, the side that is at a disadvantage often has a more powerful incentive to resort to deceptive

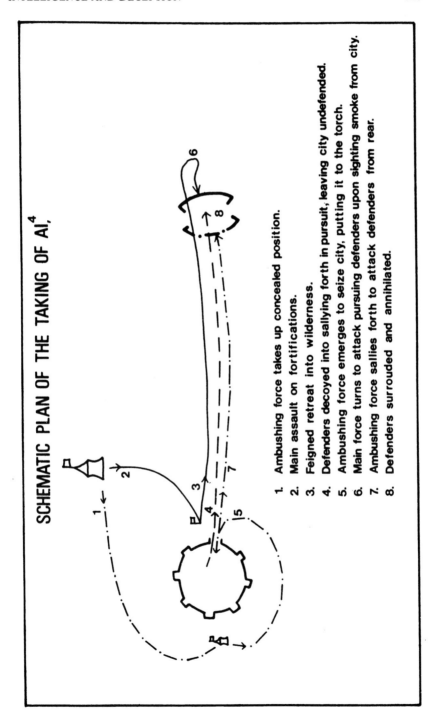

SCHEMATIC PLAN OF THE TAKING OF AI,[4]

1. Ambushing force takes up concealed position.
2. Main assault on fortifications.
3. Feigned retreat into wilderness.
4. Defenders decoyed into sallying forth in pursuit, leaving city undefended.
5. Ambushing force emerges to seize city, putting it to the torch.
6. Main force turns to attack pursuing defenders upon sighting smoke from city.
7. Ambushing force sallies forth to attack defenders from rear.
8. Defenders surrouded and annihilated.

strategy and tactics. This was recognized by Clausewitz, who cannot be said to have otherwise emphasized the importance of deception as part of war.

> The weaker the forces that are at the disposal of the supreme commander, the more appealing the use of cunning becomes. In a state of weakness and insignificance, when prudence, judgment, and ability no longer suffice, cunning may well appear the only hope. The bleaker the situation, with everything concentrating on a single desperate attempt, more readily cunning is joined to daring. Released from all future considerations, and liberated from thoughts of later retribution, boldness and cunning will be free to augment each other to the point of concentrating a faint glimmer of hope into a single beam of light which may yet kindle a flame.[7]

This implies the existence of an inverse relationship between strength and the incentive to use deception. This observation can frequently be found in military history: during World War II, the British had a more powerful incentive to use strategic deception than the Germans did; and as long as the Israelis perceived themselves as being weaker than their Arab opponents (in 1948, 1956, 1967), they often employed stratagem and deception, while the Arabs, who perceived themselves as superior, did not. In 1973, however, the reversal of these perceptions saw a concomitant change in the incentive to resort to deception: the Israelis relied more on material strength while the Arabs had to resort to deception, which they had earlier neglected.

Enjoying overwhelming material superiority in the Vietnam War or even in World War II when deception was left primarily in the hands of the British, the United States used deception rarely with a few exceptions on the tactical level. In the early stages of the Korean War (i.e. MacArthur's landing in Inchon) when the Americans were weak, they did resort to the combination mentioned by Clausewitz of readiness to take very high risks (a maximax strategy) and the use of deception and surprise. Then, as the United States increased in strength in the later stages of the Korean War, they failed to employ those elements. The landing in Inchon may, however, be related more to General MacArthur's character and style than to a real change in the US high command's approach to war.

While the tendency of more powerful states to rely more on 'brute force' can be understood, it certainly cannot be justified. The strong and powerful need not waste their strength or increase their own costs just because they are stronger. Strength not accompanied by stratagem and deception will become sterile and will inevitably decline. Perhaps for that very reason, the more powerful military establishments *must make a conscious effort* systematically to incorporate deception into their military thinking.

*   *   *

The rational use of deception can be achieved in a number of ways. One type of deception attempts to misdirect the enemy's attention, causing him to concentrate his forces in the wrong place. By doing this, the deceiver tries to make his adversary violate the principle of *concentration of forces* in space.[8]

Well-known examples of this are the Allied deception plans that diverted German attention from the beaches of Normandy to Norway and/or Pas de Calais as possible landing sites for an Allied invasion.[9] Similarly, in 1940, the Germans helped the Allies to deceive themselves by causing them to concentrate their troops in Northern France on the Belgian border rather than opposite the Ardennes.[10]

A second and related type of deception attempts to make the adversary violate the so-called principle of the *economy of force*.[11] The intention here is to cause the opponent to waste his resources (e.g. time, ammunition, weapons, manpower, fuel) in unimportant directions or preferably on non-existent targets. A simple example would be to make an adversary fire a large number of scarce and expensive anti-aircraft missiles at a cheap RPV decoy or an artificially created radar signature instead of at real attacking aircraft; during the Battle of Britain the British caused the Germans to attack non-existent airfields and factories by setting up phony targets and interfering with German electronic navigation aids. Other, much more complicated strategic or technological ploys to make the enemy waste his resources can also be designed. Information can be spread through a variety of sources that a revolutionary technological breakthrough (such as the development of 'death rays' or 'particle beam weapons')[12] has been achieved; this will induce the enemy to invest huge amounts of money, scientific man hours, and time in the wrong direction — whereas the deceiver knows it will lead to a dead end or be too costly to be useful in practice.

A third type of deception, which is also related to the two mentioned earlier, is designed *to surprise* the opponent — to create a situation that will later catch him off-guard, unprepared for action when it comes. In this case, the variety of deceptive ploys and methods most frequently employed are intended to dull his senses and create the impression that no offensive plans are entertained by the deceiver. This can be done through the maintenance — and in fact cultivation — of normal political and economic relations up to the moment of attack, as was Hitler's policy toward Russia until the eve of Barbarossa in June 1941.[13]

When two or more states are already at war it is much more difficult to launch a surprise attack out of the blue. On such occasions, the deceiver frequently tries to create the impression of *routine* activities by very gradually conditioning the adversary to a certain repetitive pattern of behavior. Just such a ruse was employed by the Germans when they jammed British radar stations in order to enable the German battle-cruisers the *Scharnhorst* and the *Gneisenau* and the cruiser *Prinz Eugen* to break out of the English Channel undetected on the night of 11 February 1942. 'The German radar officers, headed by General Wolfgang Martini, had subtly increased the intensity of their jamming over a period so that we could get acclimatized to it, without realizing that it was now so intense that our radar was almost useless.'[14]

Another way of moving large concentrations of troops towards an attack without alerting the adversary is to disguise those preparations as military maneuvers. Secrecy is further enhanced in many such cases when not even the participating troops are informed that they are about to go into action. A favorite of the Soviet Union, this last ploy was used on the eve of the Soviet attack on Manchuria in 1945 and the invasion of Czechoslovakia in 1968. A similar deception cover was carried out by the Syrians and Egyptians before their attack on Israel in October 1973.

In the final analysis all types of deception operations can be said to be directed at misleading, misinforming, or confusing an opponent on only two basic types of questions. The first is to deceive him concerning one's own *intentions,* the second is to deceive him concerning one's own *capabilities.*[15] A successful deception operation can be aimed primarily in one of these directions, although it frequently includes both at the same time. After all, intentions and capabilities are closely related to one another in the conduct of war.[16] Thus, convincing an opponent that one lacks certain capabilities may also convince him that because of the absence of such capabilities, the deceiving side also has no intention of carrying out a given type of operation. For example, the Egyptians on the eve of the Yom Kippur War spread rumors that their anti-aircraft missile systems had been short of certain spare parts (capabilities) since the expulsion of the Soviet advisors in June 1972, and that therefore they obviously were not yet ready to initiate war (intentions).[17]

Deception concerning intentions will always try to conceal the actual goals and plans of the deceiver. This can be achieved through secrecy (a *passive* mode of deception) or through a more elaborate active deception plot that diverts the opponent's attention from the real set of intentions to another. In fact, the more active type of deception must always be based on the successful concealment of one's real intentions in addition to the development of a decoy of fake intentions. Any breach of security concerning one's actual intentions will of course lead to failure and probably to self-deception, and may even become an instrument for the adversary's *own* deceptions, in that the enemy can pretend to be deceived while in fact he is anticipating the deceiver's move and planning to spring his own surprise or trap.

In complex deception operations, it is therefore extremely important to have a special unit that will try to ascertain whether the adversary has really swallowed the bait or is only pretending to have been deceived.[18] Penetration of the enemy's intelligence and/or his command echelons is essential. Through the use of ULTRA, the British in World War II were unusually successful in following up and monitoring complex deceptions. The detailed deciphering of German codes enabled British intelligence continuously to check and recheck the degree of success of its deception plans and then to modify them accordingly in order to make them even more effective.[19]

Returning to the question of deception intended to conceal one's real intentions, we find a number of examples. Before launching their first offensive against the Italian 10th Army in the Western Desert in December 1940, the British under Wavell had successfully convinced the Italians that their intentions were defensive. Here is how the official British history summarizes this deception operation.

> The fact is that in war, it is usually possible to produce some sort of evidence in support of almost every course of action open to the enemy;

the art lies in knowing what to make of it all. In this case, the Italian Air Force (in the Western Desert) had observed and reported movements and dispositions with fair accuracy — indeed, it was often intended by the British that they should. The important point is that these reports were consistent with what the 10th Army were convinced was happening. They themselves were very much occupied with their own preparations for renewing the advance, and were only too ready to interpret the air reports as indicating that the British were actively improving their defensive arrangements. The British attempt at strategic deception was therefore successful.[20]

The British and Americans did not and could not, hide their intention to invade somewhere in Southern Europe, but led the Germans to believe that they would invade Sardinia, Southern France, and Greece instead of Sicily, which was the more obvious target. Similarly, Operation Fortitude, the code name for the deception preparations for Operation Overlord (the invasion of Normandy) did not try to hide Allied intentions to invade Europe or even more specifically to cross the Channel, but focused German attention on Pas de Calais.[21] So successful was this stratagem that the Germans, anticipating a major attack in Pas de Calais, had most of their forces in that area a few days after the invasion of Normandy was well under way. There is, by the way, very little doubt that the greatest deception efforts ever invested in a military operation were part of the preparation for the invasion of Normandy, 1944. Overlord was covered by numerous complementary deception operations (not all of which are probably known even to this day) which required careful and elaborate coordination and a meticulous follow-up operation in order to estimate the extent to which the Germans were indeed deceived. This tremendous and ultimately successful investment in deception plans for D-Day is not surprising. Landing operations are notoriously tricky and involve unusually high risks. The sheer number of participants in Operation Overlord (the largest landing operation in history) made it even more essential to use elaborate deception plans in order to conceal the preparations and areas selected for attack. The success of the Allied deception plans is amazing even today, and no doubt was achieved through meticulous preparation, good luck, and the poor quality of German intelligence. The surprise achieved in Operation Overlord was total — one of the few cases of a 'surprise out of the blue' with no real warning time, any lead warning time or alert.[22]

In planning their attack on Egypt in collaboration with the British and French in 1956, the Israelis deliberately created the impression that they intended to attack Jordan by concentrating their troops closer to the Jordanian border and by escalating their reprisal raids against Jordan.[23] (Secrecy was so well kept that the British ambassador was sent to protest to the Foreign Ministry against Israeli reprisals and to warn against an attack on Jordan, while the British Government knew that the real object of the forth-coming attack would be Egypt.)

In mid-May 1967, President Nasser decided to send Egyptian troops into the Sinai thereby initiating the crisis which continued to escalate through the month. By the end of May, Israel and Egypt were fully mobilized and ready for war. By 2 June it became clear to the Israeli Government that war was unavoidable. The problem was how to launch a successful surprise attack while *both* sides were fully mobilized and alert. As part of a deception plan to conceal Israel's intention to go to war, Dayan told a British journalist on 2 June that it was both too early and too late for Israel to go to war. He repeated this statement during a news conference on 3 June:

> It is too late for a spontaneous military reaction to Egypt's blockade of the Tiran Straits ... and still too early to learn any conclusions of the possible outcome of diplomatic action. The Government ... embarked on diplomacy and we must give it a chance.[24]

Furthermore, it was decided to release a number of reservists during the weekend to create the impression that preparation and alert had been reduced. It is very possible that other plans which never became known were also implemented. In this case, the deception was simple and successful, and Israel achieved total surprise on the morning of 5 June despite the crisis atmosphere and intensified intelligence alert.[25]

It is perhaps little known that the preparations for the Israeli raid on Entebbe in July 1976 also included a deception plan intended to misdirect primarily the Americans, who were apparently watching by satellite. The deception plan indicated (mainly through spreading rumors to the press) that the Israelis planned to launch a large-scale attack on PLO targets in the Lebanon in order to capture hostages who could be traded for the hijacked passengers in Entebbe. As far as is known, this deception plan successfully directed attention away from the possibility of a direct raid on Entebbe itself. The attack was a total surprise for everyone.

During peacetime or before the initiation of hostilities, it is possible, as is well-known from the extensive literature on surprise attack, successfully to conceal the intention to attack; once a state of war and conflict already exists, the intention to attack in one place or another is already taken for granted. Under such circumstances, deception becomes much more important because it has to give the adversary the wrong expectations concerning one's inevitable and known intention to take action. The fewer the directions of possible attack, the more important a deception cover will be. Since it was almost inevitable that the Allies would have to attack across the Channel, the probability of success had to be increased by deception.

*   *   *

Deception can also be employed to mislead an opponent about the deceiver's military, primarily material, *capabilities*. The discussion of deception in this particular context is also a convenient opportunity to demonstrate some of the potential dangers and possible damage that can result from miscalculations and the wrong application of this art. It is important to emphasize that deception is by no means always a panacea for weakness or difficult situations, nor is it always as successful as most of the enthusiastic literature about it seems to indicate.

The use of deception to mislead an opponent concerning military capabilities can be divided into two types. The first is intended to create an exaggerated evaluation of capabilities in terms of both quantity and quality, the second attempts to conceal existing capabilities. The former type of bluff is normally practiced by a weaker state trying to deter a more powerful adversary, translate an imaginative superiority in military capabilities into political gains, or gain enough time to close a dangerous capability gap. The second type of deception concerning capabilities tries to hide a state's real capabilities primarily in order to create an impression that it is incapable of executing certain offensive plans, i.e. to conceal its offensive intentions. Both types of capability-oriented deceptions need not (particularly in wartime) be contradictory or mutually exclusive. A state may wish simultaneously to conceal certain capabilities and inflate others (e.g. in terms of absolute quantities or relative quantities at different places, rates of production, qualitative achievements).

The attempt to deceive by pretending to have larger than existing capabilities is well-known in time of both peace and war. As already mentioned above, the intention behind this type of ploy is normally to deter a *stronger* adversary. This was the trick played by the Germans from 1936 onwards on the French in particular and less successfully on the British and other nations concerning the real strength of the nascent *Luftwaffe*. The Germans did their utmost to impress foreign visitors such as Charles Lindbergh; Italian Air Marshal, Italo Balbo; RAF Air Vice Marshal, Christopher Courtney; and later the chief of the French Air Force, General Joseph Vuillemin. The Germans staged exciting air shows, flew in most of their latest aircraft to those airfields the guests were visiting, casually reported high production rates for advanced aircraft that in fact never went beyond the experimental stage, and gave tours of aircraft factories:

> In general, perceptions in the West of the Luftwaffe's strength were exaggerated precisely as Hitler and Goring intended. Aerial black-mailing of Germany's neighbors became an important ingredient in Hitler's diplomatic negotiations which led to his brilliant series of triumphs; the policy of appeasement was founded partially on the fear of the Luftwaffe.[26]

The exaggerated strength attributed to the *Luftwaffe* combined with the fear of British and French political leaders that 'the bomber will always get through' helped the Nazis to extract considerable political concessions from the West.[27]

Perhaps the best and also most extreme instance of an attempt by a country to inflate its military capabilities was that of Fascist Italy in the 1930s. Signor Mussolini tried to impress on all foreign observers the power of the Italian armed forces — although in this case he probably deceived no one but himself.

> By another confusing piece of legerdemain, in 1938 the composition of [Italian] army divisions had been reduced from three regiments to two. This appealed to Mussolini because it enabled him to say that fascism

had sixty divisions instead of barely half as many, but the change caused enormous disorganisation just when the war was about to begin; and because he forgot what he had done, several years later he tragically miscalculated the true strength of his forces. It seems to have deceived few other people except himself.[28]

Like Hitler, Mussolini tried — without much success — to impress foreign observers with the superior quantitative and qualitative strength of the Italian Air Force.

By 1935 Italy claimed most of the international records for flying, and this was a great achievement. The chief of the air staff informed parliament *that they had been won with ordinary machines.* It was his further boast that Italy no longer needed the help of foreign technology in this field, and indeed that Italian planes were not only 'the best in the world' but in wartime would be able to control the whole Mediterranean. Such statements were, as they were intended to be, greeted with enormous enthusiasm, and the authorities proceeded to draw the conclusion that the Italian air force was second to none, and that Italy must be impregnable.[29]

Italy did its best to exaggerate the figures on the number of Italian aircraft.

When the Second World War broke out, figures were given to show that Italy had 8,530 planes, but the air ministry privately admitted in April 1939 that there were only 3,000 front-line aircraft, and the naval information service reduced this to under a thousand. On further investigation the figure turned out to be 454 bombers and 129 fighters, nearly all of which were inferior in speed and equipment to contemporary British planes ... [Mussolini] can hardly have been intending to bluff foreign observers, because they had their own means of knowing that the official figures of the air ministry were nonsense, and indeed the British were quite sure that the efficiency of the Italian air force was growing less, not greater; the intention was to bluff Italians, and unfortunately it succeeded.[30]

The Italian navy was not in much better shape. Although its battleships and battle cruisers looked elegant and impressive, they were poorly designed. They were built for high speed and therefore were thinly armored; they had no radars or any effective anti-submarine detection capability. Their submarine fleet was the largest in the world (1939) but had no firing computers. It was ill-organized and its doctrine, training and tactics were obsolete. It was good for displays but not for war.

Mussolini successfully deceived not only himself but from May 1938 onwards Hitler also. During Hitler's visit to Italy in May 1938 Mussolini put before him a seemingly impressive military show.

The Italian military services performed much better during Hitler's visit in May 1938. An excellent one-battalion exercise combined with a superficially competent show by the navy (which included a simultaneous submerging and surfacing by eighty-six Italian submarines) to give Hitler the impression that Mussolini had revitalized Italy's military forces.[31]

Hitler was duly impressed and deceived concerning Italian capabilities until Italy's defeats in 1940. This misperception cost Germany and Italy dearly later on. Hitler's professional military advisors on the other hand were not as impressed as he was by the Italian military public relations campaign. They reported that the Italian army was poorly equipped and badly trained, and unlike Hitler, they viewed Italy as a military burden, not an asset, which they would prefer to see neutral rather than fighting on Germany's side.[32]

Another example of an attempt to deceive an adversary by inflating one's capabilities was premier Nikita S. Khruschev's boast (following the launching of the first Soviet sputnik satellite) about the tremendous superiority the USSR had obtained over the United States in the design, testing, and production of Intercontinental Ballistic Missiles (ICBMs). Initially the Soviet Union exaggerated the stage of ICBM development; later it exaggerated and in fact lied about their massive production, and finally it considerably misrepresented their capabilities and accuracy. The Russians were indeed ahead of the United States in launching satellites and their space program, but there was no *direct* connection at all between their successful space program and the military deployment of ICBMs. Western intelligence, however, could obtain little information on Soviet military ICBM strength, and the Russians used the opportunity to deceive the world (especially the Americans) concerning the advanced deployment of their ICBMs. Statements such as the following were common throughout 1957 and 1958. 'We *now have* all the rockets we need: long range rockets, intermediate rockets, and short range rockets' (Khruschev). 'I think it is no secret that *there now exists* a range of missiles with the aid of which it is possible to fulfill any assignment of operational and strategic importance' (Khruschev). 'The fact that the Soviet Union was the first to launch an artificial earth satellite, which within a month was followed by another, says a lot. If necessary, tomorrow we can launch 10–20 satellites. All that is required for this is to replace the warhead of an intercontinental ballistic rocket with the necessary instruments. There is a satellite for you' (Khruschev).[33] In fact, there was little connection between the Soviet space program and its military ICBM program, which lagged way behind. This was not so, of course, in the minds of Western political and military leaders who had little reliable information but were at first impressed by the Soviet space program.

The Americans, who initially believed Khruschev's statement, accepted the existence of a dangerous 'missile gap' and as a result redoubled their efforts to 'catch up' with the Soviet Union. By the time of the Cuban missile crisis, the United States had not only closed this fictitious missile gap but ironically had achieved a tremendous lead over the USSR in the military deployment of ICBMs. (One common explanation for the Russian planting of Medium Range Ballistic Missiles — MRBMs — in Cuba was exactly the need to close an ICBM missile gap favoring the United States.)

Successful 'inflated capability' deceptions can be too much of a good thing. Exaggerated fear of German air superiority led the British (and French) to make excessive political concessions in the short run in order to gain time to catch up with the Germans — but at the same time also to increase their own investment in air power and anti-aircraft defenses (radar in particular). By the time war broke out, the British were in much better shape to meet the German challenge. Hitler may have thus defeated his own purpose in the long run.

Khruschev's missile gap hoax created a panic in the United States and touched off such an accelerated effort to close the purported gap that within four years the United States gained a tremendous edge over the Soviet Union. This was translated into concrete political gains for the United States and a loss of face for the Soviet Union during the missile crisis in Cuba. Ultimately, Khruschev paid for his hoax with his own career.[34]

The second danger of a successful 'capability deception' is that in the end the deceiver may indeed believe his own bluff and at the same time ignore the corrective measures taken by his adversary. That is, the deceiver may see a bluff as reality or a temporary advantage as reflecting a permanent position of superiority which in fact does not exist. What may have been true in 1937 or 1938 was not true by 1939 or 1940 for the relative air strength of the British or Germans. What was true in 1957 was no longer true by 1962. The deceiver may, however, fall into his own trap when he decides to take action which is based on a past real or imagined balance of capabilities. This type of successful deception which culminates in self-deception may have caused Hitler to attack Great Britain (or even open the Second World War) believing as he did in the superiority of the Luftwaffe; it led Mussolini to his adventures in Ethiopia, Albania, and Greece, and may have convinced Khruschev that the Soviet Union was strong enough to challenge the United States in its own backyard in Cuba (whereas the United States probably never had and will never have again such an advantage in capabilities over the Soviet Union).

Thus, successful deception operations intended to inflate capabilities can create three types of serious dangers for the deceiver himself. The first is that the deceived target state will redouble its efforts to improve its own capabilities in reaction to the imagined threat and therefore will gain the upper hand even if it did not intend to do so initially; second, the deceiver's bluff might be called and his weakness will be exposed; thirdly, there is the pitfall of self-deception, i.e. accepting one's own bluff as reality and acting upon it.

The other type of capability-related deception is exactly the opposite, namely, it tries to hide and minimize the deceiver's *real* strength in order to surprise the opponent on the battlefield with unexpected capabilities that may lead to his defeat. While attempts to exaggerate one's own capabilities can often be identified with ambitious and aggressive leaders (e.g. Hitler, Mussolini, Khruschev, Nasser), attempts to conceal one's real strength are more frequently implemented by military leaders and military organizations whose standard operating procedures require secrecy and discretion.

Between 1956 and 1967, for example, the Israeli Defense Force (IDF) carefully concealed its real numerical strength and qualitative improvements. Success in concealing or camouflaging its strength is certainly one of the explanations for the astounding blitzkrieg-type victory that Israel achieved over its Arab neighbors in June 1967. Arab intelligence services completely failed to get an accurate picture of Israel's actual military strength, a fact which contributed to Nasser's decision to initiate the May crisis in 1967. But again, success in concealing one's real strength can also be a double-edged sword. The weakness Israel projected in 1967 was not the intended goal but rather the unplanned byproduct of secrecy. It diminished and weakened Israel's deterrence and tempted the Arabs to attack. Had Israel's real strength been known, deterrence might have succeeded and war could have been avoided. It can therefore be argued again that strategic deception can be too much of a good thing and must be used judiciously.[35]

A similar example is the secrecy maintained by the Soviet Union until 1941 concerning its military capabilities. Given the earlier external threats to the Soviet Union, the long-held tradition of conspiracy and its closed nature, the closed nature of the Soviet political system, and Stalin's own paranoia, the emphasis on total secrecy in the Soviet Union is not surprising. For that reason, the Germans had very poor intelligence concerning the real strength of the Soviet Union. On the eve of Barbarossa, German intelligence may have underestimated Soviet strength by as much as 120 divisions (at that time German intelligence had identified 247 Soviet divisions and soon after the war broke out as many as 360). Had the Germans known the real strength of the Soviet Union, they might have decided not to attack at all, as Hitler later told the Italian Foreign Minister, Count Ciano. Excessive Soviet secrecy had therefore led to the collapse of Soviet deterrence and to a war the Soviet Union did not want.[36] The continued closed nature of Soviet society today will have its price too. The United States may overreact to perceptions of exaggerated Soviet strength by investing huge sums in its own military machine — more than it perhaps would if more were known about current Soviet *real* capabilities and intentions.

Capabilities can normally be concealed best in closed and/or homogeneous societies which are difficult to penetrate (e.g. Soviet Union, Japan, Israel in particular until 1967), if and when the opponent's intelligence is weak. In today's world of spy satellites, electronic intelligence, and high-altitude air photography it is, of course, much more difficult to conceal material military capabilities (although one can assume that in the age of satellite intelligence new types of deception and camouflage have been developed).

At this point, it may be useful to make a distinction between *passive deception* and *active deception*. Passive deception is primarily based on secrecy and camouflage,[37] on hiding and concealing one's intentions and/or capabilities from the adversary. Some experts view passive deception as inferior and not likely to succeed against any competent intelligence organization. This, as we have already seen above, is not necessarily true. While measures of secrecy do not have the same aura of romance and intellectual excitement as that associated with active deception, they can frequently be as effective as any more elaborate type of deception operation. *Moreover, active types of deception are dependent on the success of passive deception.* What is even more important, passive deception can tremendously complicate and therefore increase the costs of intelligence work — in terms of time, money, and the like. A recent example appeared in Jack Anderson's column in the *Washington Post*. The US DIA was interested in determining the caliber of the cannon mounted on the new Soviet T-64 and T-72 tanks. It spent over 18 million dollars on this project (including computer time, satellite photographs and their development, electronic eavesdropping) and could not find the answer. The DIA finally discovered that the British and French had obtained the same information for next to nothing.[38] Given the freedom and lack of discretion of the American press, the Soviet Union can normally acquire similar information with little effort and expense (or to be more exact, at the cost of subscribing to major US publications). The number of very successful passive concealment deception operations concerning capabilities is very impressive indeed: for instance, the development of the proximity fuze by the United States (and Britain) during the Second World War, and the development of the 'window' radar jamming chaff by the British for the bomber offensive over Germany.[39] These two examples illustrate not only the decisive importance of passive deception but also the critical nature of timing — when exactly to introduce a new weapon in order to obtain the best possible results.[40] This problem is related to the study of technological surprise, a subject which has received scant attention in the open literature on intelligence so far.)[41] Finally, of course, there are the atypical examples of Ultra and the development of the atomic bomb.

In contrast to passive deception, active deception normally involves a calculated policy of disclosing half-truths supported by appropriate 'proof' signals or other material evidence. This information must be picked up by the intelligence network of the deceived. The deceived must 'discover' the evidence himself; he must work hard for it to be more convinced of its authenticity and importance. (Frequently, information that is easily obtained appears to be less credible and of doubtful value.[42] This may have something to do with human psychology, which tends to equate a better product with higher cost.)[43]

Deception operations must be tailored in each case to the deceived's unique character and conditions. To be sure that his adversary will indeed pick up the threads of evidence himself, the deceiver must prepare the bait taking into account the quality of the deceived intelligence, his methods of work and his agents, his perceptual frame of mind, his cultural framework, and other factors.

Deception should not be taken simply as a gratifying intellectual exercise. Deception that is too sophisticated and elegant may be intellectually satisfying to those who create it, but may not be picked up by the intended victim. Israel, for instance, often found that very polished and seemingly simple deception plans were not picked up by Arab intelligence organizations because they are not good enough to identify the bait offered. There is an obvious danger that 'the message developed by the deception planners is *understood by them* in the context of the endless meetings in which alternatives were weighed and details worked out. They are so familiar with their own thinking that they risk overlooking the degree to which the message is clear to them only because *they know what to look for*[44] (author's emphasis). Similarly, Ewen Montagu in in *Beyond Top Secret U* (one of the best studies of deception) repeatedly emphasizes the need to match the bait to the character and level of sophistication of the intended victim.

> It occupied a great deal of time and energy but it was fascinating work. In a way it was like a mixture of constructing a crossword puzzle and sawing a jigsaw puzzle and then waiting to see whether the recipient could and would solve the clues and place the bits together successfully, except that it was we who would get the prize if the recipient succeeded. We had no illusions about the efficiency of the German Abwehr, so we had to make sure that the puzzle was not too difficult for them to solve.[45]

Part of the art of deception is to learn to think like the adversary.[46] What may make sense for the deceiving side may not necessarily make sense to the intended victim. The bait must be designed on the basis of reliable intelligence on how he thinks and what information is available to him; this in turn requires a high degree of penetration into the adversary's most guarded secrets.

It is worth quoting Montagu on this aspect at some length. In his book he discusses a proposal for a detailed deception plan intended to ease the pressure on the Russians by creating an imaginary threat for the Germans at the Bay of Biscay area. The additional advantage of such a deception operation was that it would also force the Germans to thin out their defenses in the Channel area. Montagu proposed this deception plan on the basis of information received through Ultra (the deciphering of top secret German codes), which indicated that the Abwehr, German army and the *Luftwaffe* were particularly afraid of such a possibility (Montagu, for instance, suggested that they try to strengthen existing German fears). His plan, though, did not win the approval of the Chiefs of Staff.

> They [the Chiefs of Staff] turned it down flat on the grounds that an attack on the Biscay coast was so impossible that the deception would be incredible. With great respect, that last point usurped our function — we were the experts on deception, they were wholly ignorant about this art. If they thought, as they apparently did, that the deception would be useful, it was for us to decide whether we could put it over.
>
> Their reason was that they knew that the Biscay coast was outside the range of our fighter aircraft, so the necessary cover could not be given for a prolonged invasion, and they knew that we hadn't got enough aircraft carriers to spare to give fighter cover even for an 'in and out' operation of real magnitude — all of which was of course quite correct. But they couldn't make themselves think as Germans. The Germans did not know what our Chiefs of Staff did and, on their information, they did think that we had enough forces and material for us to risk at least a major in and out operation under Russian pressure.
>
> It was so important to deception work to be able to put oneself completely in the mind of the enemy, to think as they would think on

their information and decide what they would do — ignoring what you knew yourself and what you could do. ... We had given the Chiefs of Staff the facts about the Bay of Biscay Operation and they ought to have done better. But perhaps I am being unfair to them. Service training is not the same as that of a barrister. We have to learn throughout our career to put ourselves in our opponent's place and try to anticipate what he will think and what he will do on his information[47]

Unfortunately deception is a creative art and not an exact science or even a craft. For that reason it is difficult to teach someone how to deceive unless he has a natural instinct for it. This explains why, despite the large number of war memoirs and detailed military histories which discuss deception, little has been written on the theory of deception or how to practice it.[48] It is normally assumed that some military or political leaders are 'deception-minded' while others are not. There is probably no systematic, structured way to teach the art of deception, as it is impossible to teach someone to become an original painter. Perhaps the only way to learn the art of deception is through one's own experience.

What are some of the conditions which facilitate the development of the art of active deception? In the first place, active deception requires that an individual or an organization (preferably a small one) be able to see things from the enemy's vantage point. This will require as mentioned above, a good knowledge of his culture, language, mode of operation, procedures, and the like. To design the bait or the deception ploy, the deceiver must be both practical and imaginative, and not allow himself the temptation to be too sophisticated or enjoy deception for its own sake. He (almost every important deception operation originates and is developed in its early stages as the brainchild of one individual) must have a flexible combinatorial mind — a mind which works by breaking down ideas, concepts, or 'words' into their basic components, and then recombining them in a variety of ways. (One example of this type of thinking may be found in the game of Scrabble.) He must be able to transcend the routine type of thinking or procedures normally imposed by large organizations and bureaucracies. Barton Whaley has tried but failed to find '... some general personality type with the ability to understand and use surprise and deception and to associate its reverse type with the failure to do so'.[49] But perhaps one general pattern of personality emerges for the greatest past users of deception. They are highly individualistic and competitive; they would not easily fit into a large organization or into any type of routine work and tend to work by themselves. They are often convinced of the superiority of their own opinions. They do in some ways fit the supposed character of the lonely, eccentric bohemian artist, only the art they practice is different. This is apparently the only common denominator for great practitioners of deception such as Churchill, MacArthur, Hitler, Dayan, and T. E. Lawrence. Conversely, individuals who feel comfortable in larger groups, who prefer the democratic consensus type of agreements, and who can easily get involved in routine work will make poor candidates.

From an organizational point of view, the art of deception can be practiced only by organizations that are willing to delegate a considerable amount of authority to, and have confidence in, a small group of people.[50] In short, there must be tolerance for the existence of 'artists' among 'bureaucrats' and enough confidence and patience not to insist on immediate results. Such an organization (normally of course an intelligence organization) must be able to maintain the highest degree of secrecy. It has above all to be able to obtain the best possible information on the adversary and to penetrate his ranks by using spies, deciphering his codes, etc., in order to know what he knows, what he *wants* to know, and how he obtains his own information. Conversely, the more successful an organization is in avoiding the penetration of its own ranks, the more it will be able to carry out its own deception operations. (Barton Whaley in his extensive research on deception claims that he found no case of a deception operation that has failed or has been intercepted by an adversary.)[51] Finally, for the success of any type of deception operation, it is imperative to coordinate the policies of all other organizations that might inadvertently disclose or undermine such an operation.

It is much more difficult to advise a potential victim of deception on how to avoid or discover such a ploy. In this respect the difficulties involved in avoiding deception are very similar to the difficulties inherent in anticipating a forthcoming surprise attack. Military history shows that surprises are in fact inevitable. Whaley has therefore concluded that not only are even the most sophisticated deceivers the victims of deception (as quoted above), but that 'exhortations to *avoid* being deceived are ... as uselessly homiletic as those to use it'.[52]

Nevertheless, some evident though not necessarily effective precautions can be taken. Intelligence services must continuously ask themselves what are the most obvious and most reasonable directions from which an adversary might attack, even if the available evidence contradicts such contingencies. This can perhaps best be done by asking how one would do the same thing oneself. Such estimates can be prepared by analysts who are not familiar with the information available and who work only by trying to think as the enemy would. Only in the second stage must such an analysis be corroborated with available intelligence information.

Another, and again not very helpful, way to avoid deception is to be wary of information which falls too neatly into a single pattern that seems to exclude other, no less reasonable possible courses of action. R. V. Jones has added the following advice:

> Both for deception and unmasking, one of the personal qualities required is being able to imagine yourself in the position of your adversary and to look at reality from his point of view; this includes not only being able to sense the world through his eyes and ears, and their modern analogues such as photographic and electronic reconnaissance, but also to absorb the background of his experience and hopes, for it is against these that he will interpret the clues collected by his intelligence system. Thus it was not too difficult to convince the Germans that the

'Jay' system was going to depend on beams because they would naturally be gratified by our copying their techniques. To guard against this weakness when one is in danger of being deceived, I can only recommend Crow's Law, formulated by my late friend John Crow: 'Do not think what you want to think until you know what you ought to know.' And if a good guide to successful intelligence is Occam's razor — hypotheses are not to be multiplied without necessity — then an equally relevant guide to avoid being deceived is to multiply your channels of observation as far as possible.[53]

Although this last bit of advice may sound very reasonable, it can also create its own problems. Instead of bringing in better or more reliable information, more channels may only add more 'noise' or additional deceptions. I suspect that R. V. Jones meant that one should obtain a variety (rather than simply quantity) of opinions which may contradict his suggestion not to multiply hypotheses. Alternatively, it can be said that what is important is reliable information — but of course that is exactly the basic and unsolvable problem of all intelligence work.

Another piece of advice not unlike that of R. V. Jones' but based on psychological tests, is not to put too much confidence in conclusions drawn from a very small body of consistent data. This is because conclusions drawn from very small samples are highly unreliable. (Tests have shown that people usually tend to be overly sensitive to consistency.)[54] Heuer's final advice is very similar to that of R. V. Jones:

> As a general rule, we are more often on the side of being too wedded to our established views and thus too quick to reject information that does not fit these views, than on the side of being too quick to reverse our beliefs. Thus, most of us would do well to be more open to evidence and ideas that are at variance with our preconceptions.[55]

Alas one is tempted to say on the basis of historical evidence that — 'to be closed-minded is human'.

*   *   *

Totalitarian regimes, such as those of Nazi Germany, Fascist Italy, Japan of the 1930s, or the Soviet Union under Stalin and his successors (until this very day)[56] seem to have fewer scruples about using deception and fraud as an accepted, perhaps even common, means in the conduct of their foreign policy in times of peace.[57] This may be because they view the period of peace merely as a 'cease-fire' in a continuous and unending war over resources and ideology. In a permanent state of war and zero-sum game competition for survival, all means and methods can be justified. Hitler's foreign policy is in fact nothing but a history of deception and fraud. In times of peace, this seems to give the totalitarian states a considerable edge over the 'naïve' Western democracies; yet this very edge may be their undoing in the long run both in peace and in war. Some of the reasons for this counterproductive impact of deception are obvious while others are more subtle.

To begin with, those who frequently deceive quickly lose credibility; so what they can do one, two or three times in succession they cannot do indefinitely. Although they may continue to believe in the efficacy of deception, their peaceful adversaries have already learned their lesson. As a result, they may find themselves in a position in which no state will voluntarily seek any agreements with them, and they will force the deceived to be more alert, to have better intelligence, and eventually to resort to similar means.

Paradoxically the 'naïve', trusting states may turn out to be much better at the game of deception. One explanation for this is very simple. Someone who is known to be 'naïve' and honest will find it hard to lose his reputation and can therefore cheat and deceive much better when he wants (at least for a while). Not expecting him to play by their own rules, his adversaries may therefore be caught off guard.

This possibility can be briefly presented in the form of a 'paradox':

> The more one has a reputation for honesty — the easier it is to lie when one wants to.

or even more briefly:

> Honest people/states can deceive the best.

This may be why the Germans fell so easily for British deception. They probably could not bring themselves to believe that the same nation which let itself be deceived time and again in peacetime would develop the art of deception to new heights in times of war. While this explanation holds true for the Germans, it might not describe the attitude of the Soviet Union, whose communist ideology assumes that the capitalists will always try to deceive and that therefore they should never be trusted in the first place.[58] Stalin may have deceived himself by imagining deception behind too many moves of other states. Thus when Churchill and the British warned him on the basis of knowledge acquired by Ultra of impending German attack in 1941, he refused to believe them and viewed this information as an attempt to drag the Soviet Union into a war against Germany in order to ease the pressure in the West. Given Stalin's communist background and his paranoia, such an attitude is not altogether surprising.[59]

A second and more interesting explanation, which will require further research to subtantiate it, is that those who practise deception continuously during peace-time, as did the Germans and the Russians, usually have to establish special agencies for that purpose (normally as part of their intelligence organizations). The operation of deception by professional military men or government officials will tend to routinize the planning and execution of deception, and over an extended period of time this will in turn undermine their creativity and flair for the art of deception. By the time they reach the point where they view deception as a regular rather than special operation, their level of effectiveness will already have dropped. (This phenomenon can also be detected in the routinized deception operations of the CIA in the 1960s and early 1970s before such practises were brought to a halt in the United States).[60]

On the other hand, the Western democracies, and the British in particular, benefited considerably from their late entry into this particular field of intelligence. In both the First and Second World Wars, the British and Americans started to reorganize their intelligence organizations either immediately before the war broke out or soon afterwards. Therefore, unlike the German and Soviet intelligence organizations which were based primarily on 'professionals', the British and American intelligence organizations were staffed primarily with amateurs recruited from all sections of civilian (but mainly from academic) life.[61]

Amateurs frequently bring with them new enthusiasm, a creative imagination, informality, perhaps some academic openness, and a somewhat more detached and objective search for *veritas* — all of which are intellectual qualities highly useful for intelligence work in general and deception work in particular. This fresh start allows them to reexamine old problems from a new point of view, unlike the pre-war professional intelligence bureaucrats: they were not obliged to commit themselves to earlier, not always fully rational, traditions or old policies. The pre-war professionals certainly viewed with considerable resentment the massive penetration of their organizations by the 'professional-type' amateurs.

> The Western democracies, unlike the Germans, ... drafted civilians as intelligence officers even of army groups (i.e. military field position) with great success. First class minds became expert on the enemy; *with no worries about career,* they could both be kept in a post for the duration of the war and express their opinions more forcefully.[62]

The more conservative German officer corps strongly resisted the integration of intelligence officers into the *Wehrmacht* and all other branches of the armed forces. Their conservatism, tradition, and aversion to civilian intellectuals did not allow them to tap the enormous intelligence potential of civilian amateurs. While this type of resistance to civilians was also manifested by British intelligence professionals, this was easily quashed. It was perhaps easier for the British, given the successful contribution of civilian amateurs during the First World War.

The amateurs however did very well indeed.

> The mobilization of British intelligence for the two World Wars provides at least a partial vindication for the now unfashionable virtues of British amateurism. To a remarkable degree the British intelligence system during the First World War was the result of the brilliant last-minute improvisation by enthusiastic volunteers. That the volunteers failed to achieve more — for example, at Jutland and Cambrai — was due chiefly to the short-sightedness of the professionals. The renaissance of the British intelligence community at the beginning of the Second World War after two decades of considerable neglect was, once again, largely the work of brilliant amateurs, able in some cases to build on the achievements of their predecessors. And the man chiefly responsible for the coordination of the British intelligence effort for the first time in its

modern history was a much criticised amateur strategist, Winston Churchill.[63]

For a field such as deception, which leaves so much to imagination and creativity, the amateurs proved to be ideal practitioners who, in the final analysis, outsmarted the professionals.

This may be one of the best explanations for the curious and dismal failures of German strategic intelligence and its almost complete neglect of deception during the Second World War. David Kahn thus reaches the conclusion that '. . . Germany lost the intelligence war. At every one of the strategic turning points of World War II, her intelligence failed. It underestimated Russia, blacked out before the North African invasion, awaited the Sicily landing in the Balkans, and fell for thinking the Normandy landing a feint'.[64] These mistakes were caused not only by the inherent structural weakness of German intelligence but also by the Allied deception operations. Among others, Kahn gives the following basic reasons for German intelligence failures.[65]

(1) *'unjustified arrogance, which caused Germany to lose touch with reality'.* Early and easily attained military successes caused the Germans to feel vastly superior to their adversaries, to feel that they were immortal. This, combined with their traditional nationalism, assumed racial superiority, and ethnocentric view of the world reduced their incentive to learn about others. Such arrogance and feelings of superiority also caused the Arabs in 1948 and 1967 to wage war against Israel with almost no intelligence and knowledge about Israel. To a lesser extent, arrogance also blinded the Israelis in 1973 and the Americans vis-à-vis the Japanese on the eve of Pearl Harbor. As already mentioned, deception operations in particular require an intimate knowledge and understanding of the adversary, and perhaps even a certain degree of compassion and respect.

(2) *'Aggression, which led to the neglect of intelligence.'* This is a more subtle point based on an understanding of military strategy, in particular on Clausewitz's writings. Clausewitz viewed defense as the stronger mode of warfare and also as passive and reactive in nature (neither of which is necessarily true).

> 'What is the concept of defense?' asked Clausewitz. The parrying of a blow. What is its characteristic feature? Awaiting the blow. Now an army can await a blow only if it believes that a blow is planned, and such a belief can only be created by information about the enemy. Defense requires intelligence. There can be, in other words, no defense without intelligence.[66]

The offense on the other hand is 'complete in itself'. It can decide when, how, and where to attack. It can concentrate on a superior force at the point of its choice and can frequently dictate the early moves on the battlefield as it has planned. For that reason, the offense is *less* dependent on the availability of intelligence than the defense. 'The information about enemy intentions, while helpful and to a certain degree always present (for the offensive), is not essential to an offensive victory. . . . *In other words, while intelligence is integral to the defense, it is only contingent to the offense. As a result — and this is a crucial point — emphasizing the offensive tends toward a neglect of intelligence.*[67]

This explanation is elegant but it is not necessarily true from the military point of view, although it seems to describe existing psychological attitudes. (It is not true from a strictly military point of view because a successful offensive may require as much, perhaps even more, detailed information than the defensive. Indeed, the lack of adequate German intelligence on the Soviet Union in 1941 proved to be disastrous.)

Kahn's point on the negative incentive of an offensive-minded military to invest in intelligence work may thus be true psychologically and certainly can be accepted as an important explanation of German military behavior. It may, however, be somewhat less powerful as a general explanation. In any event, Nazi Germany's offensive and military doctrine of blitzkrieg did not stress the central contribution of intelligence to warfare. By the time the Germans were on the defensive, it was too late for them to begin building the infrastructure necessary for intelligence work. The Allies, especially the British, who were strategically on the defensive when the war broke out, greatly appreciated the importance of intelligence work and invested heavily in it. By the time they went over to the offensive, they had the advantage of a superior intelligence organization.

(3) *'The authority structure of the Nazi State, which gravely impaired its intelligence.'* Governments based on the 'führer principle', the 'cult of personality', or any other dogma which makes the leader infallible create at the highest strategic decision-making level of the state an environment which is not conducive to 'objective' and 'rational' intelligence work. The leader who always knows best, who intimidates his advisors, and who cannot be criticized will render even the best intelligence work useless. Thus, Stalin refused to listen to any intelligence indicating the possibility of a German surprise attack. Hitler frequently ignored the intelligence information given to him and refused to listen to information that contradicted his views. Later on his subordinates, on their own initiative, ceased to supply him with 'depressing intelligence' or with negative information about failures, possible dangers, or the superiority of the enemy. The fact that during the 1930s until the outbreak of war, and actually until the Battle of Britain and the invasion of Russia, Hitler's intuition was often more successful than the rational advice of the military professionals certainly made things worse. Dictators, leaders who know best, and heads of state who do not encourage their aides to express a larger variety of opinions are bad intelligence consumers. Eventually they receive only the information they want to hear and consequently lose touch with reality, creating the conditions which ultimately lead to self-deception and to their own defeat.[68] 'Successful deception' at a time of peace by totalitarian regimes may therefore not be a reassuring guarantee of similar success in times of war.[69]

*   *   *

Deception is cheap. It is neither labor- nor capital-intensive. It is among the least expensive types of modern intelligence work yet yields a high return for a relatively small investment. Even if deception were more expensive than the material and other investments in the military operation it was designed to cover, it would still be worth investment if it led to a quick and decisive victory instead of a protracted war of attrition. Even the most complicated and elaborate deception normally involves only a relatively small number of men. Barton Whaley has estimated that the total number of participants in the deception operations for the Allied invasion of Europe in 1944 — the largest deception operation in history — was 'in all perhaps 2,000 soldiers, sailors, and airmen; but none of whom were regular first line combat troops'.[70] Smaller, less intricate deception operations involve no more than a few dozen to at the most a few hundred men.

The material investment is in most cases also negligible. Making use of cheap and readily available resources, it will often require a fair amount of radio and other electronic gear to simulate or create intensified radio traffic in one direction or another, some wood and canvas, and film set experts to build dummy aircraft, tanks or other installations. It can involve the movement back and forth into an observed area during the day of already existing military equipment. More often than not it is even cheaper than this, since deception operations above all involve 'non-material' and purely verbal and intellectual activities such as spreading rumors, organizing campaigns to manipulate the publication of certain information in the press, planting agents, passing deceptive information to the enemy, and following up the planted information. The top-secret nature of deception demands a limitation of the number of participants to the bare minimum necessary.[71]

If the costs of deception are relatively small, the benefits can be considerable if not decisive. Deception will facilitate surprise, which in turn ' . . . multiplies the chances for quick and decisive military success, whether measured in terms of sought goals, ground taken, or casualty ratios'.[72] Effective deception will cause the adversary to waste his resources, to spread his forces thinly, to vacate or reduce the strength of his forces at the decisive point of attack, to tie considerable forces up at the wrong place at the worst time; it will divert his attention from critical to trivial areas of interest, numb his alertness and reduce his readiness, increase his confusion, and reduce his certainty. In short, *reducing the cost for the deceiver implies increasing the cost for the deceived.*

The possible presence of deception behind every intelligence operation, behind every piece of information obtained will cause serious problems and a degree of doubt in any important intelligence work. The ever-present possibility of deception always introduces 'noise' into the collection and analytical work of intelligence and weakens the clarity of the signals received. Consequently, there is no sense in forfeiting the use of deception or ignoring its contribution to every facet and level of planning for action in war. That would be as irrational as someone who refuses to receive interest for money deposited in the bank. In war as a rational activity, there is never a reason to make life easier for the adversary or more difficult for oneself. Therefore even if deception is not always used as part of a military plan or strategy (which would be a mistake) the adversary must *always* live under the impression that deception is being practised. As a result, deception is always a present factor whether or not it is being practiced. Deception like surprise must therefore be seen as inevitable in conflict, as an inherent part of intelligence work and war that can never be discounted.[73]

Since no effective measures to counter or identify deception have yet been developed, the inevitable conclusion is that deception — even if it does not achieve its original goals — almost never fails (see below) and will therefore always favor the deceiver, the initiating party. 'Perceptual and cognitive biases strongly favor the deceiver as long as the goal of deception is to reinforce a target's preconceptions or simply create ambiguity and doubt about the deceiver's intention.'[74] Rationality dictates that a move which involves little cost and little risk of failure should always be included in one's repertoire.

Deception as a dilemma and predicament of intelligence work has been described in the following way:

> Alertness to the possibility of deception can influence the degree of one's openness to new information, but not necessarily in a desirable direction. The impetus for changing one's estimate of the situation can only come from the recognition of an incompatibility between a present estimate and some new evidence. If people can explain new evidence to their own satisfaction with little change in their existing beliefs, they will rarely feel the need for drastic revision of these beliefs. Deception provides a readily 'available' explanation for discrepant evidence; if the evidence does not fit one's preconceptions, it may be dismissed as deception. Further, the more alert or suspicious one is of deception, the more readily available is this explanation. Alertness to deception presumably prompts a more careful and systematic review of the evidence. But anticipation of deception also leads the analyst to be more skeptical of all the evidence, and to the extent that evidence is deemed unreliable, the analyst's preconceptions must play a greater role in determining which evidence to believe. This leads to a paradox:

> the more alert we are to deception, the more likely we are to be deceived.[75]

Experience and conditioning can work two opposite ways. The first is that once victimized by deception, one finds it difficult to accept *any* information as reliable. The other is that once a source of information is thought to be trustworthy it is difficult to discredit it.

Excessive alertness to the possibility of deception can have its price too. After the success of the Allied deception operation covering their landing in Sicily (Operation Mincemeat) the Germans became overly sensitive to the possibility of being deceived. When the detailed plans of the impending landing in Normandy fell into their hands via the British Embassy in Ankara (Cicero) they were convinced that this was yet another clever Allied deception; consequently, they refused to accept the detailed plan as authentic. Conversely, a double agent who supplied the Germans with useless information was used by the Allies to supply the Germans with the *correct* date of the operation in order to discredit it. Once proven correct on such a vital piece of information the Germans continued to accept his information even if useless.

In the final analysis, whether the enemy plants a deception plan to fit our preconceptions or we perceive a deception where in fact it does not exist, it can be said that from a strictly logical and perceptual point of view, 'We are never deceived, we deceive ourselves' (Göthe).[76]

It must be emphasized that deception is not a panacea which can replace the other military factors required for success in war. Believing that deception can correct or eliminate other sources of weakness courts military disaster. The best deception is useless if it is not backed by military power or if it cannot be properly exploited. To try to manage a war (or avoid one) through over-reliance on deception is impossible and can only end in strategic failure.

Occasionally, deception operations — whether simple or complex — can fail to achieve their intended goals or even be counterproductive. This can happen as we have seen in one of three possible ways:

> (1) The enemy simply fails to catch the bait of deception offered to him. This can happen either when the quality of his intelligence work is low or when the bait has not been carefully matched to his perceptions (i.e. 'shooting over his head').
>
> (2) There is a contradiction between the short- and long-term impacts of deception. In other words, deception which is very successful and credible in the short run, can be counterproductive in the long run. In such cases, deception can be too successful. This problem will arise when a deception plan is designed to intimidate the adversary and convince him of his relative weakness. Such feelings of insecurity and weakness will usually hasten a corrective change in the adversary's policies, eventually transforming his 'weakness' into an advantage. In addition, this type of problem can often be correlated with self deception: that is, flushed by his early successes, the deceiver will convince himself that what is actually a temporary advantage is a permanent one. As a result, he will underestimate his adversary and overestimate his own capabilities.
>
> (3) The adversary has learned of the deception plan and will use it against the deceiver. This is one reason why deception plans require good intelligence and continuous feed-back from the target about what the enemy knows or does not know.

Any deceiver will be in a much more vulnerable position if he assumes his deception is working, whereas in reality his opponent is manipulating it to his advantage. I know of no such double or even infinite regression types of deception, but they cannot be discounted in theory or in practise, although the likelihood of their occurrence is very small.[77]

To deceive successfully may become more difficult, certainly much more complicated, in the future. In a world of high-altitude reconaissance aircraft, intelligence satellites with high resolution photographic equipment and a variety of other sensors, and AWACS aircraft that can trace any movements on air, sea, or land at distances up to more than 350 miles, deception will not come easy. To these factors we can add the contribution of high-powered computers to cryptoanalysis and the fact that everyone monitors his opponent's telephone, radio, and cable communications. If in the Second World War deception seemed primarily to be the game of academics from a large variety of disciplines, future deceptions will primarily require the work of electronic and computer experts. Inevitably deception will become less of an art and more of a science; this will be true chiefly in the execution of the deception plan and perhaps less so on the initiation level. Modern deception will require much greater skill in highly technical areas, as well as detailed and systematic preparations (perhaps a large number of exercises, laboratory war games, and the like). Greater efforts for the preparation of deception plans will have to be made in peace-time so that they will be available if war breaks out. Thus it appears that deception will be left less and less in the hands of amateurs and again more in the hands of professionals, intelligence bureaucrats, and 'engineers'. Such a trend may be unavoidable but may also limit the scope of deception operations primarily to super-sophisticated electronic warfare, neglecting the more traditional classical *ruses de guerre.* This should be avoided at all costs, so that the advance of the modern science of deception does not exclude the ancient art of deception.

Finally, to paraphrase David Dilks, it can be said that, 'It would exaggerate to say that successful deception by itself enables wars to be won. But it is precisely when the resources are stretched and the tasks many, when the forces are evenly matched and the issue trembles in the balance, that successful deception matters most'.[78]

NOTES

1. Barton Whaley, *Stratagem: Deception and Surprise in War* (Cambridge Mass.: MIT Center for International Studies, 1969), p. 135.

2. Ibid., p. 263.

3. Sun Tzu, *The Art of War,* translated by Samuel B. Griffith (New York: Oxford University Press, 1973), p. 133.

4. This is the schematic presentation of the plan of deception employed by the Israelites in the battle of the Ai against the Cannanites (following an earlier defeat after a direct assault on the same citadel). I used this scheme as an epigraph because it is one of the simplest and most primitive types of deception — yet it always seems to succeed.

    So Joshua arose, and all the people of war, to go up to Ai; and Joshua chose out thirty thousand men, the mighty men of valour, and sent them forth by night. And he commanded them, saying: 'Behold, ye shall lie in ambush against the city, behind the city; go not very far from the city, but be ye all ready. And I, and all the people that are with me, will approach unto the city; and it shall come to pass, when they come out against us, as at the first, that we will flee before them. And they will come out after us, till we have drawn them away from the city; for they will say: They flee before us, as at the first: so we will flee before them. And ye shall rise up from the ambush, and take possession of the city; for the Lord your God will deliver it into your hand. (Joshua 8: 3–7)

The scheme is reproduced by permission from Abraham Malamat, 'Conquest of Canaan: Israelite Conduct of War According to Biblical Tradition', *Révue Internationale d'Histoire Militaire*, No. 42, pp. 25–52. Sun Tzu expressed the same idea: 'Offer the enemy a bait to lure him; feign disorder and strike him. . . . Pretend inferiority and encourage his arrogance.' Ibid., pp. 66, 67.

5. Sun Tzu, *The Art of War*, p. 66.

6. Charles Cruickshank in *Deception in World War II* (Oxford: Oxford University Press, 1979) says 'Deception in war is the act of misleading the enemy into doing something, so that his strategic or tactical position will be weakened' (p. 1).

7. Carl von Clausewitz, *On War*, edited and translated by Michael Howard and Peter Paret (Princeton N.J.: Princeton University Press, 1976) p. 203. Clausewitz did not view deception as an important element in war and thought that frequently it was not worth the bother.

> To prepare a sham action with efficient thoroughness to impress an enemy requires a considerable expenditure of time and effort, and the costs increase with scale of the deception. Normally they call for more than can be spared, and consequently so-called strategic feints rarely have the desired effect. It is dangerous, in fact, to use substantial forces over any length of time merely to create an illusion; there is always the risk that nothing will be gained and that the troops deployed will not be available when they are really needed. (Ibid., p. 203.)

This is certainly a narrow view in more than one way. This Prussian attitude may have been accepted by the Germans but certainly not by the British or ancient Chinese. In any case the only criterion with which to judge deception is not how much it costs, but how effective it is. Will it reduce costs in terms of casualties? Will it lead to a major surprise and therefore to decisive results? As far as deception is concerned, Sun Tzu is more modern and rational than Clausewitz.

8. Ibid., p. 204.

9. For this deception plan see, for example; Ewen Montagu, *Beyond Top Secret U* (London: Corgi Books, 1979); Charles Cruickshank, *Deception in World War II*; J. C. Masterman, *The Double-Cross System* (New Haven: Yale University Press, 1972), chapter 11, pp. 145–63.

10. For the German plan of attack in the West in 1940 see: Hans-Adolf Jacobsen, *Dokumente zur Vorgeschichte des Westfeldzuges 1939–1940* (Berlin: Musterschmidt July, 1956); Hans-Adolf Jacobsen, *Fall Gelb: Der Kampf um Den Deutschen Operationplan zur Westoffensive 1940* (Wiesbaden: Franz Steiner, 1957); Ulrich Liss, *Westfront 1939/1940* (Neckargemund: Kurt Vorwinkel, 1959); Major L. F. Ellis, *The War in France and Flanders 1939–1940* (London: HMSO, 1953); Telford Taylor, *The March of Conquest: The German Victories in Western Europe — 1940* (New York: Simon and Schuster, 1958).

11. Clausewitz, *On War*, p. 213.

12. On the 'death ray', see R. V. Jones, *Most Secret War: British Scientific Intelligence 1939–1945* (London: Hamish Hamilton, 1978), p. 63. Mussolini never lost his faith in the death ray! 'In the last month of his life, Mussolini, searching for an alibi, traced the beginning of decline in his fortunes to the fact that Marconi before his death in 1937, had refused to impart the secret of a death ray which he had brought to perfection.' Denis Mack Smith, *Mussolini's Roman Empire* (New York: Penguin Books, 1977).

13. See Barton Whaley, *Codeword Barbarossa* (Cambridge, Mass.: MIT Press, 1973); John Erickson, *The Road to Stalingrad. Stalin's War With Germany*, Vol. I (New York: Harper and Row, 1975), Chapters 2 and 3; Gerhard L. Weinberg, *Germany and the Soviet Union 1939–1941* (Leiden: E. J. Brill, 1954); Vladimir Petrov, *'June 22, 1941': Soviet Historians and the German Invasion* (Columbia, South Carolina: University of South Carolina Press, 1968). Stalin told Harry Hopkins ' . . . that the Russian army had been confronted with a surprise attack; he himself believed that Hitler would not strike. . . .' *Hitler made no demands on Russia* (my emphasis) quoted in Nathan Leites, *A Study of Bolshevism* (Glencoe, Illinois: The Free Press, 1953), p. 497.

14. See R. V. Jones, *Most Secret War*, pp. 233–5. The British kept an eye on the German warships for a long while. There were a few indications of a possible German attempt to

break out of Brest between 10 and 15 February. But the continued routine watch by the British dulled their attention. Jones brings the following quote from Frances Bacon's essay *Of Delayes* in this context: 'Nay, it were better, to meet some Dangers halfe way, though they come nothing neare, than to keepe too long a watch, upon their Approaches: For if a Man watch too long, it is odds he will fall asleepe' (ibid., p. 235).

15. R. V. Jones in his essay 'Intelligence, Deception and Surprise' presented at the 8th Annual Conference of the Fletcher School of Law and Diplomacy — Tufts University International Security Studies program, April 1979. He has summarized as follows the *negative* and *positive* objectives of all deception operations. Most of the deception goals on his list can be classified under one of the two basic deception types I have suggested: (1) deception concerning intentions or (2) deception concerning capabilities.

NEGATIVE OBJECTIVES Prevent the enemy from deducing at least one of the following:	POSITIVE OBJECTIVES Persuade the enemy to deduce:
i. *Where* you are.	i. You are *somewhere else.*
ii. *What weapons* and forces you have at your disposal. (cap.)	ii. Your *weapons and forces are different* from what they are. (cap.)
iii. What you *intend* to do. (int.)	iii. You intend to *do something else* (int.)
iv. *Where* you intend to do it. (int.)	iv. You intend to do it *elsewhere* (int.)
v. *When* you intend to do it.	v. You intend to do it at a *different time.* (int.)
vi. *How* you intend to do it. (int.)	vi. You intend to do it in a different manner. (int.)
vii. *Your* knowledge of the *enemy's* intentions and techniques (cap.)	vii. Your knowledge of the enemy is either greater or less than it actually is (cap.)
viii. *How successful his* operations are.	viii. His operations are either more or less successful than they actually are.

int. = intention
cap. = capability

This table is based on his essay which can also be found in Raanan, Pfaltzgraff, and Kemp, *Intelligence Policy and National Security* (London: Macmillan, 1981). Similarly: 'Therefore, when capable, feign incapacity; when active, in activity. When near, make it appear that you are far away; when far away, that you are near.' Sun Tzu, *The Art of War*, p. 66. Katherine Herbig and Donald Daniel in their paper, 'Propositions On Military Deception', classify all military deceptions in two categories: one group is termed 'ambiguity-increasing' deception, which seeks to compound uncertainties on the deceived side, and the second is the misleading type, which is designed to *reduce ambiguity* by building up the attractiveness of one wrong alternative.
See following article p. 155 *et. seq.*

16. For a detailed analysis of this problem, see Michael I. Handel, *Perception, Deception and Surprise: The Case of the Yom Kippur War* (Jerusalem: The Hebrew University, The Leonard Davis Institute Occasional Paper No. 19, 1976); or Michael I. Handel, 'The Yom Kippur War and the Inevitability of Surprise', *International Studies Quarterly*, Vol. 21, No. 3 (19 September 1977), pp. 461–502.

17. Handel, *Perception, Deception and Surprise.*

18. On the importance of intelligence feedback from the target, see Donald Daniel and Katherine Herbig's paper 'Propositions On Military Deception'.

19. The literature on Ultra's contribution to British Intelligence operations and to the war effort in general is growing very rapidly. For a sample see: Ralph Bennet, *Ultra In the West: The Normandy Campaign of 1944–1945* (New York: Scribner's, 1980); Patrick Beesly, *Very*

Special Intelligence: The Story of the Admiralty's Operational Intelligence Centre 1939-1945 (Garden City, N.Y.: Doubleday, 1978); Ronald Lewin, *Ultra Goes to War* (New York: McGraw Hill, 1978); P. J. Calvocoressi, 'The Secrets of Enigma', *The Listener* (Vol. 97), pp. 70-71, 112-14, 135-7; David Kahn, 'Codebreaking in World Wars I and II: The Major Successes and Failures, Their Causes and Their Effects', *The Historical Journal*, Vol. 23, No. 3 (1980), pp. 618-39; Jurgen Rohwer, 'Der Einfluss Der Allierten Funkaufklarung Auf Den Verlauf Des Zweiten Weltkrieges', *Vierteljahrshefte fur Zeitgeschichte*, No. 3, Vol. 23 (July 1979), pp. 525-70. On the Polish contribution see: Richard A. Woytak, *On the Border of War and Peace: Polish Intelligence and Diplomacy in 1937-1939 and the Origins of The Ultra Secret* (New York: Columbia University Press, 1979). Ultra was of course an invaluable follow-up instrument extremely useful for the elaborate British deception operations in World War II. See Montagu, *Beyond Top Secret U.*

20. Major-General I. S. O. Playfair, *The Mediterranean and Middle East: The Early Successes Against Italy* (Vol. 1). *History of the Second World War* (London: H.M.S.O., 1954), p. 274.

21. For the success of 'Overlord' see among others: Anthony Cave Brown, *Bodyguard of Lies* (New York: Harper and Row, 1975); Gilles Perrault, *The Secret of D-Day* (Boston: Little Brown, 1965); Cornelius Ryan, *The Longest Day* (London: Gollancz, 1959). All are competent journalistic accounts. Hans Speidel, *We Defended Normandy* (London: Herbert Jenkins, 1951); G. A. Harrison, *Cross Channel Attack* (Washington D.C.: The U.S. Army in World War II, European theater of Operations, 1951); L. F. Ellis, *Victory in the West* (London: HMSO, 1962), Vol. I. The definitive history of Overlord in light of Ultra has still to be written.

22. Surprise is relative and only rarely complete or total. In most cases of sudden attack, the surprised side normally had enough information and warning signals to indicate the possibility of a forthcoming attack — its timing, place, direction, and the like. In many successful surprise attacks, the attacker achieves only a partial degree of surprise. Attacks out of the blue, i.e. achieving total surprise without *any* warning are almost non-existent. Surprise attacks preceded by a very small number of warning signals indicating an impending attack are also rare. The Allied attack across the Channel was, from the German point of view, preceded by only very few signals indicating the existence of an immediate danger and therefore comes as close as possible to an attack out of the blue. The possible degrees of surprise that can be achieved and the relativity of surprise to warning or alert can be presented on the following continuum:

THE RELATIVITY OF SURPRISE

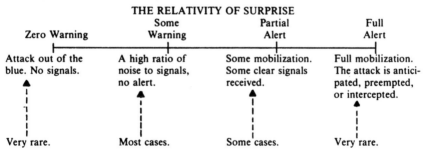

23. See Michael Handel, 'Strategic Surprise in Four Middle Eastern Wars', in Klaus Knorr (ed.), *Strategic Surprise* (forthcoming in the US, 1982).

24. Quoted in Whaley, *Stratagem, Deception and Surprise*, p. 575.

25. For a detailed analysis, see Michael I. Handel, 'Strategic Surprise in Four Middle Eastern Wars' in Klaus Knorr (ed.), *Strategic Surprise* (forthcoming in the US, 1982).

26. Quoted from Edward L. Homze, *Arming the Luftwaffe: The Reich Air Ministry and the German Aircraft Industry 1919-1939* (Lincoln: University of Nebraska Press, 1976), p. 169. See also Walter Bernhardt, *Die Deutsche Aufrustung, 1934-1939* (Frankfurt: Bernard and Grofe, 1962); Williamson Murray, 'The Change in the European Balance of Power 1938-1939' (Ph.D. dissertation, Yale University, 1975), Chapter 3, pp. 58-90; John Edwin

Wood, 'The Luftwaffe as a Factor in British Policy 1935–1939' (Ph.D. dissertation, Tulane University, 1965); Michael Mihalka, *German Strategic Deception in the 1930s* (Santa Monica, California: The Rand Corp., July 1980, N-1557-NA). David Dilks in his article 'Appeasement and Intelligence' claims there is evidence that part of the deception campaign concerning the strength of the *Luftwaffe* and the possibility of a German 'knock out' air bombardment on Britain and Holland was planted by the German anti-Hitler elements in order to force Great Britain to accelerate its reassurement and pledge itself to a continental commitment. David Dilks (ed.), *Retreat From Power: Studies in Britain's Foreign Policy of the Twentieth Century* Vol. 1, *1906–1939* (London: Macmillan, 1981), p. 158.

27.   Exaggerated strength was attributed to the *Luftwaffe* more by British civilian leaders than by British intelligence estimates. But psychology and fear proved to be more powerful than the cold intelligence calculations. See Murray, *The Change in the European Balance of Power*, pp. 71–2; also H. Montgomery Hyde, *British Air Policy Between the Wars 1918–1939* (London: Heinemann, 1976); Gerhard L. Weinberg, *The Foreign Policy of Hitler's Germany: Starting World War II, 1937–1939* (Chicago: Chicago University Press, 1980), for example pp. 22–3; 164–5; also Gordon Scott Smith, 'RAF War Plans and British Foreign Policy 1935–1940' (Ph.D. dissertation, MIT, June 1966), in particular chapter 3, pp. 71–99. The problem was that not only did the British exaggerate German capabilities, they also overestimated the devastation of strategic air bombardments. The CID (Committee of Imperial Defence) estimated in 1937 that 60 days of strategic bombing in England would result in 600,000 dead and 1,200,000 injuries (Smith, 'RAF War Plans', p. 86).

> Certainly appeasment was a consequence of a serious misunderstanding of Hitler's intentions and capabilities. This misunderstanding, however, was reinforced by the fear of the 'knock-out blow'. Had the fear of the 'knock-out blow' not been so great it might have been easier for the appeasers to see their folly in trying to meet Hitler's demands. Fear of the 'knock-out blow' made the appeasers even more prepared to accept German demands than they might otherwise have been. The consequences of war were visualized as so awful that almost any cost was worth paying if war could be avoided. From the Air Ministry poured forth the facts and figures that made war seem impossible, the true opiate of the appeasers (Smith, 'RAF War Plans', pp. 167–8).

28.   Quoted from Denis Mack Smith, *Mussolini's Roman Empire*, pp. 170; also pp. 174–5.

29.   Ibid., p. 174. During the Second World War itself the Italians and Japanese never developed new or advanced weapons. 'Their equipment was for the most part imitative and as the war continued inferior in design.' Alan S. Milward, *War, Economy and Society 1939–1945* (Berkeley: University of California Press, 1977), p. 175.

30.   Mack Smith, *Mussolini's Empire*, pp. 174, 177–8.

31.   Williamson Murray, 'The Change in the European Balance of Power', p. 213.

32.   After the war, the *Luftwaffe*'s General Plochner claimed that he had warned Hitler about the low quality of the Italian armed forces. The words he used to describe his Italian allies were unkind indeed:

> I reminded him [Hitler] that a King of Naples had once said the following about them [the Italians]: 'You can take as much trouble with the Italians as you want, you can give them the very best weapons, a mountain of ammunition to practice with, you can dress them in red, blue or green uniforms, but you will never succeed in transforming them into a useful military instrument. There are two principles to which they will always remain true. The first is: when the enemy comes in view, the best thing that you can do is to run the other way; and the second: better to be a coward for five minutes than dead all your life.' I told Hitler the only thing that had changed in Italy was Mussolini's big mouth, which was trying to convince the Italians that they had been the real victors of Vittorio Veneto.

Quoted in Murray, 'The Change in the European Balance of Power', p. 217. While the Italian philosophy of life might have seemed strange to a Prussian, there are certainly a few good things that could be said for it.

33. For the missile gap story, Khruschev's policy, and the American reaction, see: Edgar Bottome, *The Missile Gap: A Study of the Formulation of Military and Political Policy* (Rutherford, N.J.: Fairleigh Dickinson University Press, 1971); Arnold L. Horelick and Myron Rush, *Strategic Power and Soviet Foreign Policy* (Chicago: Chicago University Press, 1966) (from which the quotes were taken); Lawrence Freedman, *US Intelligence and the Soviet Strategic Threat* (Boulder Colorado: Westview Press, 1977), chapter 4. 'The Missile Gap', pp. 62–80. Another, different capability oriented deception must be mentioned in this context. Even if US intelligence was aware of the fact that no *real* missile gap existed between the US and the USSR or soon learned that it was a hoax, it was in the interest of the US Air Force or Army to maintain this myth in order to justify a greater investment in their own capabilities. Very frequently before the Pentagon budget is decided rumors of the real and imagined new strength of the Red Army are spread. This deception whether consciously or unconsciously can be expected of almost any military organization.

34. For other wartime deception operations that backfired or got out of control, see R. V. Jones, 'Intelligence and Deception', pp. 8–11.

35. The Israelis did not plan or want to go to war in 1967. The May Crisis caught them completely off-guard. The veil of secrecy concerning their real strength did involve conscious deception planning; what was *not* realized at the time was that *too much secrecy* concerning capabilities will project an image of weakness, which in turn could lead to a war no one desired. See Handel in Knorr (ed.), 'Strategic Surprises in Four Middle Eastern Wars'.

36. On the German underestimation of Soviet capabilities see among others: Lyman Kirkpatrick, *Captains Without Eyes: Intelligence Failures in World War II* (London: Macmillan, 1969), pp. 15, 51, 268; Barry A. Leach, *German Strategy Against Russia 1939–1941* (Oxford: Oxford University Press, 1973), pp. 91–4 and Appendix IV, p. 270; Albert Seaton, *The Russo-German War 1941–1945* (New York: Praeger, 1972), Chapter 3: 'A Little Knowledge', pp. 43–50; Seweryn Bialer (ed.), *Stalin and His Generals* (New York: Pegasus, 1969); Robert Cecil, *Hitler's Decision to Invade Russia 1941* (London: Davis-Poynter, 1975); David Kahn, *Hitler's Spies: German Military Intelligence in World War II* (New York: Macmillan, 1978), pp. 457–61. Herbert Goldhamer suggests that Soviet secrecy brought about the collapse of Soviet deterrence and led to a war the Soviet Union wanted to avoid:

> Soviet deterrence policy, even though combined with massive forces, failed in the end to deter the Nazis. Perhaps a continuation of past Soviet overt hospitality would have served the Soviet Union better than did the Nazi-Soviet pact. Perhaps, too, Soviet military secrecy — also a form of manipulation of perceptions — may have had an anti-deterrent effect since it led Nazi intelligence to estimate at only one half of its true value the number of Soviet divisions that would be available after the onset of war.

Herbert Goldhamer, *Reality and Belief in Military Affairs* (Santa Monica, Ca: The Rand Corp. February 1979, R-2448-NA), pp. 39, 111.

37. For 'passive deception' see: Seymour Reit, *Masquerade: The Amazing Camouflage Deceptions of World War II* (New York: Hawthorn, 1978); G. Barkas, *The Camouflage Story* (London: Cassell, 1952).

38. Jack Anderson, 'Old Fashioned Spying Methods Often the Best', *Washington Post,* 24 November 1981, p. D-15.

39. See R. V. Jones, *Most Secret War*; Alfred Price, *Instruments of Darkness: The History of Electronic Warfare* (New York: Scribner, 1978); Alfred Price, *Battle Over the Reich* (New York: Charles Scribner, 1973); Brian Johnson, *The Secret War* (London: Methuen, 1978).

40. A detailed case study of this problem can be found in Ralph Baldwin, *The Deadly Fuze: Secret Weapons of World War II* (San Rafael, Ca: Presido Press, 1980), 'Window' was also a classical case of the problem of timing in the introduction of new weapons.

41. On this see Michael Handel, 'Surprise and Change in Diplomacy', *International Security,* Vol. 4, No. 4 (Spring 1980), pp. 57–85, and Michael I. Handel, 'Avoiding Political and

Technological Surprise in the 1980s' in Roy Godson (ed.), *Intelligence Requirements for the 1980s: Analysis and Estimates* (New Brunswick: Transaction Books, 1980), pp. 85–111.

42. 'The perfect deception plan is like a jigsaw puzzle. Pieces of information are allowed to reach the enemy in such a way as to convince him that he has discovered them by accident. If he puts them together *himself* he is far more likely to believe that the intended picture is a true one' (Cruickshank, *Deception in World War II*, p. I).

43. A case in mind is 'Cicero' while operating in the British Embassy in Ankara, who supplied the Germans with detailed information on Operation Overlord, which the Germans refused to believe could be true. L. C. Mayzisch, *Operation Cicero* (London: Fitzgibbon, 1950).

44. Quoted from Richards J. Heuer, Jr., 'Strategic Deception: A Psychological Perspective', a paper presented at the 21st Annual Convention of the International Studies Association, Los Angeles, California, March 1980, pp. 17–18. An abbreviated and less exciting version of this excellent paper also appeared in *International Studies Quarterly*, Vol. 25, No. 2 (June 1981), pp. 294–327, under the title 'Strategic Deception and Counter-deception'.

45. Montagu, *Beyond Top Secret U*, p. 60.

46. For an original discussion (if somewhat exaggerated) of the need to try to see things also from the adversary's point of view, see: Ken Booth, *Strategy and Ethnocentrism* (London: Croom Helm, 1979).

47. Montagu, *Beyond Top Secret U*, pp. 138–9.

48. The only systematic discussion of deception work is to be found in Whaley, *Stratagem: Deception and Surprise in War*; Whaley, *Codeword Barbarossa*; Daniel and Herbig, *Strategic Military Deception: Perspectives on its Study and Use*. Of the published memoirs the best by far are those of Montagu; R. V. Jones, and Masterman.

49. Whaley, *Stratagem: Deception and Surprise in War*, pp. 6–12, 11.

50. Montagu claims he had more difficulties in convincing his superiors of the utility of deception than in executing the deception plans themselves. 'To deceive the German High Command was nothing like as difficult as it was to persuade their British opposite numbers that we could do that.' *The Man Who Never Was*, p. 37.

51. R. V. Jones brings one example of a German deception plan to cover the number of V-2 launching sites — which actually helped Allied intelligence to deduce the correct number and rote of fire. 'Intelligence and Deception', p. 22.

52. Whaley, *Stratagem: Deception and Surprise in War*, p. 147.

53. R. V. Jones, 'Intelligence and Deception', p. 23.

54. Heuer, 'Strategic Deception: A Psychological Perspective', p. 28. Like R. V. Jones, he suggests:

> The bias favoring a small amount of consistent information over a large body of less consistent data supports the common maxim in deception operations that the deceiver should *control* as many information channels as possible in order to reduce the amount of discrepant information available to the target. Deception can be effective even with a small amount of information as long as the target does not receive contradictory data. Not only should the notional picture be consistent, but the deceiver should actively discredit the real picture as well. To achieve maximum consistency, it is necessary to discredit the true as well as to build up the false (Heuer, ibid., pp. 33–4).

55. Heuer, ibid., p. 45.

56. On recent Soviet deception and disinformation practices see: Joseph D. Douglass Jr., 'Soviet Disinformation', *Strategic Review* (Winter 1981), pp. 16–25; 'State Department Documents Soviet Disinformation and Forgeries' in *American Bar Association Standing Committee Law and National Security Intelligence Report*, Vol. 3, No. 11, and Vol. 3, No. 12 (November and December 1981); also Ladislav Bittman, *The Deception Game: Czechoslovak Intelligence in Soviet Political Warfare* (Syracuse: Syracuse University Research Corporation, 1972).

57. See Goldhamer, *Reality and Belief in Military Affairs*; Mihalka, *German Strategic Deception in the 1930s*; and Michael I. Handel, *The Diplomacy of Surprise: Hitler, Nixon, Sadat* (Cambridge, Mass.: Harvard Center for International Affairs, 1981).

58. For a detailed analysis of Communist and Soviet attitudes to deception, see Nathan Leites, *A Study of Bolshevism*, Chapter 13. Deception, pp. 324–40.

59. Stalin's belief that every act of diplomacy (let alone war) involved deception is characterized by his statement that:

> When bourgeois diplomats prepare war, they begin with increased stress to talk about 'peace' and about 'friendly relations'. If some Minister of Foreign Affairs begins to advocate a 'peace conference' you can infer that his government has already ordered new dreadnoughts and planes. With a diplomat words *must* diverge from acts — what kind of diplomat would he otherwise be? Words are one thing and acts something different. Good words are masks for bad deeds. A sincere diplomat would equal dry water, wooden iron. (*Sotsial Demokrat*, 12 January (25) 1913, quoted in Leites, *A Study of Bolshevism*, p. 325.)

For a comment on the inevitability of at least some deception in diplomacy, see Thomas A. Bailey, *The Art of Diplomacy: The American Experience* (New York: Appelton-Century-Crafts, 1968), pp. 165–6. Also Paul W. Blackstock, *The Strategy of Subversion* (Chicago: Quadrangle, 1964); Paul W. Blackstock, *Agents of Deceit: Frauds, Forgeries and Political Intrigue Among Nations* (Chicago: Quadrangle Books, 1966).

60. For an interesting analysis of this phenomenon see: Patrick J. McGarvey, *CIA: The Myth and the Madness* (Baltimore: Penguin, 1974).

61. See Christopher M. Andrew, *The Mobilization of British Intelligence for the World Wars* (Washington D.C.: *International Security Studies* No. 12, The Woodrow Wilson Center (no date, 1981?).

62. David Kahn, *Hitler's Spies*, p. 533.

63. Andrew, *The Mobilization of British Intelligence*, p. 28. The advantage of British amateurism was also evident in the war in the Western Desert, in which British desert navigation amateurs from before the war were much better than the Germans in long-range navigation raids and commando-type operations carried out behind the German lines. See: Ronald Lewin, *The Life and Death of the Afrika Korps* (London: Corgi, 1979), in particular pp. 12–13; also W. B. Kennedy Shaw, *Long Range Desert Group* (London: Collins, 1945); Virginia Cowles, *The Phantom Major* (London); Valadimir Peniakoff (Popski), *Private Army* (London: Jonathan Cape, 1950). German professionalism under Rommel clearly had its advantages too.

64. David Kahn, *Hitler's Spies*, p. 523.

65. Ibid., pp. 524–43.

66. Ibid., p. 528.

67. Ibid., p. 528.

68. For a detailed analysis see Michael I. Handel, *The Diplomacy of Surprise: Hitler, Nixon, Sadat* (Cambridge, Mass.: Harvard Center for International Affairs, 1981).

69. David Kahn mentions two other reasons for the failure of German intelligence during the Second World War which are of less interest in this context. They are: German anti-semitism which caused the flight of knowledge and brains from Germany and simultaneously added to the Allies' pool of knowledge. The second was the poor organization and large number of competing German intelligence agencies, which caused considerable waste of resources, lack of coordination, fragmentation and hostility between the various organizations.

70. Whaley, *Stratagem: Deception and Surprise in War*, p. 233.

71. The exception is expensive and complicated cryptoanalysis and decoding operations such as Ultra which require a large number of participants. These of course relate to intelligence operations in general, not only to deception work. In retrospect, one of the amazing things about Ultra was the length of time it remained an undisclosed secret.

72. Whaley, *Stratagem, Deception and Surprise in War*, p. 234.

73. See Handel, *Perception, Deception and Surprise: The Case of the Yom Kippur War* (1976). Also in *International Studies Quarterly,* Vol. 21, No. 1 (September 1977), pp. 461–502, and Richard K. Betts, 'Analysis, War and Decision: Why Intelligence Failures are Inevitable', *World Politics,* Vol. 31, No. 1 (October 1978), pp. 61–80. The inevitability of surprise (and deception) therefore make the suggestion that the very 'knowledge that cover and deception is being deployed *must* be denied to enemy' seem to be useless. It must always be assumed in situations of war and intense conflict that the adversary will use some kind of deception in any intelligent and rational military planning. See Herbig and Daniel, 'Propositions On Military Intelligence', p. 21.

74. Heuer, 'Strategic Deception: A Psychological Perspective', p. 43. It is important not to confuse *initiative* and *passivity* (or non-use) in the use of deception, with the *offensive* and *defensive* uses of deception. Charles Cruikshank in his discussion of German deception in *Deception in World War II* seems to commit such an error when he suggests, 'Deception may help the side holding the initiative, but is not much use to the side on the defensive' (p. 206). It may be true that it is *easier* to design and implement deception on the offensive — but it is not less important on the defensive. This contradicts Cruikshank's own example of the successful deceptive measures taken during the Battle of Britain (Chapter 1). The defender should by no means give up the advantages of deception (primarily technological and scientific types of deception). This can be done by causing the attacker to waste his energy on phony targets or on heavily defended targets, by pretending to have more capabilities at weaker points of defense and less capabilities of stronger points; by interfering with the enemy's navigation aids; by pretending to launch counterattacks at the enemy's rear or to outflank him — which will force him to spread his forces, and the like.

75. Heuer, 'Strategic Deception: A Psychological Perspective', p. 47. I have suggested elsewhere the other following paradoxes (or inherent contradictions) of intelligence work:

> As a result of the great difficulties in differentiating between 'signals' and 'noise' in strategic warning, both valid and invalid information must be treated on a similar basis. In effect, all that exists is noise, not signals.

> The greater the risk, the less likely it seems, and the less risky it actually becomes. Thus, the greater the risk, the smaller it becomes.

> The sounds of silence. A quiet international environment can act as background noise which, by conditioning observers to a peaceful routine, actually covers preparations for war.

> The greater the credibility of an intelligence agency over time, the less its reports and conclusions are questioned; therefore, the greater the risk in the long run of overrelying on its findings.

> Self-negating prophecy. Information on a forthcoming enemy attack leads to counter-mobilization which, in turn, prompts the enemy to delay or cancel his plans. It is thus impossible — even in retrospect — to know whether counter-mobilization is justified or not.

> The more information is collected, the more difficult it becomes to filter, organize and process it in time to be of relevant use.

> The more information is collected, the more noise will be added.

> The more alerts that are sounded, the less meaningful they become (alert fatigue).

> Making working systems more sensitive reduces the risk of surprise but increases the number of false alarms.

76. Quoted in Handel, *Perception, Deception and Surprise,* p. 9.

77. This is very common in detective stories, films (such as the *Sting, Sleuth,* etc.) and drama (such as works by the Swiss playwright Friedrich Durrenmat) or spy versus spy in *Mad* magazines.

78. David Dilks, 'Appeasement and Intelligence', in David Dilks (ed.), *Retreat From Power,* p. 169.

Propositions on Military Deception

Donald C. Daniel and Katherine L. Herbig*

Military deception is an aspect of strategy and tactics which is often used but seldom acknowledged even long after a conflict has ended. The United States and Britain, for example, have only in the last few years declassified files on their World War II deception activities. Historians and military analysts have begun to reassess the war in the light of these new materials,[1] but, with the exception of pioneering work by Barton Whaley and William R. Harris,[2] there are as yet few systematic investigations of this topic which would further development of theory.

We have studied military deceptions of the recent past, and we wish in this paper to present concepts and propositions which would serve as a basis for formulating a theory of deception. Our analysis is divided into five sections dealing with the nature of deception, its variants, its process, factors conditioning its likelihood, and factors conditioning its success. We are primarily concerned with strategic as opposed to tactical-level deceptions. The former affect the outcome of wars or campaigns, the latter the outcome of battles or small engagements. While there are differences between both, we believe most of our conclusions apply to deceptions at either level, and in a few instances we have used tactical examples where they seemed especially apt.

The Nature of Deception

In our view deception is the deliberate misrepresentation of reality done to gain a competitive advantage. It will aid our elaboration of this definition if the reader refers to Figure 1, which illustrates how the broad concept of deception encompasses several subsidiary ideas.

At the figure's core is cover, the military term for secret-keeping and camouflage. Cover embodies deception's negative side. By this we mean that, among other things, deception entails a keeping of secrets by negating access to or withholding information. Cover is at the center of deception because, no matter what his other goals, a deceiver wishes to protect the existence of some truth, be it knowledge of an already existing reality (for example, the

*This article will be published in Donald C. Daniel and Katherine L. Herbig (eds.), *Strategic Military Deception* (New York: Pergamon Press, 1982) and appears here with the granting of permission of the publisher.

The authors express their own views in this article. What they say should not be construed as representing the opinion of the Naval Postgraduate School, the Department of the Navy, or any other agency of the United States Government. (Paper presented at the International Studies Convention, Los Angeles, 19 March 1980.)

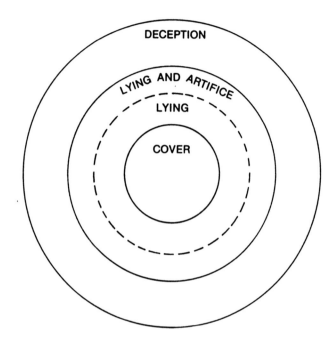

Figure 1
Deception's Subsidiary Concepts

capabilities of a weapon) or an intended reality (such as the scenario for the weapon's use).

The concept 'lying' encompasses that of 'cover'. To lie is also to withhold information, but it is something more as well: a liar *acts* to deflect his victim away from the truth, and thus lying highlights deception's positive side. Liars create and perpetrate falsities and seek to fasten a victim's attention to them. In the narrow sense, to lie simply means making an untrue statement, but in a broader sense it can also involve manipulating the context surrounding the statement in order to enhance its veracity.[3] This is what we mean by artifice, an important element of nearly all strategic deceptions.

Just as lying subsumes cover, so does deception subsume lying in both of its senses. Although the terms are often used interchangeably, deception and lying are not exact synonyms. Lying looks primarily to one side of the interaction between a liar and his audience. It stresses the actions of the teller of falsehoods. Deception is a term of wider scope because it also stresses the reactions of the receiver of those falsehoods. Someone whose false tale is not believed is still a liar, but he has not deceived. One does not fail at lying because the audience is not convinced, but one does fail at deception if the audience does not believe the lie. Eventually almost all deceptions are exposed as events unfold, but the trick for the deceiver is to insure his lies are accepted long enough to benefit him.

The question of benefits is important because they are a necessary ingredient of deception as we see it. In our view, to be labeled deception an act must be done to gain a competitive advantage. This means, in effect, that there are three goals in any deception. The immediate aim is to condition a target's beliefs; the intermediate aim is to influence his actions; and the ultimate aim is for the deceiver to benefit from the target's actions. Deceptions are often credited with success when only the first goal is achieved, but to evaluate the actual impact deception has on the course of events, its success should properly be measured against the third goal.

Two Variants of Deception

We distinguish two variants of deception which produce somewhat different effects and operate in different ways. The less elegant variety, termed 'ambiguity-increasing' or a 'A-type', confuses a target in order that he be unsure as to what to believe. It seeks to compound the uncertainties confronting any state's attempt to determine its adversary's wartime intentions. Contradictory indicators, missing data, fast-moving events, time-lags between data-collection and analysis, chance — all inhibit accurate intelligence assessments.[4] Intelligence analysts work on the assumption, however, that as an adversary moves toward his true operational goal, his preparations to do so will serve as tip-offs clarifying his intent. What A-type deceptions seek to ensure is that the level of ambiguity always remains high enough to protect the secret of the actual operation.

In order to have an impact, A-type deceptions require that the deceiver's lies be plausible enough and consequential enough to the target's well-being that he cannot ignore them. Hoping to reduce uncertainty by awaiting additional information, a target may delay decision, thereby giving the deceiver wider latitude to marshal resources and take or retain the initiative. If the deceiver can ensure that the situation remains ambiguous, then the target may be forced to spread resources thinly in order to cover all important contingencies. He thereby reduces the resistance the deceiver can expect at any one point.

Plan Bodyguard is a familiar World War II example containing numerous A-type deceptions. In support of the Normandy invasion, one of the plan's main goals was to prevent the Germans from shifting their forces from other European fronts to reinforce the Channel coast. The deceivers proposed to meet this challenge by mounting a coordinated series of deceptive invasion threats to Scandinavia, western and southern France, Italy, and in the eastern Mediterranean.[5] Some threats proved more plausible than others to the Germans but the multiple threats did increase ambiguity. Hitler and his generals were forced to consider a much greater range of possibilities than just the obvious assault across the English Channel, and this contributed to their holding in Norway and the Balkans forces better needed in France.[6]

Plan Barclay, the deception plan for the 1943 invasion of Sicily, intended to generate ambiguity about the timing of impending action as well as its location. The British raised the specter of invading plausible Mediterranean targets other than Sicily and then simulated two laborious postponements of the fake invasions. Subsequent German testimony suggests there was confusion about both where and when to expect an attack.[7]

In contrast to deceptions *increasing* ambiguity, there is a second more complicated category which we label the 'misleading' or 'M-type'. They *reduce* ambiguity by building up the attractiveness of one wrong alternative.[8] They cause a target to concentrate his operational resources on a single contingency, thereby maximizing the deceiver's chances for prevailing in all others.

A striking example of an M-type deception is *Barbarossa,* the German campaign to mislead Stalin and achieve surprise in their attack of 22 June 1941. By making their build-up along the Russian border appear to be an exercise linked to the invasion of Britain, the Germans created a plausible explanation for preparations which could not be hidden. The deception also built on Stalin's expectation that Germany would never attack Russia without first issuing an ultimatum. This 'ultimatum stratagem', according to Whaley, 'served to eliminate ambiguity, making Stalin quite certain, very decisive, and *wrong*'.[9] The overwhelming surprise achieved against the Russian defenses was a measure of how thoroughly Stalin had been misled.

Fortitude South is another well-known example. The Allies sought to portray the Normandy landings as preliminary to a much larger invasion at Pas de Calais. They did this by simulating troop concentrations in southeast England and orchestrating a symphony of agent's reports, rumors, and aerial bombing. Miscalculating badly, the Germans fatally postponed reinforcing the Normandy front. For a remarkable six weeks after D-Day, powerful Wehrmacht and Waffen SS forces remained in the Calais area preparing to repel an invasion which was never intended.[10]

Although the two variants of deception, M-type and A-type, are conceptually distinct and can be initiated with different intentions in the deceiver's mind, in practice their effects often co-exist or shade into one another as the deception evolves. In the latter case the direction of change generally appears to be from M-type to A-type. Deceptions planned to mislead a target into choosing one possibility may degenerate and instead increase ambiguity if the target resists or postpones making the choice the deceiver intends.

How one categorizes a particular deception partly depends on the perspective one takes. The variants can differ whether viewed from the deceiver's intentions or from the effect they ultimately have on the target. Strategic deceptions seem to be most often *intended* to mislead, since this form offers the largest potential payoff to the deceiver. However, one would expect pure misleading deceptions to obtain rarely because they require a target to be so sure of a false alternative that he stakes *all* on preparing for it. Prudent commanders seldom do this. They develop contingency preparations for other conceivable alternatives. Thus it may be most useful to consider the *outcomes* of the two variants as a continuum between convinced misdirection at the one pole and utter confusion, in which all looks equally likely, at the other. The *Barbarossa* deception seems to be an unusually strong example of misdirection, while immediately before D-Day *Fortitude South* would fall perhaps three-fourths of the way toward the misdirection pole. In the latter case, although quite sure the main attack would come at Calais, Hitler and most German generals continued to consider a range of invasion site possibilities along the channel. German forces, though concentrated at Calais, were disposed from Belgium to Cherbourg to cover these possibilities.[11]

The Process of Deception

In order to understand the process of deception, it is necessary to differentiate the categories of actors typically found on both sides of the interaction. Figure 2 adapts the traditional systems model to illustrate these categories and their relationships.

The deceiver's side consists of decision-makers, planners, and implementers. Regardless of who had the inspiration, a deception does not begin until a decision-maker agrees to it. Wide-ranging strategic deceptions such as *Bodyguard* are cleared only by the highest authorities. Having many responsibilities, they are unable to devote much time to planning and implementation. During World War II such tasks were assigned to small cadres in intelligence-gathering and covert action organizations as well as military staffs. These groups were often not a normal part of the civilian or military bureaucracy but rather, like the famous London Controlling Section, were specially formed during the war and disbanded or severely cut back at its conclusion. On an as-needed basis, implementers temporarily coopted regular military personnel who generated false radio traffic, set-up deceptive camouflage, simulated large troop movements or encampments and the like. National political leaders, high-level diplomats, civil servants, businessmen, and news reporters also often played starring roles in strategic deceptions.

The initial target of a military deception is usually a state's intelligence organization. It consists of channel monitors who seek out and collect information and analysts who coordinate and evaluate it. Gatekeepers within intelligence organizations and command staffs screen the information and analyses, and determine what is actually forwarded to civilian or military authorities — the ultimate deception targets. Presumably relying on information received, these leaders often make the strategic or tactical decisions which the deceivers sought to influence.

It is the links between deceivers and targets which makes deception possible. Designated as 'channels' in Figure 2, their variety is unlimited. A channel could be a foreign newspaper monitored by the target, his reconnaissance satellites, electronic intercept systems, diplomats, or spies. Through these channels the deceiver transmits signals, planted clues or pieces of evidence, which it is hoped the target will shape into indicators of the deceiver's intent or capabilities. A signal may be a paragraph in a news article on the activities of a general, a reduction in the level of military radio traffic, or a photo of ships offloading cargo. Taken together, for example, these may indicate to a target that an expected amphibious attack will not soon occur

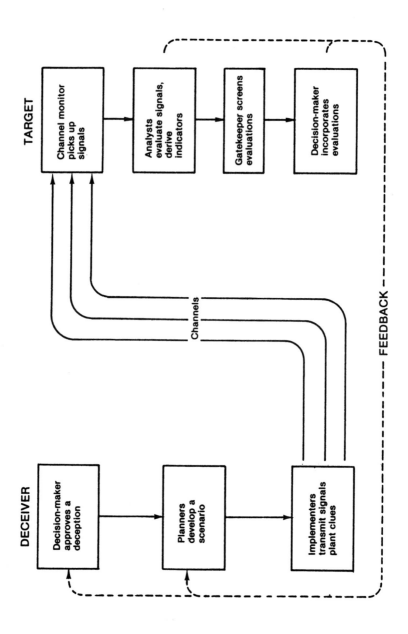

Figure 2
The Process of Deception

since the general expected to lead it is away on other business, radio traffic is too sparse to indicate impending activity, and ships preparing to carry out an impending attack usually on-load rather than off-load goods.

A deception expert has compared his task of formulating and transmitting signals to the work of a playwright. Each devises a story and seeks to put it across to an audience by means of 'scenery, props, costumes, principals, extras, dialogue, and sound effects'.[14] In order to have the story unfold in the intended manner, each must coordinate the timing, tempo, and content of his signals.

Though similar in many ways, the problems facing the military deceiver are more acute than those of the playwright. One reason is that the deceiver cannot assume that his audience is attending only to his production. He must accept that high-level target leaders have numerous responsibilities forcing them to divide their attention among numerous 'shows'. He must also accept that what a target knows about any situation is not restricted to what the deceiver is telling him. In other words, the deceiver is putting on a show but he does not fully control the number of actors on stage or all the lines being said. Few targets can be expected to be as accommodating as Stalin during the *Barbarossa* deception. Refusing to consider the possibility of a German attack, he threatened to silence forever his own agent who was correctly predicting it![15]

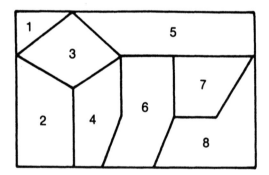

Figure 3
A Deception Puzzle

There is a second reason why the deceiver's problems are more acute: his production is being staged at some remove from his audience which at times may only dimly perceive what is going on. Hence, the deceiver must be very sensitive to the prospect that some of his signals may not make it through to the target in the intended manner and that, if they do, they may not be interpreted as he would wish. Figures 3 and 4 may aid understanding of the

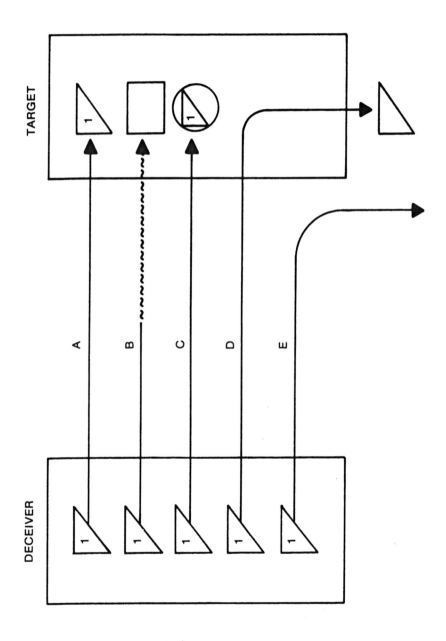

Figure 4
Possibilities During the Transmitting
and Interpreting of a Signal

difficulties he faces. Figure 3 illustrates the story of a deception as a puzzle made up of eight signals, the puzzle's pieces. The deceiver desires the target to receive each of them, interpret them as indicators, and fit them together into a story, the picture on the puzzle's face. Figure 4 illustrates what can happen to the signals during transmission and interpretation. The triangles on the deceiver's side reproduce signal number 1 in the top left corner of Figure 3. If the target has properly received and interpreted the signal, an identical triangle appears on his side. This is possibility A of Figure 4. It represents the deceiver's fondest hope. In contrast, possibility B is a signal which was garbled or modified in the channel after it left the deceiver. Hence the target received a signal different from that which was transmitted (symbolized by the square). C and D represent signals monitored intact, but the former was misinterpreted (shown as the triangle within a circle) and the latter dismissed (illustrated as a triangle thrown out from the target's side). Finally, E is a signal sent but never received by the target; perhaps the deceiver was inept in its transmission, or the target happened not to be 'listening', or chance in its many forms intervened to deflect the signal away.

One would think from the above discussion of a deceiver's problems that deceptions should seldom succeed. In fact our research leads us to conclude that the opposite is true. Targets, after all, are normally searching eagerly for indicators of enemy intent and, if the enemy is a deceiver, he is just as eager to provide his foe with indicators, albeit false ones. Hence it should not be surprising that, if properly transmitted and designed to be highly salient to a target's concerns, many signals reach the target largely unscathed. Unless his intelligence organization is inept, they are monitored and evaluated for their significance as indicators, and their underlying story (or a variant of it) usually rises to the surface. In the end the story may be dismissed, but only after it has at least been considered.

Finally, the direction of signals in a deception is not necessarily always from deceiver to target. There may be return channels from the latter to the former. This is the feedback loop shown in Figure 2. The deceiver can thereby modulate his activities if time allows. In a successful deception, of course, the target is not aware that his actions and statements constitute feedback for the deceiver. Should the target realize that his signals are being monitored to provide feedback, on the other hand, the stage is set for a further permutation in the deception process, entrapment of the deceiver by the target. By using the feedback channels to send deceptive signals to his enemy, the target becomes the deceiver and the deception channels become feedback for this new layer of deception.

Factors Influencing the Likelihood of Deception

Two groups of factors influence the likelihood of military deception: those which characterize situations confronting an actor and those which actors bring to a situation by virtue of previous conditioning or personal predilection. The factors may operate independently or in combination with one another. It is difficult to establish *a priori* which group is more important, but the second set probably has greater impact.

Of the first group, high stakes situations can certainly influence willingness to deceive. When outcomes are critical, adversaries are encouraged to make use of every capability, every advantage, to ensure victory or stave off defeat.[16]

Resort to deception can be particularly compelling if decision-makers are not fully confident of a situation's outcome because of their own military weaknesses. Desiring to compensate for them, they seek through some ruse to induce an enemy to lower his guard, dilute his strength, or concentrate his forces on the wrong objective. Plans *Bodyguard* and *Barclay,* for example, both reflected the concern that, until a beachhead is secured, amphibious landings are highly vulnerable to being pushed back into the sea. From the attacker's perspective, it is thus imperative to assure that the defender's response capability be as limited as possible. Weaker in mechanized forces, Hitler similarly wanted to limit Allied response to *Case Yellow,* the May 1940 push into France. He convinced the Allies that his main thrust would be through Holland and Belgium. While the British and French massed in that direction, the Wehrmacht's primary offensive was actually far to the south at Sedan. It then turned toward the channel encircling the cream of the Allied armies. The Dunkirk evacuation meant that the bulk of these would fight again, but for France the war was lost.[17]

Even when optimistic of the outcome of a situation, an actor may be attracted to deception as one way to lower costs. The wish to avoid being viewed as an aggressor has inspired many a nation to fabricate evidence that its victim actually fired the first shot. The wish to avoid human or material losses has resulted in schemes such as the British plan in 1943 to protect their bombers attacking Peenemunde. Though confident this German rocket facility could be destroyed, the British sought to minimize their own casualties. They succeeded in deflecting German fighters from their bomber streams by convincing the enemy's air defense that Berlin was the target instead.[18]

Situations characterized by uncertainty can also induce deception. In those circumstances, actors often seek to mislead or confuse in order to keep their options open and to test the reaction to alternative policies. A state undecided as to whether to attack another, for instance, may still wish to be ready to do so. This was the case prior to the last-minute Soviet decision to invade Czechoslovakia. Having its troops 'exercise' in border areas for the greater part of the summer allowed the USSR to proceed with preparations for an invasion while not openly committing itself to this step. It also allowed the Soviets to save face if they decided not to attack. After all, the Czechs might have backed down, making attack unnecessary, or they might have rallied the overwhelming support of the world community, making the invasion option even more unattractive.[19]

In any of these situations, not all states or individuals would resort to deception. Actors bring their own conditioned responses, their own predilections, to the problems they face. We see at least five factors possibly at play here.

First, there may be 'deception styles' which vary from culture to culture that would account for the differences in when and how nations use deception. The intriguing thought that some societies' values or expected modes of personal interaction condition individuals to understand and succeed at deception is to our knowledge largely unexplored.

Scott Boorman in his work on the Chinese does suggest that deception has traditionally been part of Chinese military strategy because it is so available in the cultural norms. The Chinese assume interpersonal deception will and should occur constantly between individuals as a means of protecting face by deflecting too-threatening truths.[20] Since at least the doctrines of Sun Tzu in the fourth century B.C., the Chinese have long prized victories gained by undermining through deception an adversary's desire or ability to give battle.[21] The potential link between a culture's expectation for interpersonal truthfulness or deceptiveness and that culture's resort to military deception is not yet well formed, but it remains suggestive. For example, does a country like the United States, with a culture noted for the openness, even the naiveté of its interpersonal interactions, find strategic deception uncongenial to its habitual ways of thinking?[22]

It is conceivable that by studying cultural norms we may learn to predict how nations will employ deception in military contexts. Harris begins such an analysis by comparing national patterns in the deceptive practices of the Soviets and the Chinese. He describes the Soviet's use of the 'false war scare' to overawe opponents, their penchant for 'disinformation', and their efforts to induce overestimation of their military capabilities. This contrasts with the Chinese preference for the 'deep lure', the multiple stratagem, and the anticipation of the enemy's intentions through acumen.[23] His work suggests that by expanding systematic comparison of national 'deception styles', we may isolate patterns that could alert counter-deception analysts sooner to the deceptive ploys of a particular culture.

Herbert Goldhamer suggests a second conditioning factor. He contends that deception may be more common in states where political leaders take a strong, central role in military decision. His argument implies that politics either attracts individuals prone to deception or conditions individuals to practice deception. As a corollary to his general argument, he adds that a tendency to deceive is particularly prevalent in dictatorships and authoritarian regimes. He reasons that the 'secrecy and total control available [in these governments], and the reduced inhibitions that accompany such exercise of power, facilitate and provide incentives for the exercise of craft, cunning, and deception'.[24]

Paralleling Goldhamer's perspective are two closely related factors. One is the bureaucratic imperative that organizations trained for particular tasks will seek to perform them. The other is the psychological trait that people tend to think in terms of what is available or familiar to them.[25] These phenomena suggest that military deception is likely to occur if a nation maintains an apparatus to plan and organize deception, or if its military preserves, passes on, or at least debates a doctrine for deception. Conversely, nations having no such apparatus or doctrine, or which allow them to atrophy, must overcome the inertia involved in creating or revivifying them — a situation characteristic of America's early strategic deception efforts in World War II.

Finally, there is the issue of a person's own predilection to deception. It is clear that even within the same cultural or organizational setting, individuals differ in this regard. Some leaders relish deception, others put up with it, still others resist it. Why this is so remains largely unexplored. Whaley searched his historical data for evidence of a 'deceptive personality type', a group of attributes or experiences that would account for these differences, but could find none.[26] At present we must be content to observe that personal reactions to deception are at least self-consistent. That is, a commander who has appreciated and relied on deception in the past is likely to do so again. Churchill was an early proponent of deception in World War I and encouraged its elaboration again twenty years later; Douglas MacArthur used serial deceptions in his campaign across the Pacific, and succeeded with it again at Inchon. In following the good advice to 'know thy enemy', a nation might be well served to evaluate its opponent's experience with deception.

Factors Conditioning the Success of Deception

The success of a deception can be evaluated in a variety of ways, none of them precise. One can consider how well the deception was implemented: were the activities outlined in the scenario carried out according to plan? Even at this narrow level defining success must be relative, since one characteristic of the most effective deceptions is that they adapt to changing circumstances and thus depart from the original plan. To evaluate the plan itself one must sort out the impact of deception activities on the target from the other influences affecting him. First, did he adopt the false understanding the deceiver intended? And secondly, did he act on the basis of that understanding in ways contrary to his true interest? Usually it is impossible to recover precisely the relative weight deception had in tipping the scale of a decision. As in most problems of historical evaluation, evidence on the priorities assigned in a decision is often lacking. Unfortunately for students of strategic deception, what seems to us as the two most common types of deceptions are also the most intractable to evaluate. Misleading deceptions which reinforce what a target believes, and ambiguity-increasing deceptions which multiply the options a target must consider, both build on what already exists. Would the target have continued undisturbed in his (false) expectations without the deceiver's reinforcement? Would his existing ambiguity have been enough to cause delay and confusion without the deceiver's adding more? One cannot know for sure.

A higher level of evaluation asks one to consider what impact the target's adverse actions, prompted to some degree by deception, had on the outcome of the encounter itself. What military and political consequences flowed from it? For example, what degree of importance should we assign to deception in the results of the invasion of Sicily or Normandy compared to force levels, or weaponry, or generalship? Would the English have bounced back more quickly from the Blitz had they escaped the delusion that Hitler's *Operation*

Sea Lion, a deception which called for an invasion of Britain, was true? Would the Israelis have rested secure in their (false) assessment of Arab intentions to attack in 1973 even without the deceptive signals of calm planted for their benefit?[27] Perhaps, but since deception did play a role of some sort in these cases, historians who will wrestle with them cannot escape the delicate task of reaching some tentative evaluation of it.

Two recently declassified documents provide an interesting starting point for discussing factors conditioning success. They reveal that experienced deceivers on either side of the conflict during the Second World War arrived at similar conclusions about how to succeed at deception. Comparing these two examples of 'lessons learned', one British, one German, helps focus on the basic requirements for success.

In September 1944, a deception planner working with the Supreme Headquarters Allied Expeditionary Forces (SHAEF), produced a top-secret report for the Allies on cover and deception procedures. His conclusions reflected 'four years of successful [deception] operations by the British'. Six years later General Hans von Grieffenberg, a German infantry officer, wrote a review of German experience with cover and deception.[28] Both of these document are intriguing, and there is considerable agreement between them.

Since the authors were writing to instruct future deception planners in 'the basics', they prescribed formulae for success in simple terms, avoiding qualifying or conditional statements. We will use their prescriptions as a foil against which we can develop and, in some cases, elaborate our thoughts on successful deceptions. The documents provide us with three useful categories: 1) secrecy, organization and coordination; 2) plausibility and confirmation; and 3) adaptability. We add a fourth, the predispositions of the target, and a fifth, factors in the strategic situation.

SECRECY, ORGANIZATION AND COORDINATION

Both the SHAEF planner and Von Grieffenberg strongly agree that 'knowledge that cover and deception is [sic] being employed *must* be denied the enemy'. (Emphasis in all quotes in original.) 'If the strictest secrecy is not observed', says Von Grieffenberg, 'all deception projects ... are condemned to failure from the very start.' Deceiving one's own troops for the sake of security, he adds, is a normal byproduct of deception.

Consistent with these admonitions, both individuals argue that deception must be well-organized and well-coordinated, else leaks may occur and the deception unravel. They are well-organized when there is 'detailed preparation' where even 'seeming trifles are not overlooked'. They are well-coordinated when directed from one central point — that being the highest headquarters controlling operational forces directly benefitting from the deception.

In one sense these prescriptions are obvious. By definition, secrecy is inherent to deception, and organization and coordination are inherent to the success of any but the most simple endeavors. Yet total security is an elusive, usually unachievable goal even in the best organized and coordinated operations. Close study of preparations for strategic operations such as the attack on Pearl Harbor or the invasion of Russia in 1941 show the numerous warnings and indications which slipped through the most Draconian security efforts.[29] The relationships between deception and security would seem to be more complex than our experts acknowledge.

There are two levels of security involved in a deception. One tries to protect the truth about what a side intends to do in an impending operation. For example, if the operational plan calls for landings at Dakar, and the related deception plans try to make it appear there will be landings on the coast of Norway or in the Middle East instead, trying to keep the actual intentions about Dakar secret is obviously important. The second level of security tries to protect the truth about the existence of the deception itself, to prevent the target's certainty that some identified possibilities are deceptive and may thus be safely ruled out.

Breaches of security at either level, commonly referred to as leaks, need not be fatal to deception's success. Some leaks may not catch the target's attention, and if they do, may only increase his ambiguity. A target's predispositions may cause other leaks to be ignored or misinterpreted as to their true significance. For example, Whaley's study of the Barbarossa campaign shows how 'leaky' the strict German security became as the invasion approached; without damaging the deception or the surprise achieved, literally dozens of clues of German intentions reached the Russians. Indeed, since Stalin apparently explained away all warnings as provocation by the Allies, here leaks actually furthered the deception.[30]

There is reason to argue that the 'bigger' the leak, the less likely the target will believe it since it seems too good to be true. One survey of ten such 'windfalls' reaching an adversary, half of them true and half deceptive plants, found that all deceptive leaks were accepted, perhaps because the deceivers made sure it was plausible that such valuable information was lost. Four of the five genuine windfalls were discounted as too blatant to be anything but plants.[31] The windfall cases illustrate that, even when a target suspects deception, his position is not necessarily improved. He must still decide which of two or more alternative scenarios is the truth.

Since leaks are an inevitable concomitant of strategic deceptions and often result from mistakes in the organization and coordination our experts from World War II recommend, we suggest that a more powerful predictor of deception success is plausibility.

PLAUSIBILITY AND CONFIRMATION OF THE LIE

The SHAEF and Von Grieffenberg documents present a number of principles to the effect that the lie must be plausible. They also imply that it must be serious; that is, the deceiver's scenario must not only be one which could conceivably happen, but also one which seems ominous enough, and likely enough, to provoke the target to forestall it. To achieve this, they recommend that the lie be woven into a skein of truth and confirmed by more than one source. As Von Grieffenberg put it, the deception 'must be brought into harmony with the *overall situation*'. His SHAEF counterpart insisted that an '*enemy will not react to information from a single source*. He will react only on information from one source confirmed by at least one other.'

Our work leads us to agree with the above propositions. As we see it, a very important factor in establishing plausibility is the deceiver's capability, as perceived by the target, to do what the lie commits him to do. A deception is doomed to fail if a target is too highly skeptical about the deceiver's capabilities. During the summer and fall of 1943, for example, the Allies tried a series of strategic deceptions, with the overall code name *Cockade* to simulate a cross-channel invasion of France for early September. German response proved disappointing: the *Luftwaffe* did not rise to the bait and avoided the needless and costly air battles the deceivers had hoped their false invasion would provoke. The Wehrmacht did not reinforce the French coast to brace for invasion; the slow drainage of German forces to the Eastern front continued. German intelligence had felt that 'the resources available in GREAT BRITAIN are insufficient to permit any attempt to invade the continent this summer'.[32] The British learned a lesson which they applied the following year in *Fortitude*: while they only had 35 to 40 divisions available for a cross-channel invasion, they built up a notional force of twice that number to convince the Germans that they really could strike at Calais.[33]

A lie is made more plausible when it has been confirmed by a variety of credible sources. The need for confirmation is a quality most people develop from their experience with the complexities of reality: truth, albeit partial, is seen to emerge from numerous points, some of them contradictory, some veiled, some obvious. The usual targets of deceptions, intelligence organizations, accentuate this issue by demanding that all claims be confirmed and evidence evaluated and ranked according to its estimated reliability. The number of sources confirming a fact and the credibility of the sources are both important, and their effects interact.

Given the expectation that an array of mutually supportive clues is likely to be true, the more channels of information a deceiver can manipulate to send signals which reinforce one another, the more credible his deception. Conversely, if he can control most of the target's channels of information, such as his double agents, the deceiver lessens his adversary's access to disconfirming evidence.[34] The latter is often as important for a deception's success as the former, since the best-orchestrated chorus of many reinforcing clues will be questioned if even a few voices sing off-key loud enough. In the Mediterranean and in Northern Africa, for example, the British deception teams could never count on complete control over German channels of information. There independent German agents persisted, sending back observations and hearsay irrespective of the British deceivers. This made deception more difficult, less precise, and more unpredictable than was achieved in England, where the island's isolation, the turning of the whole German spy network, and the decline of German air reconnaissance allowed almost complete control.[35]

Credibility of sources can be as important as their number. Intelligence analysts rank information by how credible its source is; they pay most attention to reliable sources, and a few of these may outweigh many questionable ones. The deceiver's knowledge of his target will shape how he establishes the credibility of the channels he controls. What seems credible to him may not seem credible to the target since cultural perceptions can intervene in this judgment, and it is the target's skepticism the deceiver must allay.

Furthermore, credibility itself is a relative judgment that shifts with circumstances. When one has no better available sources, those which do exist often seem better than an objective evaluation would warrant. The Germans placed heavy reliance on their agents in England during World War II in part because they had so few other choices. It seemed to the British who ran the double agent system that the Germans forgave their agents egregious errors rather than consider that they might have been turned.[36] The spymasters in Germany were paid according to how well their particular agents performed, a mercenary incentive which further undermined their skeptical evaluation of sources. On the other hand, knowing that a whole agent system could be turned, since they were doing it, did not prevent the British from being deceived by the Germans in just this way. For several years the *Abwehr* ran all the Allied agents in Holland using radio communications.[37]

Knitting the deception into many strands of truth is another part of providing the target with confirmation. By meshing many of the less-critical points of a deception scenario with the real plans, a deceiver assures that the target can verify these details as they occur. As more of the elements in an evolving explanation are confirmed, the target is likely to ignore, twist, or explain away those details which do not fit, and often these are the crucial incongruities on which the deception hinges. The British deception teams learned this early in the war. Evaluating their deception efforts for *Operation Torch,* the invasion of North Africa, they found that their scheme to explain the build-up on Gibraltar as reinforcement for Malta rather than an invasion force 'went well', while threats to more distant destinations, Norway and northern France, proved unconvincing. According to J. C. Masterman, this 'underlined the obvious fact that cover stories ought to be as near the "real thing" as was safely possible'.[38] One deception expert estimated that deception scenarios should be 80 to 90 per cent true.[39] He thereby highlighted a paradoxical quality of deception. While Churchill may have correctly defined it as the protection of truth by a 'bodyguard of lies', the execution of deception requires the protection of its lie by a bodyguard of truth.

ADAPTABILITY OF DECEPTION

Von Grieffenberg argues that deceivers should take advantage of any opportunities which arrive by chance. Implied in his argument is the proposition that the success of deception is enhanced if the deceiver adapts to changing circumstances and unplanned events. This proposition is a logical extension of earlier statements that the lie must be plausible and woven into a skein of truth. As the truth changes, so must the deception if the lie is to remain believable. Otherwise the divergence will expose the lie.

Von Grieffenberg's emphasis on unplanned opportunities is well chosen. Their 'chance' nature can help make it difficult for a target to suspect that they may be part of a deception scheme. For example, Hitler achieved complete surprise in his attack on Russia in 1941 because Stalin expected to receive an ultimatum of German demands before any action was taken. Given Hitler's previous behavior before invading Czechoslovakia and Poland, this expectation was shared by many knowledgeable observers throughout the world. Yet of all the many ploys the Germans launched to deceive the Russians about their intention to attack, this ultimatum expectation, apparently the most effective deceptive clue of all, seems to have been spontaneously generated by the churning international rumor mill. Hitler then cleverly picked up and reinforced this useful fiction in his deception campaign.[40] Similarly, the Allies expected their *Fortitude* deception to play out quickly after the size of the Normandy invasion became clear. As the days passed and evidence mounted that the Germans held to their expectations for a second invasion at Calais, the opportunity to spin out the deception, using Patton's fictional forces as a threat, was seized and milked for nearly two months, aiding the consolidation of the Normandy beachhead.[41]

The ultimate asset which allows deceivers to adapt their scenarios in these ways is *feedback* from the target. Accurate intelligence on what the adversary is intending and how he is reacting is one of the basic goals in any competition, but for deception it has particular importance. This is because the crucial effect for which deception aims occurs in the inaccessible mind of the opponent. For his miscalculations to produce actions beneficial to the deceiver, the latter ideally should be able to monitor how his opponent's ideas are evolving in response to the deceptive clues provided by him. Feedback allows deceptions to continue for a longer time, to take advantage of unexpected interpretations or unforseen events in the enemy camp, and to protect valuable resources by ending the ploy should the deception wear thin.

Since trusting one's feedback presents deceivers with the same evaluation problem that the target faces — is this information reliable, or part of a counter-deception? — the most valuable kinds of feedback are obtained through cryptanalysis, espionage, or other covert means. Such methods can bring the deceiver into the inner sanctum of high-level adversary thinking and decision-making. Revelations of the British achievement in securing feedback for their deceptions through ULTRA have recently focused attention on the importance feedback can have. Decoding relevant ULTRA messages fast enough to gain operational advantage was a 'knife-edge business', as Lewin says, but as a source of insight about how Hitler and his staff were responding to deception it was unparalleled. John Bevan, 'controller' of British deception, gave ULTRA full credit for enabling them to sustain their more complicated deception scenarios.[42]

TARGET PREDISPOSITIONS

Unaccountably, neither the SHAEF nor Von Grieffenberg reports advised potential deceivers to make use of a target's predispositions, yet this factor seems undeniably significant. Certainly deceptions which slant the target's mind-set in directions he is predisposed to take have a higher probability of convincing him than those which run against the grain of his expectations and assumptions. Conventional wisdom is supported by experimental psychology on this point: the stronger his predispositions (especially if he explicitly commits himself to them), the more a target will ignore or twist information inconsistent with them.[43]

When an adversary knows the other's predispositions, he may well choose to do the unexpected. The deceiver's task then becomes providing clues which reinforce these predispositions while minimizing or discrediting clues which contradict them. He can assume the target will do much of this work for him, however, since experiments have repeatedly shown the strong impact of expectations on perceptions and judgment. Thus the target acts as an unwitting but cooperative victim, and the distinction between perpetuated deception and 'self-deception' narrows. This is Roberta Wohlstetter's point in a recent article. She considers examples of policy-makers seeing what they devoutly wished to see, rather than what was there. For example, the United States accepted the Indian government's repeated bland assurances that their nuclear research was aimed at peaceful uses because this 'transparent cover' allowed nuclear sales to continue; when the Indians then exploded a nuclear weapon, it blew away the US' self-imposed blinders about India's goals.[44]

Determination of an adversary's expectations may be direct or indirect, through inference. Close study of an enemy's habits of thought and preoccupations provides one means, as when the Allies repeatedly played to Hitler's known fear of a Balkan invasion. Intelligence sources provide others, such as ULTRA or the analysis of German questions to their agents in England, which revealed the patterns of their concerns.[45]

Often just the indirect means of studying the strategic situation will reveal the adversary's expectations clearly enough. It was strategically almost inevitable that the Allies would eventually invade across the English channel; it was also fairly clear to both sides in 1942 that after the North African victories the next Allied target should be Sicily and the Italian Peninsula. These 'realities', which are in part a reflection of the strategic doctrine available to both sides in a given period, set bounds on what can be made to seem plausible in a deception, and define what an opponent will probably be expecting to happen.

However, the case of Sicily illustrates a different problem. Here the Allies wanted to invade precisely where the Germans expected them to; (as Churchill said, 'anybody but a damn' fool would *know* it is Sicily',) so the task for deception was to change the target's mind enough so he expected attack somewhere else, or at least at several other points instead of one.[46] This provoked the famous *Mincemeat* ruse using the corpse of a notional courier to plant false plans pointing to an attack on Sardinia. The windfall, when backed up with additional rumors and signs pointing to several other targets, led to a dilution of German forces on Sicily and confusion about where and when the attack would come.[47]

Experimental psychology tends to support the likelihood of *Mincemeat's* success. In experiments done to isolate the factors which lead someone to change his mind, results were best when subjects were confronted with a large amount of information which contradicted their expectations, and when they received this information all at once or in a short period of time.[48] The information must also be credible and salient to the problem. In our example, Hitler saw and initialed the German intelligence report on the *Mincemeat* courier's documents and altered his orders immediately thereafter to reflect this information.[49] The prediction is that only with a considerable and concentrated shock to his comfortable assumptions will the target consider giving them up and changing his mind in the direction the deceiver intends.

Examples of deceptions which successfully played on a target's predispositions are much more numerous than those which reversed a target's expectations. This suggests that the former are the norm and the latter are exceptions. How readily one can change a target's mind seems to depend in part on the pressures his environment exerts for making decisions. Experimental psychologists suggest the seemingly paradoxical proposition that if a target can be influenced to adopt a *vigilant* posture, chances increase that he can be convinced to change his beliefs.[50] Why this happens requires distinguishing between three emotional states associated with making important decisions.

The first of these is relaxation: an individual feels no tension because no such decision is required of him. The second is that of moderate tension, or vigilance: some tension arises from the need for a decision, but it remains moderate as long as the individual believes he has adequate time to evaluate alternatives before deciding on one. The third state is high tension, or rigidity. Here the individual feels great stress because time seems inadequate to properly evaluate alternatives.

Psychologists argue that individuals are *most* apt to follow their predispositions in either the first or the third emotional states: when they are relaxed, or when they are very tense. In the first case, facing no important decision, the individual sees no disadvantage in giving head to his predispositions. Pressed for important decisions in a hurry, on the other hand, individuals fall prey to 'selective exposure', defined by Janis and Mann as an 'active search and preference for supportive information and avoidance of discrepant information'.[51] In other words, the target sees what he consciously or subconsciously chooses to see. It is the second state of moderate tension, or vigilance, that elicits responses most likely to overcome predispositions. Vigilance is here defined as:

> a discriminating and open-minded interest in both supportive and opposing messages ... with no tendency towards selective exposure ... [T]he vigilant decision-maker will actually prefer to obtain nonsupportive messages in order to satisfy his need for specific information about the losses he might incur.[52]

Deceivers who need to change someone's mind should thus choose as their entry point this open-minded interest in contradictions of the vigilant decision-maker. A target confronting a potential decision with enough time can be expected to seek out, consider, and possibly accept information he would otherwise be likely to ignore or reject. A vigilant target may still consider and then reject a deceiver's slanted evidence, but faced with either more or less pressure for a decision, he might never seriously consider it at all.

A third mode for handling a target's predispositions lies open to deceivers: instead of capitalizing on or reversing existing expectations, deceivers may wish to create certain expectations. Here the deceiver sets up the target for a future surprise by conditioning him to expect something he had not considered before. Often these deceptions rely on creating the comforting illusion that the deceiver follows certain standard operating procedures which the target comes to expect and therefore to disregard. When the deceiver's intended action does occur, the target misinterprets it, and does not respond appropriately or quickly enough. An example in which the British were caught napping by such a deception occurred in February 1942. Two German ships, the *Scharnhorst* and the *Gneisenau,* dashed through the English Channel undetected because British coastal radar had been systematically hoodwinked by gradually increasing jamming. R. V. Jones admits that the Germans had 'subtly increased the intensity of their jamming over a period so that we would get acclimatized to it, without realizing that it was now so intense that our radar was almost useless'.[53]

STRATEGIC INITIATIVE

It is not surprising that our fifth category of factors affecting success is not to be found in the admonitions of either Von Grieffenberg or the SHAEF writer. This is because it concerns an element over which deceivers have little control: strategic initiative in war. While being on the defensive gives more urgent motives for resorting to deception, it limits the scale of deceptions that are likely to succeed. The initiators of action are defining the nature of the encounter and thereby have the greater degree of control over it at the outset. They act; the opponents must react. This control puts the initiators in a relatively better position to succeed at deception if they attempt it.

A major advantage which the initiative confers for successful deception is time. Being able to act when it is ready, the initiating side has the luxury of using the available time to spin deception plans if it chooses to; the defenders must respond willy-nilly to the action, ready or not. Since deceptions at the strategic level demand time to work well, it is not surprising that instances of the most elaborate sort are done by the side which can take the initiative.

Realizing that the better position from which to succeed at deception is the offensive should not lead us to underrate deception by the underdog seeking to overcome disadvantages with guile. The point is that defensive deceptions are still literally disadvantaged — limited in scope and in planning time and possibly also thin in resources needed instead for battle operations. This was the context of British deceptions in World War II from 1939 through mid-1942; most of their deceptions were passive, that is, camouflage or simulation exercises to deflect German weapons from their targets. As the tide turned against the Germans late in the war *their* ability to deceive declined as time, resources, and information ran out.[54]

Conclusion

Bacon wrote of a fly which sat on a chariot's axle and credited to itself the dust raised by the turning of the wheels. R. F. Hesketh referred to this fable in a now declassified report wherein he described the work of his deception group in 1943–44 as it implemented *Fortitude*. Hesketh's point was that he was careful in his analysis not to over-value the significance of his work to the Allied victory at Normandy. 'It is always tempting', he wrote, 'for those who set out to deceive and who see their objects fulfilled, to claim credit for their attainment when, in fact, the motive force lay in another quarter'.[55]

We applaud Hesketh's candor and would add that all deception analysts need to guard against over-crediting deception's significance. The temptation to do so is alluring because deception does seem to be such a powerful tool. *Fortitude* and other cases illustrate that the advantage in any properly executed scheme invariably belongs to the deceiver. After all, *he* knows what the truth *is,* and he can assume his adversary will search for its indicators. As a result, the deceiver can expect the victim to pick up some of the signals intended to mislead or confuse. Should they be ignored, dismissed, or misinterpreted, the deceiver is probably not worse off. Should they be interpreted as he intends, the deceiver stands to gain. The target must pay attention even to scenarios which he suspects to be untrue if they are plausible and consequential to his interests. Although the target may ultimately choose not to act on them, the additional time he spends evaluating deceptive scenarios or searching for further information should benefit his foe.

The danger in accepting an advantage to the deceiver is to assume that it will significantly contribute to victory. It may well do so, but as Hesketh would undoubtedly agree, the contribution is very difficult to measure. Hesketh proceeded as best he could, concentrating primarily on the actions of his group and on the content, timing and reasons for German beliefs. To truly certify *Fortitude's* impact, however, would have required determining not only what the victim might have believed and done in the absence of deception, but also distinguishing deception's impact from among other factors such as troop morale, quantity and quality of weapons, generalship, or effective planning. These analytical tasks are prodigious, some might say impossible; yet deception analysts must confront them. Beyond studying the use of deception in individual instances we should next try to identify a model to evaluate its relative significance across a wide range of cases.

NOTES

1. General treatments of deception in World War II include Anthony Cave Brown, *Bodyguard of Lies* (NY: Harper & Row, 1975); Charles Cruickshank, *Deception in World War II* (Oxford: Oxford University Press, 1979), and David Owen, *Battle of Wits* (London: Leo Cooper, 1978); on special topics such as Ultra: Ronald Lewin, *Ultra Goes to War. The Secret Story* (London: Hutchinson & Co. Pubs. Ltd., 1978); Ewen Montagu, *Beyond Top Secret Ultra* (NY: Coward, McCann & Geoghegan,Inc., 1978); and F. W. Winterbotham, *The Ultra Secret* (NY: Harper & Row, 1974); on electronic deception: R. V. Jones, *Most Secret War* (London: Hamish Hamilton, 1978); and Alfred Price, *Instruments of Darkness* (London: Macdonald and Jane's, 1967); on naval deception: Patrick Beesly, *Very Special Intelligence* (Garden City, NY: Doubleday & Co. Inc., 1978); on the opposing intelligence organizations: F. W. Hinsley, *et al., British Intelligence in the Second World War,* vol. 1 (London: Her

Majesty's Stationery Office, 1979); David Kahn, *Hitler's Spies. German Military Intelligence in World War II* (NY: Macmillan Publishing Co. Inc., 1978).

2. Barton Whaley, *Stratagem. Deception and Surprise in War* (Cambridge, Mass.: MIT unpublished mimeographed manuscript, 1969); William R. Harris, 'On Countering Strategic Deception', draft R-1230-ARPA, Rand Corporation (Santa Monica, Ca., 1973). Neither of these important sources has yet been published in easily accessible forms.

3. Sissela Bok, *Lying: Moral Choice in Public and Private Life* (NY: Pantheon Books, 1978), see especially 3–32 and 134–46.

4. Richard K. Betts, 'Analysis, War and Decision: Why Intelligence Failures are Inevitable', *World Politics,* XXXI (Oct. 1978), 69–72.

5. 'Plan "Bodyguard" Overall Deception Policy for the War against Germany', RG 218, Records of the Joint Chiefs of Staff, CCS 385 (6-25-43) Section 1, Modern Military Records, National Archives, Washington, DC.

6. Cruickshank, 92–7, 185–9.

7. Ibid., 52, 59–60.

8. Whaley also outlines the two variants of deception which we describe, confusion and misdirection deceptions. Since his concern is specifically with how deception creates surprise, he assumes misdirection to be the better, ultimate aim of deception. We suggest that confusion may be an equally efficacious goal and do not necessarily subordinate A-type deceptions to M-type. See *Stratagem,* 134–5, 139–42.

9. Barton Whaley, *Codeword Barbarossa* (Cambridge, Mass.: The MIT Press, 1973), 242.

10. William A. Harris, *et al.,* 'Appendix No. 1 to Informal Report to Joint Security Control. Enemy Reaction to FORTITUDE April–June 1944', RG 319, G-3, C & D file folder 27, MMR, NA; Kent Robert Greenfield, ed., *United States Army in World War II,* vol. 2 of *The European Theatre of Operations: Cross-Channel Attack,* by Gordon A. Harrison (Washington, DC: Office of the Chief of Military History, 1951), 351–2.

11. Genlt Bodo Zimmermann, *et al.,* 'OB West: A Study in Command', Foreign Military Studies, MS#B-672 US Army. Historical Division. RG-338, MMR, NA.

12. Brown, 260–74.

13- Roger Fleetwood Hesketh, 'General note giving sequence of events . . . ,' letter to William Casey, n.d., copy in the authors' possession; Cruickshank, 19–20.

14. [F. E. Fox, 1st Lt. Signal Corps], '23rd Headquarters, Special Troops, APO #655', 11 July 1944, RG 319, G-3, MMR, NA.

15. Whaley, *Codeword Barbarossa,* 213–16.

16. See Robert Axelrod, 'The Rational Timing of Surprise', *World Politics,* XXXI (January 1979), 228–46 on the logical calculation of stakes.

17. David Irving, *Hitler's War* (NY: Viking, 1977), 116–18.

18. David Irving, *The Mare's Nest* (Boston: Little, Brown and Co., 1965), 97–98, 108–15.

19. Jiri Valenta, *Soviet Intervention in Czechoslovakia, 1968: Anatomy of a Decision* (Baltimore: Johns Hopkins Press, 1979).

20. Scott A. Boorman, 'Deception in Chinese Strategy', *The Military and Political Power in China in the 1970s,* edited by William W. Whitson (NY: Praeger, 1972), 315–16.

21. Boorman, 319–23; Sun Tzu, *The Art of War,* translated by Samuel B. Griffith (Oxford: Oxford University Press, 1963).

22. See Robert Jervis, *The Logic of Images in International Relations* (Princeton: Princeton University Press, 1970), 98: 'Interestingly enough, the Americans also ignored the possibility of lying' in the pre-Pearl Harbor negotiations with the Japanese.

23. Harris, 'On Countering Strategic Deception', 98–115; for a discussion of acumen as a means of divining and predicting an adversary's future moves, see Karl E. Scheibe, 'The Psychologist's Advantage and Its Nullification: Limits of Human Predictability', *American Psychologist,* 33 (Oct. 1978), 869–81.

24. Herbert Goldhamer, 'Reality and Belief in Military Affairs: A First Draft' (June 1977), edited by Joan Goldhamer. Rand Corporation: R-2448-NA (February 1979), 107–8.

25. See Graham T. Allison, *Essence of Decision* (Boston: Little, Brown and Co., 1971), 88–95; Amos Tversky and Daniel Kahneman, 'Availability: A Heuristic for Judging Frequency and Probability', *Cognitive Psychology,* 5 (1973), 207–32.

26. Whaley, *Stratagem,* 8–12.

27. Peter Fleming, *Operation Sea Lion* (NY: Simon and Schuster, 1957); Michael J. Handel, 'Perception, Deception and Surprise: The Case of the Yom Kippur War', Hebrew University of Jerusalem, Jerusalem Paper on Peace Problems No. 19 (1976), 16–17, 57–8.

28. 'Exhibit 3. "Cover and Deception, Definition and Procedures",' 8 Sept. 1944, RG 331, SHAEF, MMR, NA; Hans Von Grieffenberg, 'Deception and Cover Plans, Project #29', Foreign Military Studies, MS #P-044a, US Army, Historical Division, MMR, NA.

29. Whaley, *Codeword Barbarossa,* 24–129 passim.

30. Ibid., 222–6.

31. Whaley, *Stratagem,* 229; see also his discussion of the relationship of security and deception, with somewhat different emphases, 225–6.

32. Maj. C. H. Bennet, 'German Appreciation of Operation Starkey', COSSAC/41 DX/INT, 1 Sept. 1943, RG 331; Maj. R. B. Woodruff, 'Conduct of Deceptive Planning, COCKADE-WADHAM', 24 Sept. 1943, RG 165; Lt. Gen. F. Morgan, letter of 25 July 1943, RG 331, MMR, NA. Morgan's plaintive tone suggests the frustrations deceivers face, e.g. 'Now for pity's sake, tell me who tells who what and when, and what he expects them to believe anyway. I refuse to see anybody in the information world [the press] about any of this until I am absolutely clear as to what it is all about, which looks to me like being never.'

33. 'Plan "Fortitude"', 23 Feb. 1944, SHAEF, RG 319, MMR, NA.; Roger FLeetwood Hesketh, 'Fortitude. A History of Strategic Deception in North Western Europe, April, 1943 to May, 1945', unpublished manuscript, Feb. 1949, 87–98, 112–29 passim.

34. Jones, 26, suggests a similar point in the context of how practical jokes deceive their victims.

35. Cruickshank, 191–4; interview with Ronald Lewin, 26 Sept. 1979, London.

36. J. C. Masterman, *The Double-Cross System in the War of 1939 to 1945* (New Haven and London: Yale University Press, 1972), 30–31.

37. H. J. Giskes, *London Calling North Pole* (NY: The British Book Centre, Inc., 1953).

38. Masterman, 110.

39. 'Exhibit 3. "Cover and Deception"', 4.

40. Whaley, *Codeword Barbarossa,* 223–4.

41. Hesketh, 113, 130–31, 139; Lewin, 317–20; Brown, 679–87 passim.

42. Lewin, 237, 316.

43. Robert Jervis, *Perception and Misperception in International Politics* (Princeton: Princeton University Press, 1976), Chapter 4 passim.

44. Roberta Wohlstetter, 'The Pleasures of Self-Deception', *The Washington Quarterly,* 2 (Autumn, 1979), 54–63, 58–60.

45. Lewin, 311; Cruickshank, 59, 93–4; Masterman, 72–5.

46. Ewen Montagu, *The Man Who Never Was* (Philadelphia and NY: J. B. Lippincott Co., 1954); also 46–50 on the problems of selecting a cover target.

47. Ibid., 134–50.

48. Jervis, *Perception,* 187–91.

49. Montagu, 142–3.

50. Irving L. Janis and Leon Mann, *Decision-Making: A Psychological Analysis of Conflict, Choice, and Commitment* (NY: Free Press, 1977), Chapter 8 passim.

51. Ibid., 205.

52. Ibid., 207.

53. Jones, 235.

54. Cruickshank, 19, 206–7.

55. Hesketh, viii.

Toward a General Theory of Deception

Barton Whaley

> Give me a good 'effect', and I'll find a way to do it.
> — David Devant, Magician

This paper gives a preliminary general theory of deception. It is pragmatic, presented as 1) a teaching tool for persons concerned with deception and counter-deception, either as practitioners or potential victims; and 2) an analytical tool or model for deception operations, specifically as a check-list to assure that all aspects have been covered, all bases touched, in the design, analysis, or detection of deception operations.

This is the first comprehensive attempt at deception theory.[1] Previous efforts, mainly classified, have been directed to specific military problems such as camouflage[2] or ECM/ECCM.[3] Even recent efforts toward special theories of military or diplomatic deception have progressed only to the stage of developing narrowly focussed and non-comprehensive maxims or hypotheses.[4] These represent, at best, proto-theory, as do some contributions from such diverse deception fields as illusions in nature, psychological misperception, and magic.

The theory is based primarily on comprehensive and systematic analyses of two major but quite separate fields in which deception predominates — war[5] and magic.[6] These fields were chosen as the first for comparative analysis because among all deceivers military deception planners and magicians have by far the most experience.

If truly general, such a theory must apply to all other fields of deceptive illusion as well. Therefore additional evidence was surveyed anecdotally for all other major occupational types that employ deception to an important degree: diplomats, counter-espionage officers, politicians, businessmen, con artists, charlatans, hoaxers, practical jokers, poker players, gambling cheats, football quarterbacks, fencers, actors, artists, mystery story writers, or you or I in our everyday lives.[7]

Even nature produces its share of deception — both physical illusions such as the mirage or the 'bent' stick in water and the perceptual illusions that have slowly evolved through genetic mutation, those kinds of hiding camouflage and/or showing lures of the zebra, the chameleon, and the anglerfish. Here too, the array of examples was surveyed.[8]

A Convergence of Traditions

All modern magicians recognize that magic is applied psychology. It is the only field where this is universally recognized to be so. However, a number of experts have implied this in asserting analogies among ostensibly separate fields where deception plays a significant role.

That spiritualism was merely 'conjuring in disguise' was first detected in 1851, three years after its introduction, by magician John Henry Anderson. Writer Raymond Chandler (in 1948) noted an analogy between sleight-of-hand and plotting a mystery story; the Roman statesman-philosopher Seneca (c. 50 AD) one between magician's sleights and the art of rhetoric; magician-stage director Henning Nelms (1969) one between magic and theater; magician Henry Hay (1949) one between magic and jokes. Magician-camouflager Major Jasper Maskelyne (1949) one between magic and both camouflage in particular and military deception in general; neuropsychologist R. L. Gregory (1970) one between psychological illusion and the scientific method. British WWII military deception planner Dr R. V. Jones (1957) argued systematically for one among the scientific method, practical joking, and military deception. British military theorist Captain Basil Liddell Hart (1929) recognized an analogy between military deception and deception in sports and subsequently (1956) added deception in international politics at the level of 'grand strategy'. But, of course, Machiavelli had long since made the even closer general connection among deception in war, politics, and (implicitly in his one work of fiction) everyday life. Finally, bringing these full circle, Brigadier-General Eliahu Zeira (1975), former Israeli Director of Military Intelligence, perceived an intimate analogy between military deception planners and magicians.

I will go further and assert that deception is the same regardless of whatever field it appears in. It is not a function of technology. All deceptions are applied psychology — the psychology of misperception — and hence are connected by more than one or two analogous points. Consequently, along psychological lines it must be logically possible to develop a general theory of deception.

Toward Theory

Theories are only statements about how separate things, whether objects or events, relate to each other. Flashes of insight, so-called sixth sense, intuition, mere hunches, presumptions, assumptions, analogies, hypotheses, principles, theorems, propositions, natural laws, and even fully articulated theories are all basically the same, distinguishable only by the degree of logical and evidential rigor by which they are stated. (I speak only of empirical theory — theory based on verifiable evidence — and not of those non-empirical theories such as are often met in religion, mysticism, psychoanalysis, and elsewhere that are incapable of either proof or disproof and must remain forever a matter of pure faith.)

In any case, to build a theory of deception we must first have a taxonomy. A taxonomy is simply a formal statement or model of the various categories included in any system, mapping the structure of that system by its types. Hence it is also called a typology. So we begin with a typology of perception and move on to examine misperception, so-called self-deception, and deception.

Misperception: Deception and Self-Deception

Deception is one form or mode of perception. Specifically, it falls in that main division of perception called misperception. These terms and the manner in which they relate are summarized in the following diagram.

A TYPOLOGY OF PERCEPTION

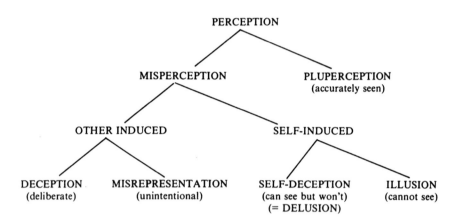

Source: Barton Whaley, *A Typology of Misperception* (draft, March, 1980), with thanks to Lewis Reich, formerly with the MATHTECH Division of Mathematica, Inc.

Because deception is a matter of misperception, it is a psychological phenomenon. All deceptions occur inside the brain of the person (or animal) deceived.[9] They take place only in the proverbial 'eye of the beholder'; we are not deceived by others, we only deceive ourselves — the 'deceiver' only intending and attempting to *induce* deception. He contrives and projects a false picture of reality; but to be deceived we must both perceive this attempted portrayal and accept it in more-or-less the terms intended and projected.

To avoid the consequent semantic bind that has bewildered many researchers when they confuse deception with self-deception and conclude that it is all 'self-deception', we will distinguish the former as other-induced deception and the latter as self-induced deception. We sometimes call such self-induced deception delusion; but, in any case, whether other-induced or self-induced, the cognitive process is, if not identical, quite similar.

Perceptions can most usefully be defined as hypotheses. The pioneering work leading to this view was published in 1867 by the influential German physicist and physiologist Hermann von Helmholtz. However his specific insight on perception as a 'conclusion' (hypothesis) based on 'unconscious inference' was overlooked during the next hundred years by his fellow scientists who concentrated instead on uncovering the intermediating biological mechanisms that feed sensory data to the brain. These scientists have given us a wealth of understanding of how and with what specific distortions information reaches the brain, but they have remained bogged down in Immanuel Kant's 1781 theory of perceptions as 'intuition' (*Anschauung*). Now this is convenient shorthand for explaining how we perceive, but it is useless for explaining how we misperceive. This is why Gestalt psychology, wedded to both Kantian intuitionism and the now totally discredited 'isomorphic' or 'brain-trace' theory of physiology, seemed so promising but has proved such a disappointment in helping us understand how we misperceive.[10]

Then, in 1970, British neuropsychologist R. L. Gregory, picking up on Helmholtz's century-old lead, first proposed that 'perceptions are hypotheses'.[11] Professor Gregory combined evidence from physiology, neurology, and the philosophy of science to conclude that sensory inputs simply provide 'data for hypotheses' about the environment; the selected hypotheses being what psychologists and Everyman alike have been more-or-less loosely calling 'perceptions'.

The process of perception (including misperception) is crudely as follows: 1) The environment continuously transmits a chaotic cascade or spectrum of discrete data (the 'information bits' of communications theorists). 2) Our sensors (intrinsic such as eye and ear as well as extrinsic such as seeing-eye dogs or radar sets) detect certain portions of some of these spectra. 3) These bits and scraps of received data are transmitted (with slight delay but often considerable distortion) to the brain. 4) The brain discards most of these data but processes some immediately and stores it in memory. 5) The brain then develops hypotheses about the environment by drawing inferences from new as well as stored data.[12]

It would seem that everything we call 'thinking' is the cognitive process of testing hypotheses about incoming and stored data. This is true of all human brains, from the highest IQ to the lowest, from the most rational or logical to the most deranged and intuitional, from the child to the adult.[13] It has also been demonstrated for certain bigger-brained animals and seemingly applies even to the reflexes (responses to perceptions) found in the primitive nerve systems of brainless creatures. Similarly, 'learning' is the accumulation of more and more interrelated hypotheses.

Leaving the Helmholtz-Gregory theory aside, we must define the process whereby hypotheses are generated. They are built entirely by a process of comparison. At the simplest level, the individual, discrete information bits (raw data) are distinguished as *categories* (Plato's 'ideal types'), that is, hypotheses about their sameness or difference. These hypotheses are stored in memory. At the next higher level of aggregation sets of related bits combine into characteristics ('charcs' for short),[14] which are hypotheses about the interrelatedness of categories. These too are remembered. New bits of data are then compared with these hypothetical charcs and incorporated if perceived as congruent or discarded if incongruent. At the highest level of aggregation, charcs combine into *patterns,* which are hypotheses about the interrelatedness of charcs. Again, these are remembered; and newly perceived charcs will be compared with the old pattern and either incorporated if congruent or rejected if incongruent.

More than one hypothesis can, of course, be erected upon any given set of sensory inputs. This is a logical requirement of scientific hypothesis building in general, but each specific builder (brain) has its own bias. While it would be useful to know more about such biases, considerable recent work has shown some of the different types of memory and styles of thinking[15] including cultural biases.[16] Nonetheless these are only the trees in the forest of theory, necessary for fine-tuning any deception plan or operation but not essential for understanding the overall theory.

Turning from perception to misperception, Gregory concludes that 'illusions are failed hypotheses' and suggests that they occur whenever either 1) our physiological perceptual input mechanisms malfunction, or 2) our cognitive hypothesis-generating strategies are inappropriate. The first circumstance accounts for all physiological illusions, the second for all psychological ones.

Gregory's is an elegant theory because it cuts through the previous turgid or inchoate speculations of psychologists.[17] Nor need we sit and wait until physiologists and neurologists discover all the physical mechanisms of perception.[18] Gregory's theory says in effect that while these other theories may tell us how we *receive* information, they are irrelevant for explaining how we *process* it.

The Structure of Deception[19]

The taxonomic structure and operational process of misperception applies equally to all four of its sub-types (p. 181) but we will now focus in on only one — deception.

In this section, each term will be defined both descriptively by its role in the structure of deception as well as operationally by its role in the process. Each term will also be compared with its standard usage by both magicians and soldiers.

Deception is the distortion of perceived reality. Operationally, it is done by changing the pattern of distinguishing characteristics (charcs) of the thing (whether object or event) detected by the sensory system of the target. The task (purpose) of deception is to profess the false in the face of the real.

* Magicians call this generally 'magic' or occasionally and privately 'deception' and specifically a 'trick' or 'illusion'.
* Soldiers and practitioners of intelligence call it 'deception'. Some military camouflagers call it 'strategic camouflage'.

Reality is distorted, deceptively portrayed, by both nature and man. Nature's deceptions are either without purpose (as with such familiar physical illusions as a mirage or the apparently 'bent' stick in water) or purposeful and, then, always to the advantage of the species involved (as with all evolutionary bits of camouflage that have survival value).[20] Man's deceptions are also either without purpose (unintentional misrepresentations) or purposeful — with intent to deceive. Nature does this unconsciously; man does it either unconsciously (as with self-deception and some deceptions of others) or consciously and, then, always to some perceived advantage.

Every deception operation, whether of man or nature, is comprised of only two basic parts: dissimulation and simulation.[21] *Dissimulation* is hiding the real. It is covert, that part of a deception concealed from the target. Its task is to conceal or at least obscure the truth. Operationally, dissimulation is done by hiding one or more of the characteristics that make up the distinctive pattern of a real thing.

- ★ Magicians speak of the 'method', the means or procedure by which a trick is done, the part that must be hidden from the audience. Some also use the word 'dissimulation' itself.
- ★ Military deception specialists call this variously 'cover', 'cover and concealment', or simply 'dissimulation', defining the latter as 'hiding the real'. Practitioners of intelligencers speak of 'cover' and 'covert'; and some camouflagers call it 'negative camouflage'.

Simulation is showing the false. It is overt, that part of a deception presented to the target. Its task is to pretend, portray, profess an intended lie. Simulation is done by showing one or more characteristics that comprise the distinctive pattern of a false thing.

- ★ Magicians speak of the 'effect' and define it as that part of a trick the audience is meant to perceive. Many also use the word 'simulation'.
- ★ Some military deception experts also call this 'simulation' and define it explicitly as 'portraying the false'. Some camouflagers call it 'positive camouflage'. The term 'notional', meaning the false thing shown, was coined in its military sense around 1941 by Brigadier Dudley Clarke, the head of British World War II deception planning in the Middle East.

Both simulation and dissimulation are always present together in any single act of deception. Nothing is ever 'just' hidden; something is always shown in its stead, even if only implicitly — the housewife who hides her money in the cookie jar is pretending (showing) she has no money at home. It is the two in combination that misdirect the attention and interest of the target, inducing it to form misperceptions (false hypotheses) about the real nature of what is impending.

Basically there are only three ways to dissimulate and only three to simulate. The three procedures by which real things (objects or events) are hidden are masking, repackaging, or dazzling:

Masking hides the real by making it invisible. It either interposes a screen, shielding it from the senses (and any intermediating sensors) of the deceivee so it is truly covert, or integrates it with its environment so it is unnoticed, blending into its background, literally overlooked, hiding in plain sight. Operationally, masking is done either by concealing all distinctive characteristics (at least those thought to be available to the target's sensors) or by matching them to surrounding characteristics. This is done in order either to conceal or blend its original pattern.

* The magician shields by hiding his gimmicks out of sight — backstage, behind mirrors, under the table, or in his hand. He integrates the Fake Finger by blending it in among the five real fingers of his hand. He also blends by 'black art'. Biologists call this 'crypsis', meaning concealment or camouflage.
* The soldier shields with smokescreens or electronic jamming; he blends into jungle or desert with mottled camouflage. German aircrews hid in captured American B-17s in 1944 to spy close-up on US bomber formations. And statesmen often feign diplomatic normalcy to mask their intent to go to war, as with Japan vs. the US in 1941 or Russia vs. Japan in 1945, Czechoslovakia in 1968, and Afghanistan in 1979.

Repackaging hides the real by disguising. It wraps a thing differently, modifying its appearance. It is simulated metamorphosis. Repackaging is done by adding or subtracting characteristics to transform them into a new pattern that resembles something else.

* Magicians repackage when they exchange costumes with an assistant in various 'substitution' illusions.
* A general may have a new unit in the line wear the distinguishing patches of the old to disguise the changeover. An admiral disguises a warship as a harmless freighter. General Dayan repackaged the opening stroke of the 1956 Sinai Campaign by publicly calling the seizure of the Mitla Pass a mere 'reprisal' to delay an all-out Egyptian counter-attack.

Dazzling hides the real by confusing. It bewilders, confounds, baffles, perplexes, reducing certainty about the real nature of a thing. Dazzling is done by randomizing or otherwise partially obscuring the characteristics of an object (its precise location, size, color, etc.) or an event (its exact timing, method of operation, etc.) in order to blur their distinctive pattern. Ideally, this modified pattern carries less conviction, conveys less certainty, than the real but underlying one.

* Magicians bewilder their audiences when they use the 'equivoque' to 'force' an object.
* The Royal Navy used zig-zag 'dazzle painting' on its warships in WWI to confuse German U-boat commanders; and General Bradley had his radio net simulate Patton's Third Army five times over to confuse the Germans about Patton' crucial move to relieve the Battle of the Bulge in 1944. All military codes and ciphers are a type of dazzle, jumbled mathematically so that they remain unreadable, although fully recognizable as encrypted messages.

Conversely, the three procedures by which false things are shown are mimicking, inventing, or decoying:

Mimicking shows the false by having one thing imitate another. It duplicates a sufficient number of aspects of the other to give a passable replica. The ideal example is the double (*döppelganger*). Operationally, mimicking is done by copying one or more of the distinctive characteristics of the thing to be imitated to approximate its distinctive pattern.

* ★ The magician thus uses only the 'talk', the characteristic clinking sound of coins or the snapping of cards, to simulate the presence of the entire object; or, at the other extreme, introduces a double in the form of an identical twin to enhance a 'vanish'. Biologists specifically call this 'mimicry'.
* ★ General Otto von Emmich attacked the great Belgian fortress of Liège in 1914 with six brigades totalling only 20,000 troops; but, because this was a mixed force drawn from five corps, Belgian intelligence concluded from prisoners taken that they faced all five corps, an overwhelming force of 150,000 and accordingly withdrew their infantry screen. A more charc-filled ruse was that involving the British Army actor who played 'Monty's Double' in 1944.

Inventing shows the false by displaying another reality. Unlike mimicking which imitates an existing thing, inventing creates something entirely new, albeit false. Inventing is done by creating one or more new characteristics to create an entirely new pattern.

* ★ Magicians create dummy objects for certain 'substitution' effects such as forged billets in mind-reading acts or a complete dummy magician in Maskelyne's Levitation Extraordinary.
* ★ Generals create rubber tanks, wooden guns, canvas aircraft, and dummy radio traffic; admirals create dummy warships. Major Frederick Funston dressed his Philippino troops in Moro costume to capture their leader, Aguinaldo, in 1901.

Decoying shows the false by diverting attention. It offers a distracting, misleading option and is therefore a matter of feints and diversions, literally misdirection. Decoying is done by creating alternative false characteristics that give an additional, second pattern. Ideally this alternative pattern carries more conviction, conveys more certainty, than the real one.

* ★ For the magician, this is 'misdirection' in its most literal sense. Thus decoying occurs during every sleight-of-hand 'pass', as in the French Drop where an empty fist moves away from the other hand as if it had just taken an object from it.
* ★ And generals, like football quarterbacks, fake left and run right. By creating a successful diversion on one flank, at one point, or from one direction while attacking another, Sherman took Atlanta in 1864, Allenby took Palestine in 1918, the US Marines took Tinian in 1944, and MacArthur took Inchon in 1950.

Also, just as the two overriding categories of dissimulation and simulation are opposites, their separate sub-categories also stand opposing one another as mirror-image antonyms — shown schematically as follows:

DISSIMULATING $\left\{ \begin{array}{ll} 1. & \text{masking} \\ 2. & \text{repackaging} \\ 3. & \text{dazzling} \end{array} \right.$ $\left. \begin{array}{ll} \text{mimicking} & 1. \\ \text{inventing} & 2. \\ \text{decoying} & 3. \end{array} \right\}$ SIMULATING

Therefore, masking has its counterpart in mimicking, repackaging in inventing, and dazzling in decoying. Although this schema is logically elegant, it is an artifact, a logical consequence of the fact that the basic categories of dissimulation and simulation are already defined as opposites. In practice as in theory, all three ways of hiding the real can accompany the three ways of showing the false in any of their possible combinations.

Because both dissimulation and simulation are always present together in any single deception operation, we can take the pair of separate but parallel three-fold parts of the taxonomy and create a 3×3 matrix that will encompass all acts of deception. Thus the following table, which draws its examples from magic tricks.

THE STRUCTURE OF DECEPTION
(with process defined)

DECEPTION (Distorting Reality)	
DISSIMULATION (Hiding The Real)	SIMULATION (Showing The False)
MASKING Conceals One's Own } Matches Another's } Charcs (to eliminate an old pattern or blend it with a background pattern).	MIMICKING Copies Another's Charcs (to recreate an old pattern, imitating it).
REPACKAGING Adds New } Subtracts Old } Charcs (to modify an old pattern by matching another).	INVENTING Creates New Charcs (to create a new pattern).
DAZZLING Obscures Old } Adds Alternative } Charcs (to blur an old pattern, reducing its certainty).	DECOYING Creates Alternative Charcs (to give an additional, alternative pattern, increasing its certainty).

This matrix seems to provide a close fit for the multitude of magical tricks. Should all such effects and methods fit, then it is truly a special structural or taxonomic model of magic. If they fit with ease and without ambiguity, it is a useful model as well. If much torturing is required to make the example fit the matrix, then the model is an intellectual Procrustean Bed of limited value. But even if only *most* tricks fit easily, the model is still perhaps worthy of further development.

Observe in the matrix that the three ways of dissimulation and the three of simulation are each arrayed in ostensibly descending order of effectiveness. Bell's assumption (hypothesis) was that masking would be the most effective way to dissimulate. Therefore, if *masking* fails to confer sufficient invisibility to the real object or event and it is noticed, the deceiver can then resort to *repackaging* to disguise it. And if repackaging fails and the thing is recognized for what it is, then *dazzling* can be used as a last-ditch measure at least to confuse the target about some characteristics. Conversely, Bell assumed that mimicking would be the most effective way to simulate. Therefore, should *mimicking* fail to show the false by a convincing imitation, the deceiver can resort to *inventing* to create an alternative reality. And if inventing also fails, *decoying* can still be used at least to attract the otherwise undivided attention of the target away from it.

Consequently, it seemed to me that, in theory, the most effective deceptions will dissimulate by *masking* and simultaneously simulate by *mimicking,* while the potentially least effective would be those that combine *dazzling* with *decoying* to achieve only a mere razzle-dazzle effect. Therefore, while dazzling-decoying deceptions might get invented, few if any would survive frequent operational experience and consequently would get dropped from repertory.

To test Bell's hypothesis and my subsidiary one, I chose to use the tricks of magicians, because among all professional deceivers, they have by far the most frequent experience of both failed and successful deceptions. Generals, like card cheats, would be more likely simply to *prefer* certain types of deception without having much hard evidence of their effectiveness. Accordingly, all magic tricks that had been collected to illustrate a previous paper were fitted to the matrix. As can be seen in practice or at least in magician's practice, both hypotheses were substantially verified.[22] Masking and mimicking are not only overwhelmingly the most common methods used for dissimulation and simulation respectively; but also they are the two used most often in combination. Conversely, only one example of dazzling-decoying was discovered (the 'Thought Force'), despite an even wider search among the repertory of magic.[23] Thus, this is an apparently useful procedural model or guide for the planner to follow in designing the most effective deceptions.

Magical tricks are the magician's deception operations. If this model can be as effectively applied to deception outside the special field of magic, it then takes on the character of a general theory. In fact, as noted above, work to this end has already been done not only somewhat systematically on military deception but, albeit with less rigor, also on the other major fields that employ it.

THE MATRIX OF DECEPTION
(as applied to 60 magic tricks)

DISSIMULATING	SIMULATING		
	Mimicking	Inventing	Decoying
Masking	19	10	10
Repackaging	4	3	1
Dazzling	10	2	1

Source: Whaley (1981), table, based on an opportunity sample of 60 tricks.

The Process of Deception[24]

The deception process is implicit in the preceding section, which gave operational definitions of all relevant terms. Here this process is made explicit. Its ten steps are:[25]

First, in planning a deception, the planner must know its *strategic goal.* For the magician, this is always 'simply' to provide the audience with a pleasing and surprising effect or puzzle, for that is all they expect if he is to earn his keep. For the military commander it may be to launch a surprise invasion of another country, effect a landing on an enemy beach with minimum initial opposition, get the jump on the enemy with a new attack or counter-attack, or simply get a reconnaissance or rescue party in and out of hostile territory with sufficiently low casualties to assure success. These goals pose the kinds of problems the planner initially faces; they are the 'givens' he must work within.

Second, the planner must decide how he wants his target to *react* in such a given situation. The magician requires only that his audience concentrate their attention and interest on the portrayed effect to the exclusion of the secret method. For the military deception planner, however, the problem is more subtle, as best put by Britain's most experienced WWII deception planner, Brigadier Dudley Clarke, head of the so-called 'A' Force deception planning team in Cairo:[26]

> In the first Deception Plan I ever tackled I learned a lesson of inestimable value. The scene was Abyssinia ... Gen. Wavell wanted the Italians to think he was about to attack them from the south in order to draw off forces from those opposing him on the northern flank.
> The Deception went well enough — but the result was just the opposite of what Wavell wanted. The Italians drew back in the South, and sent what they could spare from there to reinforce the North, which was of course the true British objective.
> After that it became a creed in 'A' Force to ask a General 'What do you want the enemy to *do*?', and never 'What do you want him to *think*?'.

Third, only then must the planner by himself — whether general or magician — decide what he wants the target to think about the facts or event, precisely what it is they should *perceive.*

Fourth, he must decide specifically what is to be *hidden* about those facts or impending events and what is to be *shown* in their stead. In doing this he should remember the caveat that hiding and showing ideally take place simultaneously, as any deviation from simultaneity gives the target more time to discover the switch. (In military practice hiding usually takes place prior to showing, only sometimes simultaneously, and fortunately because most riskily rarely afterwards.)

Fifth, the planner now analyzes the *pattern* of the real thing to be hidden so as to identify its distinguishing characteristics ('charcs'), specifically which of these charcs must be deleted or added to give another pattern that suitably *masks, repackages,* or *dazzles.*

Sixth, he does the same for the false thing to be shown to give another pattern that plausibly *mimicks, invents,* or *decoys.*

Seventh, at this point the planner has designed a desired *effect* together with its hidden *method.* He must now explore the means available for presenting this effect to the target. The magician may be limited by the type of apparatus he has at hand, his ability to purchase or construct appropriate new apparatus, or his theatrical ability. Military commanders or practitioners of intelligence may be limited by their available deception assets and will often have too little time to acquire additional ones. They must make do or go back to Stage Four planning and try for an alternative design.

Eighth, having the effect and the means, the planning phase has ended and the operational phase begins. In magic, the planner is usually also the performer. In the military and intelligence fields, the deception planner usually hands over to operational units to present ('sell') the *effect.*

Ninth, the *channels* through which the false charcs (and patterns) are communicated must be ones open (directly or indirectly) to the target's sensors. A magician should not use a 'false count' of clicking coins before a deaf spectator. An intelligence officer should not plant disinformation in a newspaper unless he has reason to believe the enemy monitors that paper.

Tenth, and last, for the deception to succeed, the target must accept ('buy') the *effect,* perceiving it as an *illusion.* Deception will fail at this point only if the target takes no notice of the presented effect, notices but judges it irrelevant, misconstrues its intended meaning, or detects its *method.* Conversely, the target will:

* ★ take notice, if the effect is designed to attract his *attention*;
* ★ find it relevant, if the effect can hold his *interest*;
* ★ form the intended hypothesis about its meaning, if the projected pattern of charcs is *congruent* with patterns already part of his experience and memory; and
* ★ fail to detect the deception, if none of the ever-present charcs that are *incongruent* are accessible to his sensors.

Effective deception planning must anticipate all four of these contingencies. And a wise deceiver will seek feedback, monitoring the target's responses, to assure that these four contingencies are being met.

Counter-deception

Counter-deception[27] is the detection of deception. As just implied (point 10, above) its own special theory flows smoothly from the general theory of deception.

Several experts have argued that surprise is inevitable, particularly if deception is employed to gain it.[28] While acknowledging the grave difficulties that the intelligence analyst (particularly the counter-deception analyst) faces, I would argue that counter-deception, like deception, is in theory possible — always.

The possibility of detecting deception, any deception, is inherent in the effort to deceive. Every deception operation necessarily, inevitably, leaves clues. The analyst requires only the appropriate sensors and cognitive hypotheses to detect and understand the meaning of these clues. The problem is entirely one of technology and procedures and never one of theory.

Because everything (whether objects or events) can to some extent be both simulated and dissimulated, deception is always possible. However, because this can *never* be done to the *full* extent, counter-deception is also always possible. In other words, incongruent characteristics (clues) inevitably are present in every deception operation. These incongruent charcs form alternative patterns (hypotheses) that themselves are incongruent (discrepant, anomalous, paradoxical) with reality. As there are no paradoxes, no ambiguities, no incongruencies in nature, to detect incongruency is to detect the false.

Conclusion

In sum, everything that exists can to some extent be both simulated and dissimulated. Therefore deception is always possible; any thing and any event is meat for the deception planner. The planner — whether magician, general, or anyone else — can take courage from magician David Devant's motto: 'Give me a good "effect" and I'll find a way to do it.' And his is no idle claim, as proven time and time again by Devant and other magician-innovators faced with this challenge to deceive.

Finally, although we now have a preliminary theory of deception, we might also wish a theory of counter-deception — the detection of deception. Here too a study of magic can be helpful because magicians — master deceivers themselves — have proven themselves the best detectives of the deceptions of three of the main types of deceivers: psychic frauds, gambling cheats, and other magicians. But that is another story, a promising one because while anything can be either simulated or dissimulated to some extent, it can never be done so to the *full* extent. Therefore counter-deception, like deception, is in theory always possible.

NOTES

1. This paper is an elaboration and refinement of work begun in 1979 by J. Bowyer Bell and Barton Whaley. See Bell and Whaley (1979) and Bell and Whaley (1982).

2. For example, Solomon J. Solomon, *Strategic Camouflage* (London: Murray, 1920), the pioneering work on camouflage theory.

3. Beginning in World War II with Dr R. V. Jones' 1942 paper on 'The Theory of Spoof'.

4. Donald C. Daniel and Katherine L. Herbig, 'Propositions on Military Deception', in Daniel and Herbig (eds.), *Multidisciplinary Perspective on Strategic Deception* (Monterey: US Naval Postgraduate School, 1980), 5–44.
   L. Daniel Maxim, Mary C. Walsh, Carl Leaver, and Barton Whaley, 'Deception Maxims' (Washington, D.C.: Mathematica, Inc., and ARM/ORD/CIA, 1980); and Robert Jervis, *Perception and Misperception in International Politics* (Princeton: Princeton University Press, 1976).

5. Barton Whaley, *Stratagem: Deception and Surprise in War* (Cambridge, Mass.: Center for International Studies, MIT, 1969) which, with updates, surveyed 232 battles from 1914 to 1973.

6. Barton Whaley, *The Special Theory of Magic: Conjurers as Deception Planners* (draft 1981), which surveyed 60 magic tricks.

7. J. Bowyer Bell and Barton Whaley (under psudonym of 'J. Bartos Bowyer'), *Cheating* (New York: St. Martin's Press, forthcoming, spring 1982), surveying several examples from each of these fields for a total of about 200.

8. H. E. Hinton, 'Natural Deception', in R. L. Gregory and E. H. Gombrich (eds.), *Illusion in Nature and Art* (New York: Scribner's, 1973), 97–160.

9. Colin Blakemore, 'The Baffled Brain', in Gregory and Gombrich (1973), 9–47. See also John P. Frisby, *Seeing: Illusion, Brain and Mind* (New York: Oxford University Press, 1980).

10. Gregory (1973), 51–3.

11. See Gregory (1973), 53–69, 74–90. See also Frisby (1980), 156. Professor Frisby, a perceptual psychologist, reaches a similar conclusion in speaking of 'descriptions inside our heads' or 'object recognition' arrived at by 'computational strategies'.

12. Gregory (1973), 51, 55.

13. Peter Bryant, *Perception and Understanding in Young Children: An Experimental Approach* (New York: Basic Books, 1974).

14. To use a convenient term coined by Dr J. Bowyer Bell in 1980.

15. Particularly relevant is: Karl E. Schiebe, 'The Psychologist's Advantage and Its Nullification', *American Psychologist*, October 1978, 869–81. See also his *Mirrors, Masks, Lies, and Secrets*.

16. Jan B. Deregowski, 'Illusion and Culture', in Gregory and Gombrich (1973), 161–91. The thin literature on cultural style in military deception is summarized in Daniel and Herbig (1980), 16–17.

17. Neatly summarized in Richards J. Heuer, 'Cognitive Factors in Deception and Counterdeception', in Daniel and Herbig (1980), 45–101.

18. This work is summarized in Colin Blakemore, 'The Baffled Brain', in Gregory and Gombrich (1973), 9–47.

19. This section is a refined and elaborated account of the material in Bell and Whaley (1982), Ch. 2, which in turn was based on the authors' draft paper, 'A Taxonomy of Deception', written in 1979 for Mathematica, Inc. This taxonomy was primarily the work of Dr Bell.

20. H. E. Hinton, 'Natural Deception', in Gregory and Gombrich (1973), 97–159.

21. While the systematic analysis of these two terms as a dichotomy goes back at least as early as the early 17th century essay 'On Simulation and Dissimulation' by Sir Francis Bacon, its first application to military theory (and using these two words) was made by the painter who became head of British camouflage in the Great War, Solomon J. Solomon, in his pioneering book, *Strategic Camouflage* (London: Murray, 1920).

22. Although this sample was not a random selection (much less a 'universe') of tricks, the *relative* values in the separate cells of the table probably hold, the bias having been to search out more diligently the rarer categories.

23. Indeed, the only example found in any other field of deception is the old carnival game called, appropriately, Razzle-Dazzle in which the 'flat-joint' operator false-counts the sucker's score to make him a loser. See Scarne (1974), 582-9.

24. This section is a simplified summary of the model of deception planning given in Bell and Whaley (1982), Ch. 2. The preliminary version was a draft paper, 'A Deception Planning Model', done in 1979 for Mathematica, Inc.

25. An alternative but not contradictory process model is given by Daniel and Herbig (1980), 8-14.

26. Brigadier Dudley Clarke, 'Some Personal Reflections on the Practice of Deception in the Mediterranean Theatre from 1941 to 1945' (memo dated 6 Sept. 1972), as reproduced in Mure (1980), 274. See also Mure (1980), 9, 81-2; and Daniel and Herbig (1980), 4.

27. This now standard term was coined in 1968 by Dr William R. Harris.

28. Notably Roberta Wohlstetter, *Pearl Harbor: Warning and Decision* (Stanford: Stanford University Press, 1962); and Michael Handel, 'Perception, Deception and Surprise: The Case of the Yom Kippur War', *Jerusalem Papers on Peace Problems,* No. 19 (Jerusalem: The Hebrew University, 1976).